WALKING EASY

in the

SWISS AND AUSTRIAN ALPS

Third Edition

Chet and Carolee Lipton

The
Globe
Pequot
press

Guilford, Connecticut

To Barbara, Arnie, Dustin, Sue, and Steve—
the next generation of *Easy Walkers*

Page design: Lisa Reneson
Photographs by Chet Lipton, except the following: pp. 17, 19: courtesy of Fritz Lauener; p. 25: courtesy of the Swiss Tourist Office; and p. 64: courtesy of the Zermatt Tourist Office.
Maps and pen and pencil illustrations by Chet Lipton

ISBN 0-7627-2314-9

Manufactured in the United States of America
Third Edition/First Printing

Contents

BECOMING AN EASY WALKER

SWITZERLAND

AUSTRIA

Acknowledgments

A special thank you to Gabriele Wolf, Austrian National Tourist Office, New York, and Evelyne Mock, Switzerland Tourism, New York, for their invaluable support and assistance.

Our thanks also to the Austrian Tourist Information Office directors and their staff: Renate J. Danler, Alpbach; Badgastein; Hans Wallner, Kaprun; Robert Jank, Kitzbühel; Mieming; Gertrude Santeler, Neustift; Markus Tschoner, Seefeld; Robert Pramstrahler, Zell am Ziller.

We also thank the Swiss Tourist Information Office directors and their staff: Guido Buob and Willy Raes, Appenzell; Arosa; Rolf Wild and Brigitte Bucher, Central Switzerland (Lucerne); Engelberg; Joe Luggen, Grindelwald; Gstaad; Jerun Vils, Kandersteg; Beatrice Dolder, Lauterbrunnen; Yvonne Mark, Lenk; Frank Bumann, Saas-Fee; Andrea Parolini, Samedan; Patrick Messeiller, Verbier; Jörg Gnotke, Wengen; Andrea Hardmeier, Zermatt.

Another note of thanks goes to all the hotel owners and their staffs for providing the authors with local village history, general background information, and helpful hints about the best walking trails.

We wish to acknowledge the support of the Swiss Travel System and Rail Europe.

BECOMING AN *EASY WALKER*

Lush green valleys filled with the clanging bells of placidly grazing cattle. Dramatic snow-covered peaks. Pine forests surrounding crystal-clear glacial lakes. These are part of the landscape of the Swiss and Austrian country-side, but it is the gentle townspeople who are the vibrant heart and soul of the villages tucked into these valleys and alps. A varied network of summer hiking trails and cableways complete this pastoral scene, attracting walkers from around the world. This is the setting of *Walking Easy in the Swiss and Austrian Alps,* written for active adults who enjoy walking, prefer the exhil-arating outdoors, and have the need to fulfill a quest for discovery. This is a how-to book, filled with carefully detailed day walks based out of charming villages and towns; sight-seeing excursions for lazier days, including special side-trip itineraries to Vienna, Salzburg, Innsbruck, and Lucerne; sugges-tions for comfortable accommodations; and helpful hints to benefit the recreational walker.

Every activity described in the following chapters has been experienced and edited by the authors to meet the needs of the active adult walker (and perhaps those juniors who think they can keep up). Travelers of all ages walk on the intricate and fascinating network of alpine hiking trails and use the clean and efficient Swiss and Austrian public transportation systems.

Each section in this guide is devoted to a particularly beautiful village or mountain area and includes a brief description of its location, access by public transportation and car, excursions to nearby points of interest, and detailed instructions for each walk. In Switzerland, our base villages are Ap-penzell, Arosa, Engelberg, Gstaad, Kandersteg, Lauterbrunnen/Wengen, Lenk, Saas-Fee, Samedan/St. Moritz, Verbier, and Zermatt. Base villages in Austria include Alpbach, Badgastein, Kaprun, Kitzbühel, Mieming, Neustift, Seefeld, and Zell am Ziller. These mountain areas were selected because of their proximity to great walking and exciting excursions, local charm, avail-ability of public transportation, and comfortable accommodations.

Every walk in the book is preceded by an overview, followed by direc-tions on how to arrive at the start of the walk from the base village. Many walks begin with a mountain railway or thrilling cable car ride; others are gentle walks through the forest or around a tranquil lake. Some are above the tree line or across a glacier, while others descend through alpine meadows resounding with the harmonious ringing of cowbells—all within the capability and range of most active adults and planned to give *Easy Walkers* maximum visual and physical pleasure.

The walks are graded into one of three classifications: **gentle**—low-level walks with few ascents and descents through valleys and around lakes and rivers; **comfortable**—ascents and descents over mixed terrain; **more challenging**—steeper and longer ascents and descents on narrower, rockier trails. All walks can be accomplished in two to six hours by recreational walkers of any age and in good health.

Walk at a pace you are comfortable with, depending on the terrain and your own reaction to the altitude. Hiking in the Alps should not be treated as a fitness test. Enjoy the spectacular scenery and rest as often as needed. Most *Walking Easy* hikes are under 7500 ft. (2285 m.) altitudes that most walkers find comfortable. Each walk description includes the degree of altitude change and the ratings reflect these conditions. Generally, it's a good idea to walk more slowly at higher altitudes until your body adjusts. There are easy-guide maps in some of the more detailed walks. They are not drawn to scale but act as a general guide to major trail markings. You will also find a recommended hiking map listed at the beginning of each village's Walks section. These and other maps can be purchased at the local Tourist Information Office or newspaper/magazine stores. While a detailed local hiking map and a whistle for emergency use are necessities, you may also find it fun to carry a compass to check direction and a pedometer to keep track of walking distances.

The *Walking Easy* time listed before each walk is time spent actually walking. It does not include time spent for lunch, resting, photography, scenery breaks, sight-seeing, and transportation. This additional time is left to the discretion of each *Easy Walker*, so an average day with a four-hour walk could begin at 9:00 A.M. and end back at your hotel in the late afternoon.

The Swiss and Austrian Alps have thousands of miles of trails—*wanderwege* (comfortable walking paths) and *bergwege* (narrower, rockier mountain trails)—most well signed, well maintained, and easily followed. But be warned: Not all hikes are easy. Many will challenge your capabilities with ascents and descents over mixed terrain. However, it is not uncommon for people of all ages to be steadily wending their way along a favorite trail, and it is said that the first pair of shoes that proud Swiss and Austrian parents purchase for their children is a pair of tiny hiking boots. Europeans love to walk—and love walkers. The Swiss and Austrians have created wonderful trail systems—it is the best way to see the countryside—and walkers are welcome almost everywhere in their hiking boots and backpacks.

You can do it—just tuck a copy of *Walking Easy in the Swiss and Austrian Alps* in your backpack, and you're on your way!

Timing Is Everything

The weather can vary tremendously within the small countries of Switzerland and Austria. The tree line is about 6500 ft. (1980 m.) and the snow line in summer can be at 9000 ft. (2745 m.) or lower.

Deciding the best time of year to walk in the Alps depends on what you enjoy most in the way of scenery and weather. The alpine flowers begin to bloom in late May and are at their peak from mid-June through July. Snow can still cover some of the high trails in mid-June, but the riotous colors of alpine wildflowers, framed against the white mountain peaks, are breathtaking.

July and especially August are the most popular tourist months. September offers fewer tourists, lower temperatures, and clearer skies. Hiking season usually begins mid-June and lasts through the end of September, but it is *very* important to check lift schedules in each village—some stay open until October, while others close after the first week in September. Whichever month you choose, walking on the network of alpine trails will be an exhilarating experience.

Hint: *Insulated or Polartec-type jackets are a necessity in mountain areas, even during summer.*

Europe by Auto

If you are planning a trip to Europe of seventeen days or longer and prefer to travel by car, Auto France offers a cost-saving vacation plan. A new Peugot is delivered to your airport or city of choice, and insurance is included. There is no value added tax or maximum age restrictions. For full details call Auto France at (800) 572–9655; Web site: www.auto-france.com.

Switzerland and Austria by Train and Bus

The efficient Swiss and Austrian public transportation systems are among

> **Hint:** *Train cars are marked with a large 1 or 2 to denote travel class. Second-class rail travel is as clean and almost as comfortable as first class—we recommend taking advantage of second-class savings.*

the best in the world, linking trains, buses, and boats.

Buses are one class and can take *Easy Walkers* to trail heads, across remote valleys, and through high alpine passes. Boats traverse major lakes and rivers from May to October.

> **Hint:** *Gëpack, or baggage forwarding, is an invaluable and reliable traveler's aid. Bring your luggage to the train station and, for a small fee, have it sent on to your next destination. However, it may be necessary to check your luggage through the night before to ensure timely arrival.*

Discount Travel

Swiss Pass: This is the most convenient of the Swiss discounts. It entitles users to unlimited travel on the entire public transportation system—including trains, buses, and lake steamers—and to purchase 25 percent discount tickets on selected lift systems and mountain railways. You can choose a period of consecutive days—four, eight, fifteen, or twenty-one days or one month—with savings for two adults traveling together (Swiss Saverpass) and free travel for children under sixteen when traveling with adults. Ask for the family card.

Swiss Flexi-Pass: Within a one-month period you can travel on any three days of your choice without restrictions, with the same privileges as the Swiss Pass. You can also purchase up to six additional days of unlimited transportation. There are additional savings for two adults traveling together (Swiss Saver Flexipass) and no charge for children under sixteen traveling with adults.

> **Hint:** *If you're planning a* Walking Easy *trip to Switzerland, we recommend buying a Swiss Pass. These passes can be purchased only in the United States. Call Rail Europe (888–382–7245), or visit www.raileurope.com.*

Swiss Card: You travel free of charge from the border or airport to your destination and back. In other words, one free round-trip, plus 50 percent discount for all additional trips by train, bus, or boat and 25 to 50 percent discount on most cableways. This card is valid for one month, and children under sixteen travel free with you.

Austrian Railpass: This pass is valid for any three days of unlimited travel, without charge, in a given fifteen-day period; you can also buy up to five extra days of travel. It's sold in the United States through Rail Europe.

Hint: Travel with extra passport-size photos, as some local discount passes may also require them.

Comfortable Inns and Hotels

Accommodations in Switzerland and Austria range from five-star, deluxe hotels to comfortable rooms in rural farmhouses. The quality of a hotel, or *pension,* and its prices can be judged by the number of stars awarded to it: Five stars denote deluxe; four stars, first class; three stars, superior; two stars, standard; and one star, minimum. The recommended *Walking Easy* three- and four-star Swiss and Austrian hotels listed for each base village have been used by the authors on their walking trips. All hotels offer half-board (breakfast and dinner) unless otherwise noted, and all have excellent kitchens. For convenience, quality, and savings, we suggest making hotel reservations *with* half-board. All listed three-star hotels offer comfortable rooms with private facilities and buffet breakfast, and are scrupulously clean and well located. Our recommended four-star hotels, while more expensive, generally feature more luxurious accommodations, a wider menu choice at breakfast and dinner, and a variety of other guest services. Many of these three- and four-star hotels have been owned and operated by the same families for generations.

Hint: For best rates when making reservations, fax, write, e-mail, or call the hotel directly and ask if a "Walking Easy Special Hiking Package" is available. All taxes and gratuities are included in the room rate.

To call or fax Switzerland or Austria from the United States, first dial the international access number (011), followed by the country code—41 for Switzerland, 43 for Austria—followed by the telephone or fax number. Every listed hotel can be reached by a phone and fax number, and many have e-mail.

Hint: All Walking Easy *hotels accept credit cards, unless otherwise noted.*

Where to Eat and Drink

Hotels: Hotels in the Alps offer a buffet breakfast and a three- to five-course meal for dinner, if you take *halbpension* (half-board). Hotel food is usually excellent, and *Easy Walkers* can take advantage of lower costs by booking with dinner.

Hint: Always carry bottled water in your backpack when hiking, even when planning to lunch in a restaurant.

Restaurants: If you decide to eat in a restaurant outside your hotel, check the special of the day (*tagesteller* or *plat du jour*). A 15 percent service charge is always included in your bill. A few coins should be left on the table if you were pleased with the service.

Picnicking: When planning a day of walking, we recommend taking along a picnic lunch. Many local supermarkets will prepare sandwiches for you.

Dressing for the Trail—from Boots to Backpack

Walking Easy clothing should be lightweight and layerable. All clothing is not suitable for all types of walking—climate, altitude, and time of day during the alpine hiking season are points to consider.

Hiking Boots: The most important item for a successful *Walking Easy* experience is a pair of broken-in, medium-weight hiking boots, preferably waterproof and above the ankle, providing more support. Do not wear sneakers or sneakers that look like hiking boots; they do not provide the foot/ankle support and traction needed.

Hint: Wear your hiking boots for overseas and intercity travel—they can be heavy and bulky to carry or pack. You can remove them on the plane for comfort. Custom dictates that hiking boots are never worn in a hotel dining room. Sneakers, sandals, or even slippers are preferred.

Socks: Socks worn closest to your skin should *not* be made of cotton. Cotton absorbs perspiration and holds it, encouraging blisters. A lightweight undersock made of a hydrophobic synthetic will wick sweat away and keep your feet drier. When purchasing hiking boots, be sure to wear the type of socks you will wear on the trail.

Outerwear: An insulated or Polartec-type jacket or vest may be essential for walking or sight-seeing.

Rain protection is best provided by a good-quality waterproof poncho large enough to fit over your backpack, or a waterproof jacket. Don't let a light rain cancel your walking plans.

Hint: Rain gear should always be stored in your backpack until needed.

Hat: A hat with a brim provides protection from sun as well as rain and should always be worn.

Pants: Our favorite walking apparel in the Alps is hiking knickers, for both men and women. They are worn with high socks, which protect the legs but can be rolled down in warmer weather. Hiking knickers can be bought in most sporting goods stores in the Alps. In warmer weather, hiking shorts are a good alternative.

Sweaters: A medium-weight sweater is essential for cool evenings in the mountains, even in summer.

Sweatshirts: A medium-weight sweatshirt can be layered over shirts for hiking.

Shirts: A cotton/polyester blend can be used for ease of laundering. Short-sleeved knit shirts, along with long-sleeved knits and turtlenecks, are essential for layering under sweaters or sweatshirts, for both day and evening.

Backpack: Each *Easy Walker* should carry a lightweight backpack with wide, adjustable, foam-padded shoulder straps. Roomy, outside zipper compartments are necessary to organize daily hiking essentials.

Waist Pack: Use a roomy, comfortable waist pack to carry money, passports, etc.

Walking Stick: Walking sticks are an indispensable aid to balance when hiking downhill or on rocky terrain. They come in many sizes and styles and can be bought at an alpine village sporting goods store. The newest walking stick innovation telescopes so that it fits into your backpack when not in use. We think this item is a must.

Rules of the Trail

Paths are generally well signed and marked. Signs may indicate the time it takes to walk to the destination—1 std. indicates one hour. (*Std.* is the abbreviation for the German *stunde,* or hour.)

Most *Easy Walkers* should allow about 25 percent more time than the signpost estimates.

In Switzerland, yellow diamond-shaped signs represent *wanderwege,* lower level paths through easy hills and lower mountain slopes. Red-and-white signs and blazes denote higher level *bergwege*—narrower, rockier mountain trails.

1. Plan the route by checking this book and local hiking maps before beginning each walk. *Always* carry a local hiking map with you.
2. Ask about local weather conditions, and adjust the day's activities accordingly.
3. Tell someone about your planned route, either a friend or one of the hotel staff.
4. Take your time, especially at higher altitudes.
5. *Never* leave the marked trail.
6. Turning back is not a disgrace if you feel the trail is too difficult or the weather looks threatening. Return on the same path, or check available public transportation.
7. Be sure your hiking boots are in good shape and your backpack holds the needed items, plus lunch and a snack in case you are delayed. *Always* carry bottled water in your backpack. Longer and more strenuous hikes require more water.
8. *Never* start a hike without stowing a special energy treat in your backpack. We prefer one or two of the many varieties of **"Ritter Sport"** chocolate bars.
9. In case of an accident, send for help. If this is not possible, use the standard alpine distress signal with your whistle: Make six signals, spaced evenly within one minute, pause for one minute, then repeat.
10. Appreciate the beauty of the wildflowers but do not pick them.
11. Do not litter. Take out what you bring in.
12. Alpine meadow gates work in wondrous ways—some are turnstiles, some have spring-attached hooks, some feature sliding boards, and others are meant to be ducked under or stepped over. Whichever the case, be sure you leave the gate the way you approached it—closed.
13. Always check current timetables when using public transportation.

14. Sunscreen and high-quality sunglasses are very important at high altitudes and on glacier walks.

The purpose of any walking trip is to have fun. Tuck a copy of *Walking Easy* in your backpack and take a hike . . . you can do it!

SWITZERLAND

GRUEZI from Switzerland Tourism

Let's take you on a **SWISS HIKE**.

Switzerland—your walking Easy vacation paradise—with 31,000 miles of well-marked trails.

Wander through high Alpine pasteurs past grazing cows, into quiet woods leading to rustic villages beneath you.

In the Swiss Alps, you can stand on glaciers, looking through green ice, hearing the icy water gurgle beneath you.

Stroll on the shores of a sparkling lake—in Switzerland, a lake is never more than 10 miles away.

Sleep soundly under down comforters in a mountain chalet after a day of invigorating hiking.

Hip and healthy people enjoy hiking the Swiss Alps, dogs tag along—it's tradition.

Ice grottoes fascinate visitors on the Jungfraujoch, Mount Titlis, and Mittelallin.

Knapsacks are a must for a day hike—carry food and drink for a picnic—and a sweater or windbreaker.

Edelweiss is the mountain flower you may find in hidden places, but please do not pick this beautiful flower—it's rare and protected.

Enjoy *Walking Easy* in the Swiss Alps.

—Urs Eberhand
Director, North America
Switzerland Tourism

SWITZERLAND

Modern Switzerland is a federation of more than 3,000 communes. Years ago, neighboring communes formed twenty-three cantons, each with its own constitution, laws, and government, leaving only foreign policy, national defense, economic policy, etc., to the federal parliament. Although Switzerland is a small country, it has four official languages: German, spoken by 65 percent of the population; French, 18 percent; Italian, 12 percent; and Romansch, spoken by only 1 percent of the people in the southeastern mountains. The German language of the native Swiss is called *Schwyzer Deutsch*, a dialect different in vocabulary, pronunciation, and grammar from classical German. However, English is usually spoken in even the smallest village. Tourist information offices in Switzerland are designated by an **i** sign and are a valuable friend to the hiker. You'll usually find them on the main street in even the smallest village and the personnel are multilingual and friendly.

From high, panoramic trails at the foot of the snowcapped peaks to peaceful rambles around lakes and through pastures, the Swiss Alps offer *Walking Easy* at its best.

BERNESE OBERLAND

LAUTERBRUNNEN/WENGEN

(GRINDELWALD, MÜRREN, MEIRINGEN)

The Bernese Oberland villages of Lauterbrunnen, Wengen, Grindelwald, Mürren, and Meiringen form the hub of some of the finest hiking in Switzerland. Lauterbrunnen and Wengen, the preferred *Walking Easy* base villages, welcome you with snowcapped peaks towering over a deep glacial valley.

Lauterbrunnen, at 2625 ft. (800 m.), sits in the middle of a picturesque valley near convenient rail connections that can take *Easy Walkers* throughout pocket-sized Switzerland. The Lauterbrunnen train station is a great jumping-off place—for a shopping visit to Lucerne, to Interlaken and a steamer outing on Lake Thun or Brienz, to Wilderswil for a cogwheel railway ride to scenic Schynige Platte, or to the medieval arcades and bear pits of Bern.

Car-free Wengen, at 4160 ft. (1275 m.), Lauterbrunnen's upstairs neighbor, is perched on a sunny plateau with enchanting views of some of the Bernese Oberland's most imposing peaks—the Eiger, the Mönch, and the Jungfrau.

Neighboring Grindelwald, also boasting myriad hiking trails, is easily reached by train or gondola from Wengen and Lauterbrunnen. A car-free hamlet with a population of 350, Mürren is perched on a terrace above the Lauterbrunnen Valley, facing the Jungfrau massif. At 5400 ft. (1646 m.), it is the highest village in the Bernese Oberland. Meiringen, home of Reichenbach Falls, where fictional detective Sherlock Holmes plunged to his death along with evil Professor Moriarty, is the center of several not-to-be-missed hikes.

Transportation

By Train - To arrive in Lauterbrunnen and/or Wengen, take the train to Interlaken Ost and change to the Lauterbrunnen train. To continue to

Wengen, change trains in Lauterbrunnen for the twenty-minute trip by cog railway.

By Car - Drive toward Interlaken and pick up the local road through Wilderswil, into Lauterbrunnen. To Wengen, park your car in the garage at the Lauterbrunnen station and continue the trip to Wengen by train.

> **Hint:** *In Interlaken Ost, be sure to sit in the front cars marked* LAUTERBRUNNEN *in the A and B track sectors— the back cars in C and D marked* GRINDELWALD *drop off in the village of Zweilütschinen for the trip to Grindelwald.*

Favorite *Walking Easy* Hotel

Hotel Silberhorn

Three-Star; Owners—Familie Christian von Allmen

CH-3822 Lauterbrunnen; **Tel:** 33 855 14 71; **Fax:** 33 855 42 13

E-mail: silberhorn@bluewin.ch

A breathtaking view of the Lauterbrunnen Valley and Staubbach Falls can be seen from the balconies of many rooms, as well as the newly renovated dining room. A full Swiss buffet breakfast is served, along with a salad bar and excellent regional cooking at dinner. The Silberhorn caters to walkers of all ages and nationalities, and it is a convenient and comfortable jumping-off place for hiking and sight-seeing in the Bernese Oberland.

Excursions

The Lauterbrunnen Tourist Information Office is across from the train station.

Fax: 33 855 36 04

Internet: www.lauterbrunnen.ch

E-mail: lauterbrunnen.tourismus@bluewin.ch

The Wengen Tourist Information Office is on the main street, near the post office.

Fax: 33 855 30 60

Internet: www.wengen-muerren.ch

E-mail: information@wengen.ch

A Jungfrau train and cable car pass **(Jungfraubahnen Pass)**, available at tourist offices and train stations, is valid for unlimited use of most trains and lifts in the Jungfrau area, including Interlaken, Grindelwald, Mürren, and Wengen/Lauterbrunnen. This pass also offers a 50 percent reduction on the excursion to the Jungfraujoch from Kleine Scheidegg.

1. **Trümmelbach Falls (Trümmelbachfälle)** - The ten glacier-fed waterfalls, cascading inside a mountain, have been made accessible by a Swiss engineering miracle. Remember, it's cold and damp inside the mountain, so dress warmly.

   Directions: Take the bus to the falls at the Lauterbrunnen train station, or walk through town and follow walking signs to the falls.

2. **The Schilthorn** - A cable car ascends to 9750 ft. (2972 m.) to an incredible panorama (See Walk #1.)

3. **The Jungfraujoch** - The "top of Europe" is reached by the highest rack railway (and probably the most expensive) on the continent, climbing to an ice wonderworld at 11,333 ft. (3454 m.). (See Walk #3.)

4. **Schynige Platte** - At 6500 ft. (1981 m.), the Schynige Platte's remarkable panorama overlooks mountains and lakes from Grindelwald to Interlaken.

   Directions: Take the train to Wilderswil. Change to the Schynige Platte Railway for the fifty-minute scenic ride.

5. **Grindelwald** - This tourist mecca lies at the foot of several imposing mountains and serves as a central point for many walks. (See Walks #6 and #8.)

6. **Interlaken** - Named for its location between Lake Thun and Lake Brienz, Interlaken is a busy tourist center surrounded by a superb mountain panorama. The Höhweg is a wide main street bustling with stores and restaurants. Lake steamer excursions can be boarded from Interlaken to Lake Thun or Lake Brienz—the piers are only a minute's walk from either the Interlaken Ost or the Interlaken West train stations.

   a. **Heimwehfluh** - The Heimwehfluh funicular's top station, a five-minute walk from the Interlaken West station, features an elaborate scale-model railroad.

   b. **Harder Kulm** - The top of Harder Kulm is reached by a fifteen-minute funicular ride; the base station is only a few minutes' walk from the Interlaken Ost station.

   Directions to Interlaken: Take the train to Interlaken Ost and change for Interlaken West, a three-minute ride.

7. **Meiringen** - A visit to **Reichenbach Falls** strikes right at the heart of the mystique surrounding Meiringen. Take the funicular up to the falls to view the place where Holmes and Moriarty fell to their death. The

Sherlock Holmes Museum is located on the main street, with the first authentic replica of Holmes's front room at 221B Baker Street. The **Aareschlucht**, just outside Meiringen, is a natural wonder, with towering rock walls lining both sides of the gorge.

Directions: Take the train to Interlaken Ost and change for the train toward Lucerne, exiting at Meiringen.

Trail from Mänlichen to Grindelwald

8. Brienz - If you're interested in woodcarving or violinmaking, be sure to visit Brienz, a lake village offering local artisans' work.

Directions: Take the train to Interlaken Ost and change for the train to Brienz. An alternate means of transportation is by steamer. The docks in Interlaken Ost and Brienz are just outside the railroad stations.

9. Swiss Open-Air Museum in Ballenberg - This beautifully landscaped area provides fascinating insights into Swiss lifestyles of the past.

Directions: Take the train to Interlaken Ost and change for the train toward Lucerne, exiting in Brienz. Take the connecting bus to Ballenberg at the Brienz station.

10. Thun - (See Kandersteg, Excursion #3.)

Directions: Take the train to Interlaken Ost and change for the train to Thun.

11. Bern - The capital of Switzerland is a delightful city of medieval arches, fountains, and towers. (See Kandersteg, Excursion #4.)

Directions: *Take the train to Interlaken Ost and change for the train to Bern.*

Lauterbrunnen/Wengen Walks

(Grindelwald, Meiringen, Mürren)

Recommended Maps:
- ❖ Wanderkarte—Lauterbrunnental Jungfrau Region
- ❖ Wanderkarte—Grindelwald Jungfrau Region
- ❖ Wanderkarte—Oberhasli, Meiringen-Hasliberg, Haslital

Walk #1

Introductory Walk—Lauterbrunnen to Stechelberg, Mürren to Grütschalp (Excursion to the Schilthorn)
Walking Easy Time: 2½ hours
Rating: Gentle

Today's walk introduces *Easy Walkers* to the lovely Lauterbrunnen Valley. The level path parallels the Lütschine River, leading past Staubbach and Trümmelbach Falls. Before Stechelberg, take the cable car to Mürren and, if the weather is clear, to the Schilthorn. Return to Mürren and continue on the gentle path from Mürren to Grütschalp, taking the funicular back to Lauterbrunnen.

Start: Walk through Lauterbrunnen toward Staubbach Falls, ahead and on the right. Follow a paved path signed STECHELBERG—1 HR., 15 MIN. As you approach Staubbach Falls, note the sign ZUM STAUBBACHFALL and a path ascending up to the base of the falls—take this detour for a closer look.

Continuing to the hamlet of Buchen, a bridge crosses the river to Trümmelbach Falls. (See Excursion #1.) Today, however, continue ahead on the main path. You soon arrive at a small bridge leading to the lift station. Cross the bridge and walk to the Schilthorn lift. Buy a ticket from Stechelberg to the Schilthorn, with a return to *Mürren only*. After changes in Gimmelwald, Mürren, and Birg, the cable car lifts you to the Piz Gloria restaurant of James Bond fame. Visit the terrace with its incomparable views and, when ready, take the cable car down to Mürren to explore this tiny hamlet. Mürren is car-free and perched on a hillside high above the valley.

When ready, follow the sign to Grütschalp, the gentle mountain trail paralleling the railroad tracks. Don't be tempted by signs pointing directly to Lauterbrunnen; these paths are usually steep. You may encounter friendly cows, sheep, or goats along the path, and the typically alpine sound of their echoing bells is a fitting accompaniment to the spectacular mountain scenery. At the Grütschalp funicular station, return to Lauterbrunnen, changing for the train to Wengen if necessary.

Walk #2

Allmendhubel to Grütschalp

Walking Easy Time: 2½ hours

Rating: Comfortable

Today's outing will take you by funicular to Allmendhubel, 6257 ft. (1907 m.) above the charming village of Mürren at 5374 ft. (1638 m.), with outstanding views of the peaks that make this Bernese Oberland area so famous. As you walk from Allmendhubel toward Grütschalp on the Höhenweg, or high trail, the panorama includes the Jungfrau, the Eiger, the Mönch, Männlichen above the village of Wengen, and all the way to the Schynige Platte.

At Grütschalp you will take the funicular down to Lauterbrunnen.

Directions: Take the Grütschalp funicular to the top and board the little mountain train to Mürren. At Mürren, follow the sign to the Allmendhubel funicular, riding it to the top.

Start: After exiting, follow the sign GRÜTSCHALP—1 HR. 20 MIN. The trail—with spectacular views of snowcapped Eiger, Mönch, and Jungfrau peaks—rises to the top of a hill and descends quickly. You will meander on this red-and-white blazed mountain *bergweg* through the alp, always following signs to Grütschalp. After about seventy-five minutes, you can turn down the mountain to Mürren at Pletschenalp, if necessary. Descend the

Staubbach Falls and the Lauterbrunnen Valley

mountain, following signs to the Grütschalp funicular. As you walk to Grütschalp, this path becomes a bit steep but manageable. At the road, turn left toward the station, taking the funicular down to Lauterbrunnen.

Walk #3

Männlichen Top Station to Männlichen Gipfel to Kleine Scheidegg to Wengen (Optional Walk to Lauterbrunnen)
Walking Easy Time: 3 to 4½ hours
Rating: Comfortable

This walk, one of the most popular in the Bernese Oberland, begins in the shadow of some of Switzerland's most famous mountains, including the Eiger, the Mönch, and the Jungfrau.

Directions: If starting from Lauterbrunnen, take the train to Wengen. The new Wengen-Männlichen cableway is a short walk. Follow signs on the main street. Buy a one-way ticket to the top station. This plateau is at 7313 ft. (2229 m.) and offers many options, such as riding on the 4-mile-long Männlichen/Grindelwald gondola, the longest in Europe.

Start: From Männlichen Top Station, follow the sign to MÄNNLICHEN GIPFEL—20 MIN.—the Männlichen peak, clearly visible up the hill to your left. The short climb to the top is worth the effort. You'll be able to see Interlaken, the Schynige Platte, and the surrounding mountains and glaciers of the Bernese Oberland. When ready, return to the cable station and follow the sign KLEINE SCHEIDEGG—1 HR., 20 MIN. (There may be a few signs that vary a bit in walking time. Don't be put off—follow the main path to Kleine Scheidegg.)

As you walk toward the Eiger, the mountain used by Trevanian for the setting of his best-selling book and movie *The Eiger Sanction*, you are hiking one of the most traveled paths in the Bernese Oberland. Grindelwald is on the left in the distant valley, as you walk easily down toward Kleine Scheidegg and its railroad stop, bustling with hikers, climbers, and tourists changing for the train to and from the Jungfraujoch. (See Walk #4.)

Cross the railroad tracks at Kleine Scheidegg to the sign WENGEN—1 HR., 45 MIN. *NOTE: Two trails at this point lead to Wengernalp and Wengen, one taking about two and a half hours to Wengen via Stalden. You have the option here of taking the longer way to Wengen or following the trail closest to the railroad tracks.*

If you choose the shorter option, Wengernalp is an easy, thirty-minute walk from Kleine Scheidegg, with the railroad tracks on your right and the Jungfrau peak on your left. At Wengernalp, walk past the station and follow signs to Wengen.

If you wish to take a longer route, follow the sign WENGEN—2½ HRS. This path leads through the meadow and forest toward Stalden at 5515 ft. (1681 m.), with its exceptional views of the Lauterbrunnen Valley. At Stalden, take the middle path toward Wengen, eventually meeting the railroad and the main path above Schiltwald at Allmend. Turn left and follow the path into Wengen.

Easy Walkers can continue down to Lauterbrunnen (if your hotel is not located in Wengen) by following the signs marked LAUTERBRUNNEN. This walk will take another one and a half hours. Or take the short train ride from Wengen to Lauterbrunnen.

Walk #4

Excursion to the Jungfraujoch, Walk to Mönchjochhütte, and Return (Optional Walk Eigergletscher Station to Kleine Scheidegg)

Walking Easy Time: 2 to 3½ hours

Rating: More challenging

Reserve the better part of a clear day, making an early start, for a visit to Europe's highest altitude railway station. You will find that the Jungfraujoch train station is more than a stop on the rail line. It houses a high-altitude weather observatory and research station, several restaurants, a post office, a busy souvenir shop, an Ice Palace, and a snowfield where visitors can ski, take a sleigh ride pulled by huskies, bask in the sun, and take a two-hour round-trip hike to the Mönchjochhütte across a snowfield.

The Jungfraujoch rail station is at 11,333 ft. (3454 m.) between the imposing peaks of the Mönch, at 13,449 ft. (4099 m.), and the Jungfrau, at 13,642 ft. (4158 m.). This ice world features a multitude of glaciers tucked in between jagged, snow-covered peaks in a pristine and dazzling environment that defies the imagination.

Directions: Take the train from Lauterbrunnen or Wengen to Kleine Scheidegg and change for the special Jungfrau train. After station Eigergletscher, at 5524 ft. (2320 m.), the train enters a mountain tunnel, with stops at Eigerwand and Eismeer, where viewing windows have been cut into the face of the mountain. At the Jungfraujoch station, signs direct you to all the possible activities.

Start: After taking in all the sights, walk on the wide, well-signed snow trail for about an hour, ascending to the Mönchjochhütte along with dozens of other hikers, and return along the same path. (Make sure trail is open.) At the beginning of the snow trail, it is possible to ride on a sleigh pulled by a team of huskies.

When ready, walk back to the complex. *NOTE: The return train stops at Eigergletscher, one stop before Kleine Scheidegg. You can take a one-hour hike down to Kleine Scheidegg, where you pick up the train again.*

Walk #5

The Eiger Trail—Eigergletscher Station to Alpiglen
Walking Easy Time: 2¾ hours
Rating: Comfortable

One of the major attractions in the Jungfrau Region of the Bernese Oberland is the notorious north face of the Eiger, site of many climbing expeditions. Close-up views of this awesome mountain face are now available from the new Eiger Trail, which begins at the Eigergletscher station. The trail meanders past fascinating rock formations and over small streams to Alpiglen. While this hike can be taken in either direction, *Easy Walkers* may prefer beginning at the Eigergletscher station, ending at Alpiglen.

Directions: Take the train to Kleine Scheidegg and change trains, getting off at Eigergletscher, the first stop on the train to the Jungfraujoch.

Start: Cross the railroad tracks, following the sign EIGER TRAIL, leading up past the stone house and on to the well-blazed *bergweg*. After a short ascent, the trail reaches a vantage point with an imposing view of the north wall of the Eiger. This trail, winding along the mountain's base, provides views from Kleine Scheidegg and Männlichen down through the meadows and peaks above Grindelwald. You ascend and descend over scree and alp, first to the "cow line," then down to the tree line. The final half-hour descent through the forest can be steep and muddy—take it slowly, and soon the restaurant at Alpiglen appears. At Alpiglen you have a number of options, depending on the time:

1. Follow the signs to Grindelwald and walk ninety minutes to town, returning by train to Lauterbrunnen or Wengen.
2. Take the train from Alpiglen to Grindelwald, returning by train to Lauterbrunnen or Wengen via Zweilütschinen.
3. Take the train from Alpiglen to Kleine Scheidegg, returning by train to Lauterbrunnen or Wengen.
4. Take the train to Kleine Scheidegg and walk to Wengen (about two hours by the shorter path by the railroad tracks, as in Walk #3).

Walk #6

Grindelwald "First" Top Station to Grosse Scheidegg (Excursion to Grindelwald)

Walking Easy Time: 1½ hours

Rating: Comfortable

Today's excursion is particularly interesting because it includes a visit to the famous town of Grindelwald, with a hike on its surrounding mountains. This walk provides excellent views of the Wetterhorn, whose dark cliffs seem to loom directly above tiny Grosse Scheidegg, your trail destination.

Directions: Take the train from Lauterbrunnen to Zweilütschinen and change for the connecting train to Grindelwald. Walk through town, following the sign to First, and buy a one-way ticket to the top.

Start: Follow the sign indicating GROSSE SCHEIDEGG—1½ HRS. This trail is entirely in the open, with nothing to block the magnificent views. A sign directs you ahead and slightly up to the left on the Panoramaweg.

This trail brings you directly to Grosse Scheidegg. Check the bus schedule outside the restaurant for the return to Grindelwald. The bus ride—on a steep, narrow, winding road—is an appropriate ending to a magnificent day. Take time to explore Grindelwald before returning to Lauterbrunnen or Wengen, via a change of train in Zweilütschinen.

Walk #7

Männlichen Top Station to Grindelwald
Walking Easy Time: 4 hours
Rating: Comfortable

Today's hike begins in Wengen, ascending to Männlichen by cable car. The downhill walk to Grindelwald through alpine meadows and pine forests is in the shadow of the great Bernese Oberland mountain peaks.

Directions: Follow the signs through Wengen to the Männlichen cable station and buy a one-way ticket to the top.

Start: As you leave the lift station, take the path marked GRINDEL-WALD—3 HRS., 10 MIN., but plan on four hours to complete this hike. Begin walking on a paved, descending road, under the Grindelwald–Männlichen gondolas. The path is blazed in red and white, and a red-and-white marker takes you to the right, from the paved path to a grassy trail across a meadow.

The trail crisscrosses the paved path—always follow signs and blazes to Grindelwald and Holenstein, the mid-station on the gondolas. In about ninety minutes you will have walked down 2000 ft. (610 m.) on a scenic meadow path to the middle station, where you have the option of proceeding to Grindelwald by gondola or continuing the walk (about two and a half more hours).

To continue, at Holenstein follow the signs to the right to Grindelwald Grund and Grindelwald Dorf. In about ten minutes you'll reach a paved road. Turn left and you'll see another paved road. Facing you, on a barn in a small pasture, is a Grindelwald *wanderweg* sign. Follow this sign on to a forest path. As you get closer to Grindelwald, follow signs to Grindelwald Dorf and the main railroad station. If you prefer not to walk up the hill to the main train station at Grindelwald Dorf, walk down to Grindelwald Grund and wait for the next train or bus leaving for the main station. At the main station, take the train to Zweilütschinen and change for the train to Lauterbrunnen or Wengen.

Walk #8

Pfingstegg Top Station to Stieregg to Pfingstegg to Café Milchbach to Hotel Wetterhorn—A Double Glacier Visit (Optional Walk to Grindelwald)
Walking Easy Time: 4 to 5 hours
Rating: More challenging

There is a double treat in store for *Easy Walkers* today. After taking the cable car from Grindelwald to Pfingstegg, the trail will ascend 984 ft. (300 m.) to Stieregg, at 5577 ft. (1700 m.), for a close look at the Unterer Grindelwaldgletscher. After returning to Pfingstegg, the path descends 1500 ft. (457 m.) to Café Milchbach and the Oberer Grindelwaldgletscher—the second glacier to be visited—with the possibility of walking into the glacier's ice caves. The hike ends with a walk to the Hotel Wetterhorn and a bus ride back to the Grindelwald station, or another hour's pleasant hike into Grindelwald from the hotel.

Directions: Take the train to Grindelwald (with a change in Zweilütschinen) and walk up the main shopping street, following the sign PFINGSTEGG BAHN. Purchase a one-way ticket to the 4564 ft. (1391 m.) Pfingstegg station.

Start: Follow STIEREGG—1 HR. to the right, heading toward the glacier, the trail blazed in red and white. The leading edge of the glacier becomes visible, and Männlichen can be seen on top of the mountain to the right. Within ninety minutes you'll reach the plateau overlooking the glacier; descend to Restaurant Stieregg, completing the first part of today's double glacier hike.

Return by retracing your steps to Pfingstegg and continue by following signs to Milchbach and Hotel Wetterhorn. The rest of today's hike is mostly downhill, except for a short rise before reaching the Café Milchbach. This path to Milchbach and Grindelwald is highlighted by rock formations revealing deposits representing a time span of eighty million years.

Unterer
Glacier

Stieregg
1700m.

Pfingstegg
1391m.

(S)

Oberer
Glacier

Milchbach
1348m.

(E)

Hotel Wetterhorn
1229m.

Grindelwald
1034m.

Follow directions to the Milchbach, with a terrace overlooking the glacier. From the cafe you can walk down to the Hotel Wetterhorn in twenty minutes by way of the Blue Grotto Ice Caves. The small admission charge allows you to walk through man-made tunnels into the glacier itself, with its brilliant blue color.

Continue on the path to the Hotel Wetterhorn, crossing a wide gravel auto road leading into the parking area across from the hotel. Buy a bus ticket for the short ride back to the Grindelwald station. Or, if you still feel fit, walk through the parking area to your left and follow a sign directing you through meadow and forest for a pleasant one-hour walk back to Grindelwald.

Walk #9

Grosse Scheidegg to Schwarzwaldalp to Rosenlaui to Zwirgi to Reichenbach Falls (Excursion to Gletscherschlucht Rosenlaui and Reichenbach Falls)

Walking Easy Time: 4½ hours (including forty-five-minute gorge walk and excursion to Reichenbach Falls)

Rating: Comfortable

Meiringen (home of the *meringue*) is not only rich in history, culture, and great walks, it also boasts the spectacular gorge at Rosenlaui and Reichenbach Falls, made famous as the spot where the evil Professor Moriarty "done in" Sherlock Holmes. Get an early start for today's excursion and hike because of the transportation involved on both ends of the trip. *NOTE: Check all train and bus schedules carefully and coordinate times before leaving. This trip is worth the extra effort involved.*

Directions: Take the train to Grindelwald (changing in Zweilütschinen). Walk 1 block from the train station to the bus *bahnhof* and take the bus to Grosse Scheidegg, an exciting ascent on a winding mountain road.

The trail above Wengen

Start: Follow the path with signs pointing through the meadow to Schwarzwaldalp, then to Rosenlaui—first on the road, then through a wide meadow along the Reichen River. Today's walk is particularly pretty in early summer, when the meadows are filled with wildflowers and gently meandering herds of bell-clanging cows. A half-hour from Schwarzwaldalp you'll arrive at Gletscherschlucht Rosenlui. The gorge walk begins at 4430 ft. (1350 m.) and rises over the torrent on stone steps through dark, cave-like tunnels, close to the wild and stormy rush of the glacial waters—climbing to 4922 ft. (1500 m.) at the top—and followed by a fifteen-minute descent.

Resume the walk down the road, reaching the old Rosenlui Hotel, with a sign pointing toward KALTENBRUNNEN—35 MIN. At Kaltenbrunnen, with a small restaurant, you have two choices:

1. Take the bus to the Meiringen train station.

2. Walk on to Zwirgi, where you can descend to the top of Reichenbach Falls for a visit; then take the ancient funicular down to Meiringen, where you follow signs to the *bahnhof*.

Either way, take the train to Interlaken Ost and change for the train to Lauterbrunnen and Wengen.

Walk #10

Planplatten Top Station to Balmeregghorn to Tannenalp to Engstlenalp
Walking Easy Time: 4 hours
Rating: More challenging

Use the Meiringen hiking map today. One of the most popular high-level walks in the Meiringen area—and a favorite of ours—is from Planplatten to Engstlenalp. You'll leave Meiringen on the Meiringen–Hasliberg lift, changing for the lift to the Planplatten peak, at 7366 ft. (2245 m.). You'll walk along the spine of the mountain, crossing over the Balmeregghorn, past the Melchsee and the Tannensee, and down to Engstlenalp, at 6070 ft. (1850 m.), where you'll return to Meiringen by bus.

Directions: Take the train to Interlaken Ost and change for the train to Meiringen. At the Meiringen bus station, make a reservation for the return from Engstlenalp to Meiringen. Walk up the main street to the Sherlock Holmes Hotel, turn left to the lift station, and take the cable car to Reuti, transferring to a gondola to Magisalp. Exit the station and take the lift to Planplatten, where the walk begins.

Hint: Plan a full day for this hike—it will be necessary to get an early start if you're coming from the base villages of Lauterbrunnen or Wengen. Make bus reservations for your return from Engstlenalp to Meiringen at the bus bahnhof in Meiringen (at the Meiringen train station) upon arrival.

Start: A sign directs you left— ENGSTLENALP—3 HRS. Be careful **not** to follow the sign to Engstlenalp Steiler Absteig—a lengthy, steep trail. The views from this path are exceptionally beautiful; after about forty minutes, you'll arrive at the Balmeregghorn for a climb to the peak (this takes from thirty to sixty minutes, depending on your pace). Walk down the other side of the peak, following signs to Engstlenalp and Tannenalp. When the path divides, take the mountain path up to your right, as the wider path continues down to Melchsee. The trail continues to be blazed white and red as you walk along the spine of the mountain. Follow the main trail to the right and down toward the Tannensee, following a sign indicating ENGSTLENALP—35 MIN. The rocky trail descends to Engstlenalp, at 6070 ft. (1850 m.). The bus stop is past the hotel, with the last bus leaving about 5:20 P.M. When you see the crowd at the bus stop, you'll be delighted that you made reservations.

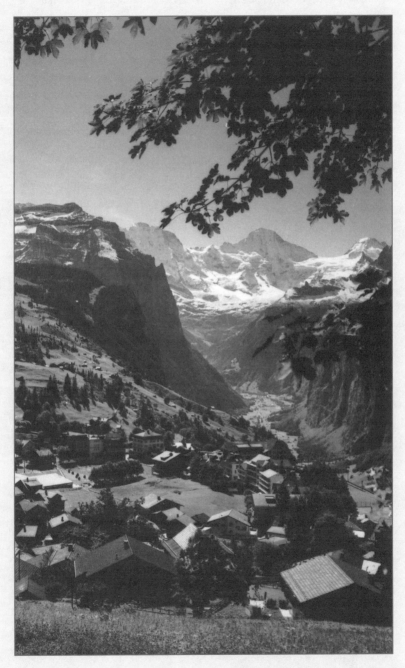

Wengen and the Lauterbrunnen Valley

Walk #11

Lauterbrunnen to Zweilütschinen to Wilderswil to Interlaken (Excursion to Interlaken)

Walking Easy Time: 3½ hours

Rating: Gentle

This walk can be reserved for a day when clouds or drizzle are not conducive to high-altitude exploration. The trail begins at the Lauterbrunnen train station. Walk down the station steps, turn right under the tracks, and follow the yellow *wanderweg* signs. The gentle path passes through the villages of Zweilütschinen and Wilderswil, then into Interlaken for an excursion. (See Excursion #6.) The appeal of today's low-level walk is that it can be shortened or extended at each train station, depending on the weather.

LENK

Lenk, at 3543 ft. (1080 m.), is nestled near the end of the bucolic Simmental, or Simmen, Valley, surrounded by lush, undulating alps filled with placidly grazing *Milka* cows, a special breed of cattle. The area is interlaced with comfortable paths in the shadow of snow-covered peaks, including the 10,640 ft. (3243 m.) Wildstrübel, with lifts bringing hikers to scenic mid- and high-level trails. Zweisimmen, the small village at the entrance to the Simmental, is headquarters for the Rinderberg lift, the beginning of a sensational high-level trek to Schönried, a neighbor of fashionable Gstaad. The hike from Iffigenalp to dramatic Iffigfall, through meadow and forest to Lenk, is another not-to-be-missed experience for *Easy Walkers*.

Lenk is off the beaten path, yet close enough to public transportation for day excursions to the castles at Spiez and Thun, steamer rides on Lake Thun, and shopping trips to Bern and Interlaken, along with panoramic rail excursions to Gstaad and Montreux. Lenk is also home to the New Orleans Jazz Festival and the Lenk Music Academy. If you appreciate good walking, we recommend Lenk, a village far from main roads and exhaust fumes, a beautiful corner of Switzerland.

Transportation

By Train - You always change in Zweisimmen for the local train to Lenk.

By Car - From western Switzerland, drive east to Zweisimmen. Turn south on the local road, driving through the Simmental to Lenk. From eastern Switzerland or the Bernese Oberland near Interlaken, drive to Spiez, then to Zweisimmen, picking up the local road into Lenk.

Favorite *Walking Easy* Hotel

Hotel Kreuz
Three-Star; Director—Familie Ischi-Michel
CH-3775 Lenk; **Tel:** 33 733 13 87; **Fax:** 33 733 13 40
Internet: www.kreuzlenk.ch
E-mail: kreuz.lenk@bluewin.ch

The outstanding, three-star Hotel Kreuz, located in the heart of the peaceful village of Lenk, is a charming, chalet-style hotel with large, modern guest rooms and public sitting rooms. The Kreuz boasts several restaurants—one for casual and bar service; another for the special, themed buffet dinner of the day, always accompanied by a full salad and appetizer bar. Half-board guests have the choice of any menu in any of these restaurants—a terrific bonus for Kreuz clients and *Easy Walkers.*

Excursions

The Lenk Tourist Information Office is located in the middle of town, between the train station and the Hotel Kreuz.

Fax: 33 733 20 27

Internet: www.lenk.ch

E-mail: info@lenk.ch

1. **Gstaad** - At an altitude of 3543 ft. (1080 m.), the chic village of Gstaad lies at the junction of four valleys. The area around Gstaad, called Saanenland, offers a 200-mile (322 km.) network of hiking trails and a variety of cable lifts. (See Gstaad section.)

   Directions: Take a train from Lenk to Zweisimmen and change for the train to Gstaad (about a one-hour trip).

2. **Spiez** - This charming town on the shore of Lake Thun boasts a medieval castle overlooking the lake and vineyards. (See Kandersteg, Excursion #2.)

   Directions: Take a train from Lenk to Zweisimmen, where you change for the train to Spiez (about a one-hour trip).

3. **Thun** - The medieval city of Thun, with its cobblestoned streets and famous castle, lies at the northern end of Lake Thun. (See Kandersteg, Walk #8.)

   Directions: Take a train to Zweisimmen, changing for the train to Spiez. Change again in Spiez for the train to Thun (one stop toward Bern).

4. **Interlaken** - Interlaken is a busy tourist center, surrounded by a superb mountain panorama. (See Lauterbrunnen, Excursion #6.)

   Directions: Take a train to Zweisimmen, changing for the train to Spiez. In Spiez, change for the train to Interlaken West—a trip of less than two hours.

Lenk Walks

Recommended Map:

   ❖ Lenk Wanderkarte Trail Map

Walk #1

Introductory Walk—Lenk to the Lenkersee along the Obersimmentaler Hausweg to Simmenfälle to Metsch Lift, Metsch Mid-Station to Lenk

Walking Easy Time: 3 to 3½ hours
Rating: Comfortable

If you arrive in Lenk early enough to spend about three hours on a low- to mid-level walk on your first day, this is a good introduction to the region. You'll walk past the Lenkersee (the tiny lake outside central Lenk), to the hamlet of Ey (Oey), all the way to Simmenfälle and its cascading waterfall, passing old, wooden farmhouses, some dating back to the seventeenth century—along the Obersimmentaler Hausweg. The Tourist Office can provide an English description of these landmark buildings. You'll then walk to the Metschbahn and take the cable car up to Metsch Mid-Station for the hike back to Lenk.

Start: Walk past the church, following the OBERSIMMENTALER HAUSWEG sign. A wide path leads past tiny Lenkersee on your left, a breeding ground for birds and waterfowl, and continues around the end of the lake. Turn right, following the signs for Hausweg. After passing through tiny Ey, proceed on the Hausweg path along the rapids of the Simme, through the forest. After walking about ninety minutes you'll reach the Hotel Simmenfälle. Walk past the hotel to the viewpoint overlooking the falls.

When ready, return to the hotel and walk for a half hour on the small, paved auto road, through Oberried, passing other houses on the Hausweg, all the way to the Metschbahn. Buy a one-way ticket to Metsch Mid-Station at 4856 ft. (1480 m.); on exiting, turn left, following the sign to Lenk. After about ten minutes, a sign directs you to Lenk through the forest on a somewhat steep trail. We prefer to pass this trail; walk straight ahead on the road for open views of the Simmental and note the sign reading LENK—50 MIN. After walking a half hour from Metsch, pass a sign indicating BRANDHUBEL 1295 M., and continue walking on the road. At the sign FUSSGANGER (footpath), turn left, then right, down the steps in the direction of the red-and-white arrow. Take the *bergwanderweg*, shortcutting the road through the meadows and forest, eventually leading to a wagon path. This descending path brings you into the center of Lenk.

Walk #2

Iffigenalp to Iffigfall to Schroand to Ey to Lenk

Walking Easy Time: 2½ hours

Rating: Comfortable

This fabulous hike should not be missed by *Easy Walkers*. Part of the fun is the bus ride from Lenk on a steep, winding mountain road to the start of the walk at Iffigenalp, at 5197 ft. (1584 m.), then descending on a forest trail to Iffigfall, at 4397 ft. (1340 m.), and hiking down along the waterfall. This hike is a favorite, offering many kinds of trails with views of the rolling alps of the Simmental and a bonus of dramatic Iffig Falls.

Directions: Take the private bus across from the *bahnhof* to Iffigenalp. Purchase your one-way bus ticket at the train station. The bus ascends 1693 ft. (516 m.) on a winding, narrow mountain road to Iffigenalp.

Start: Several hikes begin at this location. More adventurous walkers can continue up from Iffigenalp, at 5197 ft. (1584 m.), to the Iffigsee, at 6844 ft. (2086 m.), returning back to Iffigenalp (a four-hour round-trip hike) for the walk back to Lenk by way of the falls. Another hike that can be taken by *Easy Walkers* is the popular three-and-a-half-hour mountain hike to Simmenfälle. (See Walk #3.)

Today, *Easy Walkers* will follow the sign IFFIGFALL—40 MIN., passing a trail on the right marked SIMMENFÄLLE, and walking ahead on the auto road. About ten minutes from Iffigenalp, follow a *wanderweg* sign directing you down steps to the right, into the forest. This trail takes you along the river on your right, crossing the road several times; always continue on the marked *wanderweg*.

At one point, after crossing the road, you pass in front of a 600-year-old farmhouse. Stay on the main trail, walking past the bus stop sign, descending into the forest and crossing the bridge for a view of the falls. Follow the trail to the left to Poschenried, at 3937 ft. (1200 m.), where it is possible to depart from the trail to the Alpenrosli Restaurant and bus stop, if the weather turns bad. Return to the main trail, following the sign LENK—1 HR. 10 MIN. The trail narrows and ascends through a meadow, then enters the forest for the final descent into Ey. Follow signs past the Lenkersee into Lenk.

Centuries-old Swiss barns

Walk #3

Iffigenalp to Langermatte to Rezliberg/Sibe Brünne to Simmenfälle

Walking Easy Time: 3½ to 4 hours

Rating: More Challenging

Another popular walk from Iffigenalp, reached by bus as in Walk #2, is the hike that ascends from Iffigenalp, at 5197 ft. (1584 m.), along the Langermatte, at 6090 ft. (1856 m.), descending somewhat steeply to Rezliberg/Sibe Brünne, at 4610 ft. (1405 m.), along the Simme River, to the bus stop at Simmenfälle, at 3616 ft. (1102 m.).

Directions: See Walk #2.

Start: After exiting the bus at Iffigenalp, walk down the road for a few minutes to the sign directing you right, to Simmenfälle. The first ninety minutes ascends steadily from 5197 to 6090 ft. (1584 to 1856 m.), a rise of 892 ft. (272 m.), to Langermatte. This portion of the hike, under the Oberlaubhorn, should be taken slowly until you reach Langermatte, the high point of today's hike.

At this point the trail descends, somewhat steeply in areas, to the Rezliberg mountain restaurant, at 4610 ft. (1405 m.), along the Simme rapids. A short diversion to Sibe Brünne, the source of the Simme River, is a worthwhile stop. As you continue to descend, walk in the signed direction of Simmenfälle. At the falls, take the path down to the hotel, restaurant, and bus stop at Simmenfälle for the ride back to Lenk. If you feel fit, pick up the gentle path to Lenk behind the restaurant.

Walk #4

Zweisimmen/Rinderberg Top Station to Parwengen to Horneggli, Lift down to Schönried (Excursion to Gstaad)
Walking Easy Time: 2½ hours
Rating: Comfortable

Be sure to reserve the better part of a beautiful day for this lovely hike and excursion to the famous resort of Gstaad—this is one of the most scenic walks in the Bernese Oberland. You'll take the train from Lenk to Zweisimmen, ascend by gondola to Rinderberg, at 6575 ft. (2004 m.), and hike up to an exciting viewpoint for an incredible panorama. The hike continues on a comfortable trail along the spine of the mountain to Parwengen, where you'll walk in the direction of the next valley, home of the sophisticated mountain resort of Gstaad. The hike ends at the Horneggli chairlift for a descent to the Schönried train station and the short train ride to Gstaad. After visiting Gstaad, you'll return to Lenk by train via Zweisimmen.

Directions: Take a morning train to Zweisimmen and exit the train station, following signs to the Rinderberg Gondelbahn. Buy a one-way ticket to Top Station Rinderberg.

Start: See Gstaad, Walk #5.

Walk #5

Leiterli Top Station to Stüblenipass to Leiterli to Stoss Mid-Station
Walking Easy Time: 3½ to 4 hours
Rating: Comfortable

After taking the Betelberg Lift to Leiterli Top Station, at 6431 ft. (1960 m.), you will continue ahead to the Stüblenipass, at 6562 ft. (2000 m.), and return via the same trail to Leiterli Lift Station.

Although it is possible to take the gondola back down to Lenk at Leiterli, you might enjoy continuing the hike to Stoss Mid-Station, at 5361 ft. (1634 m.), then taking the lift down to Lenk.

Directions: At the church, follow signs to the Betelberg Lift, about a ten-minute walk. Purchase a one-way ticket to Leiterli Top Station.

Start: After exiting at Leiterli, walk ahead, following the sign STÜBLENI-PASS—1 HR., 15 MIN. (Flower lovers might wish to detour to the Alpenblumenweg, a signed alpine garden trail.) The trail winds comfortably around the mountain and passes a "geologically protected" area below, on the right. This marshland was formed millennia ago and is one of eighty-seven protected marsh areas in Switzerland. An ancient sea, it is now the highest marsh area in the Alps. Views are spectacular, with remote dairy farms dotting the alpine landscape above the tree line. There are some splinter paths along the way; stay on the main *bergweg* all the way to the pass at Stübleni. Here, *Easy Walkers* can continue as far as they wish, then continue back on the same path to Leiterli Lift Station. At Leiterli, you have a couple of options:

1. Continue the walk down to the mid-station by following signs to Stoss, taking the gondola to Lenk from there.
2. Take the gondola from Leiterli all the way down to Lenk.

Walk #6

The Luchs (Lynx) Trail—Leiterli to Wallegg to Lenk
Walking Easy Time: 3½ hours
Rating: Comfortable

Two lynx were caught near the Betelberg cable car and were fitted with transmitters in order to trace their activities. These shy, elegant animals choose only the most attractive areas for their home. Today's Lynx Walk is along a similar trail, and six lifelike fake lynx have been hidden close by. They are well camouflaged—so look carefully and see if you can spot them! You'll take the Betelberg Lift and return to Lenk through Siten and Wallegg.

Directions: Walk past the church, following signs up to the Betelberg Lift, and purchase a one-way ticket to Leiterli Top Station, at 6375 ft. (1943 m.).

Start: After exiting the lift, walk down in the direction you came from toward LENK, WALLEGG—2½ HRS. Follow red-and-white posts left, through the meadows to a small farmhouse and the sign *bergwanderweg*. Pass the farmhouse and walk on a little jeep road toward Siten and Lenk.

After passing Siten, walk down the steps toward Wallegg and Lenk. After crossing the bridge over the gorge, continue left along the gorge to the Hotel Wallegg, 4331 ft. (1320 m.) (closed on Wednesday). At the restaurant you have several options:

1. Take the bus back to Lenk.
2. Take the *schlucht* trail alongside the gorge to Lenk.
3. Continue down the road to the sign BÜEL, LENK, and turn right, into the forest on a mountain *bergweg*. Return to Lenk by following the LENK BAHNHOF signs.

Walk #7

Metschberg Top Station to Hahnenmoospass to Bühlberg to Simmenfälle to Lenk

Walking Easy Time: 2 to 5 hours

Rating: Comfortable

Today you'll visit the heights over the Simmental by taking the Metsch lifts to the top station at Metschberg, 6198 ft. (1889 m.), hiking to the Hahnenmoospass and continuing down to Bühlberg, at 5443 ft. (1659 m.). From Bühlberg there are several options to return to Lenk.

Directions: Take the private bus from the back of the *bahnhof* to the Metsch Lift Station. Buy a one-way ticket to the top and take the cable car to the mid-station, transferring to the purple *Milka* chairlift.

Start: After taking in the views, follow HAHNENMOOSPASS—30 MIN., directing you on a mountain path to the left. More adventurous walkers might wish to hike up to Metschstand and continue on to Hahnenmoospass by the high-ridge route—a bit more challenging. The lower route offers views of the soft, green alps overlooking the Simmental, while the high route to Hahnenmoospass gives you a 360-degree panorama.

There's a mountain hotel at Hahnenmoospass and a gondola descending the mountain in the direction of Adelboden. Today, however, you should follow the sign BÜHLBERG—45 MIN. At Bühlberg, you can exercise any one of three options:

1. Continue walking forty-five minutes from Bühlberg to the Metsch Mid-Station, taking the lift down to the base station for a gentle, half-hour valley walk back to Lenk. Or, if you wish, there's always the bus.

2. Continue to walk three hours from Bühlberg to Simmenfälle—through Metsch, Nessli, and Stalden—taking the bus back to Lenk.

3. Continue from Bühlberg to Mid-Station Metsch and return to Lenk, walking gently down the mountain, as described in Walk #1, another one and three-quarter hours from Bühlberg.

We recommend option #2—the hike from Bühlberg to Simmenfälle—an additional three hours of "more challenging" walking. Follow the signs to Simmenfälle, continuing ahead at the cutoff to the mid-station of the Metsch Lift. At the Simmenfälle bus stop near the hotel, take the bus back to Lenk.

KANDERSTEG

(Adelboden, Lötschental)

The village of Kandersteg has everything going for it—a central location in Switzerland's majestic Bernese Oberland, a profusion of quality hiking trails, and proximity to the Lötschberg Tunnel for quick access to southern Switzerland's impressive mountains, glaciers, and centuries-old villages. The charming lakeside towns of Thun, Interlaken, and Spiez are only a short train ride away, with Zermatt, home of the Matterhorn, an easy day excursion.

Kandersteg, at 3858 ft. (1176 m.), sits in a narrow valley sandwiched between towering mountain peaks. Hiking around Kandersteg includes a large network of trails—a gentle walk to the remarkable Blausee, a small, crystal-clear lake; a hike on the heights around Kandersteg, with views of the snow-covered Blümlisalp mountain range; a ramble through the Kander Gorge along the raging Kander torrent; and a trek to marvel at the unspoiled beauty of the Gasterntal (Gastern Valley). The mountain trails above Kandersteg lead from the Gemmi Pass down to the spa village of Leukerbad or up to Oeschinensee, a glacial lake set under high cliff walls. Walkers return year after year to comfortable hotels and breathtaking scenery around Kandersteg—a hiker's paradise and a perfect setting for *Walking Easy* in the Swiss Alps.

Transportation

By Train - From Zurich and the Zurich airport there are a few direct trains to Kandersteg. From points south of Kandersteg, change trains in Brig and ride north through the Lötschberg Tunnel.

By Car - From the north, drive to Spiez and follow signs south to Kandersteg. From the south, follow signs north to Goppenstein, where the car-train leaves every thirty minutes through the Lötschberg Tunnel. You'll remain in your car for the 9.5-mile (15 km.) trip, detraining in Kandersteg.

Favorite *Walking Easy* Hotel

Hotel Adler

Three-Star; Owners—Familie Fetzer

CH-3718 Kandersteg; **Tel:** 33 675 80 10; **Fax:** 33 675 80 11

Internet: www.chalethotel.ch

E-mail: info@chalethotel.ch

Kandersteg can be nominated as the hiking capital of Switzerland, and the Hotel Adler is in the center of this walkers' paradise. Cozy and comfortable, the Adler is under the caring eyes of the Fetzer family. Many rooms have balconies and hot tubs and are decorated with Swiss wood paneling. New amenities include spacious apartments and spa facilities and an indoor pool. The kitchen serves regional food, with a salad bar at dinner and Swiss buffet breakfast. The Adler is proud of its repeat clientele and caters to walkers. The Hotel Adler is always busy, so try to make reservations early. Ask for a quiet room in the back.

Excursions

The Kandersteg Tourist Office is located diagonally across the street from the Hotel Adler.

Fax: 33 675 80 81

Internet: www.kandersteg.ch

E-mail: info@kandersteg.ch

1. **Blausee (Blue Lake)** - The translucent, azure color of the Blausee is exceptionally beautiful. This small lake sits amid a network of paths winding through the surrounding forests. (See Walk #2.)

2. **Spiez** - This charming town on the shore of Lake Thun boasts a medieval castle, now a museum. Paths take walkers along Lake Thun, with a lovely waterside trail from Spiez to Faulensee, where you catch the boat back to Thun or Spiez or ahead to Interlaken West.

   Directions: Trains to Spiez run hourly from Kandersteg.

3. **Thun** - The medieval city of Thun, with its cobblestoned streets and famous castle, lies at the northern end of Lake Thun.

   Directions: Take the train to Thun through Spiez.

4. **Bern** - The capital of Switzerland is a delightful city, declared a "world landmark" by the United Nations. The Bern Tourist Office, inside the railroad station, can supply you with maps and sight-seeing suggestions. Walk into the Old Town, or *altstadt*, with its 3.5 miles (10 km.) of ancient

arcades, fountains, towers, and shops. Visit Theaterplatz and the **Clock Tower (Zytgloggeturm)**, Kornhousplatz and its much-photographed **Ogre Fountain**, and, of course, the famous **Bear Pits** for which the city is named.

Directions: Trains to Bern leave hourly for the one-hour ride.

5. **Interlaken** - Interlaken, named for its location between Lake Thun and Lake Brienz, is a busy tourist center, surrounded by a superb mountain panorama. (See Lauterbrunnen/Wengen, Excursion #6.)

Directions: Take the train to Spiez and change for the train to Interlaken West.

6. **Zermatt** - Zermatt is a tourist and hiking mecca encompassing some of the world's most magnificent scenery, including the mighty Matterhorn. (See Zermatt section.)

Directions: Trains leave hourly from Kandersteg to connect in Brig with the train to Zermatt.

Kandersteg Walks

Recommended Maps:

- ❖ Kandersteg Wanderkarte—Blausee, Leukerbad mit Üschintal, Gemmigebiet, Gasterntal, Oeschinensee, Hohtürlipass
- ❖ Kümmerly+Frey Wanderkarte—Lötschental
- ❖ Kümmerly+Frey—Adelboden

Walk #1

Selden to Heimritz to Selden to Waldhaus to Kandersteg—through the Gasterntal

Walking Easy Time: 3 to 4 hours

Rating: Comfortable

The Gasterntal, or Gastern Valley, was formed millennia ago, well before Walt Disney created his Magic Kingdom, but it surely must mean that Mr. Disney visited this dream valley for creative inspiration. The magic kingdom you will visit today ends at the leading edge of a great glacier, the source of the Kander River, which flows into Lake Thun. After arriving at Selden, you'll walk into the valley to Heimritz, with its tiny *gasthaus* and views of the glacier. You'll return to Kandersteg, walking through forests and over meadows, never far from the rushing Kander River, the Kander Waterfall, and the spectacular Kander Gorge.

Directions: A day before this trip is planned, make reservations through your hotel with the minibus for riding to Selden and walking back to Kandersteg. We recommend the 9:30 A.M. minibus across from the Kandersteg railroad station. Exit the bus in front of the Hotel Steinbock, after a ride on a narrow, one-way mountain road.

Start: Follow the sign to Heimritz, leading toward the distant mountains, gradually ascending from 5043 to 5364 ft. (1537 to 1635 m.). The view on the right is of the Kander River, with high mountains on

A church in Kandersteg

either side of a long, narrow, fertile valley. Within twenty-five minutes you'll reach Gasthaus Gletscher Heimritz. Walk past the *gasthaus* and around the bend for a magnificent view of the Alpetligletscher. *NOTE: If you wish, continue along the trail toward Kanderfirn and the glacier, remembering to leave enough time for the return walk to Kandersteg.*

When ready, retrace your steps to Selden for the two-and-a-half-hour hike to Kandersteg. Begin walking on the car road, but after fifteen minutes, follow signs pointing left toward Eggenschwand, Waldhaus and Kandersteg, on a *wanderweg*, blazed with a yellow diamond. The trail descends through the forest and empties on to a path signed KANDERSTEG AND WALDHAUS to the left. Crossing the river on a small bridge as directed, follow the path through an open meadow, passing through a sea of larch trees. The Balmhorn is on the left, with high, jagged peaks reflecting the sun and casting dancing images across the valley floor. Continue through the valley, passing a statue of a Swiss climber pointing to the Balmhornhütte. Follow the signs to Waldhaus and Kandersteg, and within ninety minutes from Selden you'll reach the Hotel Waldhaus, at 4456 ft. (1358 m.). A refreshment stop here is a must; the beer is cold, the *kuchen* is tempting, and the views are unforgettable.

Continue on the trail behind the hotel, toward Kandersteg. Reenter the forest and follow *wanderweg* blazes. Walk with the now raging Kander River on your right, and after fifteen minutes of descending, the rocky path recrosses the river as you enter the Kander Gorge. Walk on the auto road for a few minutes, but as the road turns left to enter a tunnel, follow signs to Eggenschwand and Kandersteg and turn right on a descending mountain path. This is an exciting part of the trail—traversing the gorge, feeling the power and the spray of the torrent. The path is rocky, so watch your step as you descend. The tranquil, green valley beyond Eggeschwand soon appears.

Cross the bridge to the right, and turn left as the path becomes a car road and enters the parking area of the Sunnbüel cable car. *Easy Walkers* have the option of returning to Kandersteg by bus or continuing on a half-hour stroll to the village.

Walk #2

Kandersteg to Blausee to Kandergrund (Excursion to Blausee)
Walking Easy Time: 2½ hours
Rating: Comfortable

The hike to Blausee from Kandersteg is a gentle walk along the Kander River, leaving Kandersteg, at 3858 ft. (1176 m.), and walking easily down to beautiful Blue Lake, at 2910 ft. (887 m.). About 15,000 years ago an avalanche shook the Kander Valley, and enormous chunks of ice thundered down the mountain. These ice blocks left crevices in the rocks, and the resulting hollows filled with water as the ice melted, forming tiny Blausee, or Blue Lake, famous for its trout.

Start: Walk to the railroad station and follow the sign marked BLAUSEE—1 HR., 15 MIN., through the parking area. As you head north in the direction of Blausee and Frutigen, the Kander River is on the right. In about ten minutes the path splits—stay on the right path, along the river. Continue on this *wanderweg*, walking under the railroad tracks and past the power station, following signs to Blausee. Continuing ahead on the main path, turn right as directed and follow the trail to Blausee, leaving the path continuing on to Frutigen. Crossing over the river, you reach the main auto road, with signs pointing to Blausee across the highway and left. Within ten minutes, note the sign announcing BLAUSEE—THE BLUE LAKE, back across the road to the left.

Pay an admission fee entitling you to visit the trout nursery and take a boat ride. You should plan to spend an hour or two visiting this lovely park—enjoying your picnic lunch and wandering on some of the forest paths.

Leave Blausee by the Rock Path and walk back to the road. Turn left on the sidewalk and continue down the hill toward Kandergrund. A few minutes after passing the Zoo Tierpark, a sign across the road points to Wanderweg Kandergrund. Take this *wanderweg*, walking through the meadow, in the direction of Inner Kandergrund Kirche. As you pass the church and arrive at intersecting paths, walk up the hill to the right, following the sign FRUTIGEN, SPITZRUTELI, AND KANDERGRUND.

This trail ascends into the forest, with spectacular views of the valley below. Follow the KANDERGRUND STATION—20 MIN. sign and turn sharply left on a narrow meadow path. This path continues to be blazed with the *wanderweg* diamond. The trail takes you through a turnstile and soon meets an auto road. Turn left through a tunnel, where the road enters the area of the rarely used Kandergrund railroad station. Follow the sign pointing down a paved, zigzagging path to the Kandergrund bus stop. Cross the road to wait for the bus to Kandersteg.

Walk #3

Kandersteg to Höhwald to Kandersteg (Excursion to Allmenalp)
Walking Easy Time: 2½ hours
Rating: Comfortable

Today's walk entices *Easy Walkers* with some of the dramatic scenery surrounding Kandersteg. You'll take the gondola up to Allmenalp, a plateau under the Bundespitz with a cheese-making dairy and restaurant. After returning by gondola to the valley floor, the walk will continue on the *höhweg* (high trail), along the Kandersteg heights.

Start: Facing the Kandersteg station, turn left and walk through the tunnel under the tracks. Turn left again so that you're walking with the tracks on your left. This signed path goes directly to the Allmenalp *luftseilbahn* (cable car). Buy a round-trip ticket. At the top, visit the cheese-making dairy and walk to the lookout point for spectacular views of the Kander Valley all the way to the Oeschinensee. Return by gondola to continue walking along the heights bordering Kandersteg.

Leave the base station and retrace your steps on the paved road. Make

A gentle *Walking Easy* trail

a left turn on the first road, marked PRIVAT STRASSE. Proceed through the meadow, passing the Waldrand ski lift on the right, walking in the direction of the waterfall. The road empties into a small parking area with a large, flower-bedecked house inscribed BUDDHIST KLOSTER, DHAMMAPALA. This charming, weathered *kloster* (monastery) is run by Buddhist monks.

A path enters the forest on the left side of the *kloster,* marked with the sign HÖH PANORAMAWEG. After ascending through the forest, the trail breaks out of the woods, passing a small wooden barn. Continue walking to an intersection and turn left to the Höh Panoramaweg. Within a few minutes, the mountain ranges that give this valley its special flavor come into view, including the jagged peak of the Doldenhorn up on the right, overlooking the valley. The trail continues through the alp.

Take a narrow mountain trail to the left, marked HÖH AND GOLITSCHENALP. Walk around a farmhouse and up the hill on a narrow trail leading to a high point for all-encompassing views. Follow this *wanderweg*, a grassy path through the meadow, passing through several wooden gates and crossing from one pasture to another.

Take the path down to the right marked KANDERSTEG WALDWEG—30 MIN. Cross the wagon road and pass to the right of a small cabin, entering into a forest area. Within a minute the yellow, diamond-blazed trail splits. Take the left trail for a ten-minute descent through the forest to the road below. Turn left on the road in the signed direction of Bühl and Kandersteg. The road winds around the mountain, and at a major intersection marked KAN-

DERSTEG to the right and BLAUSEE to the left, turn left, as if walking to Blausee, then make an immediate right turn. Walk through the power station and tunnel, under the highway, continuing on the path back to Kandersteg.

Walk #4

Kandersteg to Eggeschwand, Sunnbüel to Spittelmatte to Schwarenbach to Sunnbüel

Walking Easy Time: 3½ hours
Rating: Comfortable

Your first part of the trip is the thirty-minute walk from Kandersteg to Eggeschwand, where you'll board the cable car for the ride up to the 6345 ft. (1934 m.) Sunnbüel Station. You'll walk through the Spittelmatte meadows and then ascend to Schwarenbach, at 6759 ft. (2060 m.), with a restaurant, returning to the lift station on a new path.

Directions: Follow the sign STOCK GEMMI, walking past the Hotel Schweizerhof to Eggeschwand. Buy a round-trip ticket.

Start: At the top follow the sign SCHWARENBACH—1 HR., 15 MIN. Proceed down and through the Spittelmatte meadow, as if walking through the center of a large punch bowl. After about forty minutes, you can picnic at the working dairy farm on your right with a snack of fresh milk and cheese.

The path ascends, with directions HOTEL SCHWARENBACH—30 MIN. painted on a rock. Don't believe it! Fifty minutes is more realistic for *Easy Walkers*, as this path ascends more steeply to reach Schwarenbach, at 6759 ft. (2060 m.).

Take the same path back toward Spittelmatte and the lift station, but just before the dairy farm you passed earlier in the day, note the sign pointing left to Arvenseeli. This *bergweg* is blazed red and white and meanders around the Arvenwald and its small lake (Arvenseeli—usually dry in late summer), ending at the lift station. Of course you can also stay on the main path all the way to the lift station. The Sunnbüel cable car descends to Eggeschwand, and you can walk back to Kandersteg or take the bus outside the lift station.

NOTE: *Another version of this walk is an exciting and rewarding full-day's excursion and three-and-a-half-hour hike over the Gemmi Pass from Leukebrad. You would not want to do both walks—just one or the other. This alternate version starts from Leukerbad, taking the lift up to the Gemmi Pass, walking past the Daubensee to Schwarenbach, then to the Sunnbüel Lift. It's best to take this version on a Saturday or Sunday, when a morning bus goes directly to Leukerbad from the train station at Goppenstein, one stop south of Kandersteg. Ask at the Tourist Office for a Gemmi Pass hiking map and transportation details.*

Walk #5

Schwandfeldspitz Top Station to Adelboden (Excursion to Adelboden)
Walking Easy Time: 2 hours
Rating: Comfortable

(Use the Adelboden map.) Today's hike is a good way to become acquainted with Adelboden, a resort in the Bernese Oberland. You will take a lift to the top of the Schwandfeldspitz, then proceed along Tschenten Alp. The trail follows the Hornliweg, and at Hörnli you will descend on a comfortable wagon path into Adelboden for the bus ride back to Frutigen and the return train to Kandersteg.

Directions: Take a morning train one stop from Kandersteg to Frutigen. Catch the connecting bus outside the Frutigen train station for the thirty-minute scenic ride to Adelboden. Arriving in Adelboden, exit the bus station, turn right, and walk toward the center of town, where a sign directs you to the Schwandfeldspitz Lift. Purchase a one-way ticket for this gondola, rising to 6400 ft. (1951 m.).

Start: Outside the top lift station, follow the signs TSCHENTENEGG—15 MIN., HÖRNLI—50 MIN., and ADELBODEN—1 HR., 50 MIN. Walk to the right, up and over a small grassy meadow, following the trail down the ridge of Tschentenegg. After about twenty minutes, *ignore* a sign indicating ADELBODEN—1 HR. Do *not* take this steep trail, but walk ahead following HÖRNLI—30 MIN., ADELBODEN—1 HR. You are now at Tschentenegg, and within a short time you'll arrive at a split in the path—the left marked LECHTERWEG and the right marked STEILERWEG. *Steiler* means steep in German, and while we have descended this trail, we recommend taking the easier path to the left. Both forest trails eventually lead to a small grassy plain, the entire valley visible in front of you. The level of descent eases on a path now marked not only with the familiar *wanderweg* diamond but, in rockier spots, with white-and-red blazes. You'll soon reach an overlook with benches and signs pointing to Adelboden.

Turn right and follow the sign ADELBODEN—30 MIN., UNTER HÖRNLI—which means "to Adelboden by the lower trail." This blazed path descends gently through the forest, eventually reaching the meadows and suburbs around Adelboden. Within another ten minutes you'll reach the bottom of the road. Turn right for the bus station and the return to Frutigen, where you catch the train to Kandersteg.

Walk #6

Lauchernalp Top Station to Weissenreid to Blatten—through the Lötschental
Walking Easy Time: 3 hours
Rating: Comfortable

The day we took our hike, the little handmade weather sign at the Kandersteg train station ticket office showed a happy, sunny face in *die Lötschental*—the Lötschen Valley—while the weather in Kandersteg was marginal, with low, ominous clouds. You, too, may find this a great opportunity to visit the other side of the mountains. The Lötschental appears to be lifted from another century. In fact, it was isolated for centuries, until roads and the Lötschberg Railway were built in the early 1900s. Each small village has managed to maintain much of the culture and character of the region, including many of the old wooden barns, some in the traditional Valaisian *mazot* style.

Today you'll depart from the more traditional trail walks in order to wander by road through one of these old mountain villages, filled with centuries-old barns and homes. The walk begins at Lauchernalp Top Station, then winds up and around on the Höhenweg to Tellialp. Here you will take a mountain road through the charming old hamlet of Weissenried and continue down to Blatten, another traditional village.

Directions: Catch the morning train (before 9:30 A.M.) from Kandersteg to Goppenstein, the first stop after a short ride through the Lötschberg Tunnel. Leave the station, following signs to the Lötschental–Lauchernalp bus, and take the bus marked LAUCHERNALP–WILER to Wiler, where you take the Lauchernalp cable car. Buy a one-way ticket to the top.

Start: At the top station, at 6562 ft. (2000 m.), follow the signs toward FAFLERALP—2 HRS., 30 MIN. on the Lötschentaler Höhenweg. Look north to see the impressive Langgletscher and the Lonza River flowing through the long, narrow valley below. Continue on an ascending, yellow-blazed trail as it turns and rises gently around the side of the mountain.

After you reach a high point of 6760 ft. (2060 m.), the path begins to descend for the remainder of the walk. It winds through the mountain town of Weritzalp, narrowing here and taking on more of the *bergweg* character of a traditional mountain trail. Enter onto a shaded forest path, rocky at times, and continue to descend along this trail toward Fafleralp. The blazes turn red and white, alerting walkers to be more cautious, as you proceed to Tellialp, easily recognized by a small bridge and a rushing waterfall. At Tellialp, with a new restaurant, a sign indicates the way to Fafleralp, up to the left, or to Blatten and Reid, descending to the right on a wagon path. *Easy Walkers* have two options at this point:

1. Walk on to Fafleralp, catching the bus to Goppenstein.
2. Walk down to Blatten through Weissenried, our suggestion for today.
   If you decide on Option #2, turn right and walk on the small road, rejecting a path going down the mountain on a trail to your left. Stay on the main wagon road to Weissenried—the reason we took you in this direction. Walk slowly through this tiny mountain hamlet, with its chapel built in the 1700s. The village is filled with marvelous photographic opportunities; walking through Weissenried is like strolling through a small Swiss museum. When you're ready, follow signs to the picturesque village of Blatten, where you catch the bus back to Goppenstein, timed to meet the return train to Kandersteg.

Today was spent walking through one of the most beautiful and isolated valleys in Switzerland, with a tantalizing glimpse of the Switzerland that used to be—and still is in many areas of *die Lötschental*!

Walk #7

Oeschinensee Lift Top Station to Oeschinensee to Kandersteg (Excursion to Oeschinensee)
Walking Easy Time: 2 hours
Rating: Comfortable

Kandersteg is blessed not only with glaciers, snow-covered peaks, and fabulous walking trails but also with one of the prettiest mountain lakes in the Bernese Oberland. You will visit the Oeschinensee by taking a chairlift from Kandersteg to the top station, at 5519 ft. (1682 m.). A thirty-minute walk to the lake descends to 5177 ft. (1578 m.), where you can boat, swim, picnic, or *spazier* (ramble) before the return walk to Kandersteg. A new option is to take a horse-and-wagon ride from the top lift station to the lake, which is surrounded by the Doldenhorn and Blümlisalp and their glaciers.

Directions: Walk past the Tourist Office to the second sign directing you to the Oeschinensee Chairlift. Purchase a one-way ticket to the top station.

Start: Follow the path to Oeschinensee. All trails lead down to the lake. From the lake you can meander on trails on either side, rent a boat, and enjoy the spectacular views.

When ready, walk up and around the Hotel Oeschinensee to a group of signs. Follow directions KANDERSTEG—1 HR. along the gravel path. After about five minutes, a *wanderwege* enters the forest on the right. You can continue on the road (the easier way down), or follow the *wanderweg* paths all the way into Kandersteg.

Walk #8

Excursion to Thun and Walk to the Lake Towns
Walking Easy Time: 1 to 3 hours
Rating: Gentle

The small city of Thun is an ideal location for a visit, not only when the weather is fair but also when it is cloudy or drizzling—conditions not conducive to high-level walking. Thun is the largest and most important town in the Bernese Oberland, situated on the beautiful Thunersee (Lake Thun) and easily reached by train. It has a delightful Old Town section, with a castle currently serving as a museum. While there are high-altitude walks around Thun, we are bringing you there in less than ideal weather because the lakeside walks around Thun can help to brighten an otherwise dreary day.

Directions: Take the train through Spiez to Thun. The Thun Tourist Office is located outside the train station and to the left. City maps are available.

Start: As you leave the railroad station and enter the main shopping district, follow signs with a symbol of a castle. After a fifteen-minute walk, enter the castle area through ancient fortress walls dating back to the twelfth century. The main center of attraction is the Knight's Hall, a large room paneled in tapestries, with a fine collection of fifteenth-century weapons.

After exploring the castle and Thun's many shops, walk down and around the hill, back toward the railroad station and the canal you crossed earlier. Note a group of signs with directions for walks along scenic Lake Thun. Turn left, in the direction of Oberhofen, and walk on the path along the canal, leaving the center of Thun. After walking forty minutes, note the steamer stop at Hunibach, with several options, again depending on the weather:

1. You can follow the same lake path back to Thun and take the train back to Kandersteg.

2. On leaving Hunibach, walk in the direction of Hilterfingen, where another castle awaits you—Castle Hünegg—more elaborate than Thun castle. It's situated in a parklike setting, with the small village and its mountains as a backdrop. From Hilterfingen, follow signs to Oberhofen and another medieval castle. Hunibach, Hilterfingen, and Oberhofen are all regularly scheduled steamer stops for the return to Thun, where you change for the train to Kandersteg.

3. From any lake village, take the boat to Interlaken West and the train to Spiez, where you change for the Kandersteg train.

GSTAAD

(Saanenland)

Sophisicated Gstaad, Switzerland's "Aspen of the Alps," enjoys a unique, worldwide reputation—*the* place to be for Europe's jet set. Situated in a quiet alpine location in southwestern Switzerland, Gstaad is close enough for one-day excursions to Montreux and its summer Jazz Festival on the shores of Lake Geneva, Lausanne with its Olympic Museum, the formidable peaks and glaciers of Les Diablerets at the Col du Pillon, and the picturesque cheese-producing village of Gruyères and its medievel castle.

Gstaad boasts exclusive shops, gourmet restaurants, two world-renowned five-star hotels, a well-maintained car-free walking street, and the Swiss Open Tennis tournament—usually held the second week in July. But most important to *Easy Walkers* is the little-publicized fact that the Gstaad area has an outstanding network of lifts and more than 185 miles (300 km) of summer hiking trails tailored for all levels of ability.

Gstaad is recognized as the unofficial capital of Saanenland—the last outpost of the Bernese Oberland, the valley adjacent to the Simmental and the *Walking Easy* base village of Lenk. Saanenland's traditional villages of Saanen, Saanenmöser, Gsteig, Lauenen, Turbach, and Schönried are all part of the impressive Swiss public transportation system—frequent trains and buses tied into the beginning and ending points of *Walking Easy* trails. Switzerland's alpine heritage is nurtured in Saanenland; its mountain farming, cheese-making, and chalet-style architecture are still a way of life, along with a lively music scene—a perfect combination for *Walking Easy*.

Transportation

By Train - From Geneva (two and a half hours) take the train to Montreux and change for the train to Gstaad. From the Bernese Oberland area, take the train from Spiez to Zweisimmen and change for the train to Montreux, stopping in Gstaad.

By Car - From the north and Spiez, head southwest on Route 11. From the south you can pick up Route 11 outside Aigle.

Favorite *Walking Easy* Hotel

Hotel Bernerhof

Four-Star; Owners—Claudia and Thomas Frei

CH-3780 Gstaad; **Tel:** 33 748 88 44; **Fax:** 33 748 88 40

Internet: www.bernerhof-gstaad.ch

E-mail: bernerhof@gstaad.ch

The Hotel Bernerhof is located in the center of town on Gstaad's main walking street. All rooms and suites have private facilities, balconies, minibar, and TV; every guest has the use of a plush terry robe to wear around the indoor pool, sauna, and steam rooms. Book with half-board, as guests can choose from three excellent restaurants in the hotel, one of which offers outstanding Oriental specialties. The hotel is open year-round and is geared to *Easy Walkers*, offering daily walking tours and the use of Lowa hiking boots. Many *Easy Walkers* will appreciate special discounts for senior guests.

Excursions

The Gstaad Tourist Information Office is located on the main walking street.

    Fax: 33 748 81 33

    Internet: www.gstaad.ch

    E-mail: gst@gstaad.ch

1. **Les Diablerets** - From the Col du Pillon, or Pillon Pass, cable cars transport visitors up to a spectacular panorama of ice and snow, with snow bus tours available on Glacier 3000.

   Directions: Take the bus to Col du Pillon and the cable lifts to the top station.

2. **Montreux** - Stretching along the shores of Lake Geneva in what is called the Vaud Riviera because of its exceptionally mild climate, Montreux is home to **Chillon Castle**, made famous by the poet Lord Byron. Above Montreux is **Rochers-de-Naye**, at 6700 ft. (2042 m.), reached by rack railway. Montreux is also home to the world-famous **Jazz Festival**, beginning the first Friday in July and lasting two and a half weeks.

   Directions: Take the train to Montreux—the Panoramic Express with its special windows and comfortable seats, if possible.

3. **Gruyères** - This tiny fortified village is perched on a hillside dominated

by a fifteenth-century castle. The cobblestone streets are lined with ancient houses, and the village is car-free between Easter and November. A model dairy, making the famed Gruyère cheese, is in operation at the entrance to the town, at the foot of a hill near the train station.

Directions: *Take a morning train from Gstaad to Montbovon. Change for the train to Gruyères—about a seventy-minute ride.*

Gstaad Walks

Recommended Map:
- ❖ Wanderkarte Saanenland—Gstaad Saanenland

Walk #1

Introductory Walk—The Menuhin Trail
Walking Easy Time: 1 to 2 hours
Rating: Comfortable

Today's short, low-level walk from Gstaad to its neighboring village of Saanen is a fine introduction to the Saanenland if you arrive too late in the day to attempt a longer and more strenuous hike. The return to Gstaad can be along the same path or by train. Violinist Lord Yehudi Menuhin was an integral part of the summer music community for many years and is the commune's honorary citizen. This trail is dedicated to him—with panels in three languages reflecting the thoughts and philosophy of this world-famous musician.

At Alpenruhe, the halfway mark, walkers can visit a Yehudi Menuhin room to view books, CDs, and videos about his philosophy and works. The walk ends in Saanen at the Mauritius Church, in which Lord Menuhin played and conducted many concerts.

Start: In Gstaad, leave the Kapälliplatz in the direction of Saanen. Pass the Atelier d'Artiste and walk under the train tracks. Continue toward Gschwend and follow the Saane River to the Bellerive restaurant, where you pick up a pleasant, shady path that follows the river. Turn right to the Alpenruhe, and visit the Menuhin Room. Walk across the area called Salzwasser as far as the Chouflisbach. By following this stream you reach the river again—head for Saanen and end the walk at the Saanen church. This path recalls the great artist and is intended to stimulate quiet reflection. To return to Gstaad, return on the same path, or take the train or bus at the *bahnhof.*

Walk #2

Lauenensee to Gstaad
Walking Easy Time: 3 hours
Rating: Comfortable

Today you'll take a bus to the far end of the valley that rises easily from Gstaad, at 3416 ft. (1041 m.), to the Lauenensee, at 4137 ft. (1261 m.). After rambling around the lake, you'll walk back to Gstaad by way of Lauenen. The path is never far from the rushing Louisbach and is generally made up of a *wanderweg* through meadow and forest, close enough to the road and bus to Gstaad, if needed.

Directions: Take a morning bus from the Gstaad bus station, next to the train station, to Lauenensee. (If you are using a Swiss Pass, there is a small supplement from Lauenen to Lauenensee.)

Start: After exiting the bus at Lauenensee, follow the sign LAUE-NENSEE—5 MIN. As you pass the lake on your left, the path splits. Take the wider path ahead, marked HINTEREMSEE, and you will be walking to Lauenen. It takes about an hour to reach the outskirts of Lauenen, with the path emptying to the Hotel Alpenland and its wonderful restaurant, the Rösti Factory, offering many delicious variations of the famous Swiss national dish.

When ready, walk up the gravel path next to the restaurant. Cross the little bridge and immediately take the trail on your right into the woods, following a sign marked *wanderweg* GSTAAD—2 STD. This path alternates between a *wanderweg* (always signed) and a small country road. You can remain on the road, but for a more scenic walk, follow the yellow *wanderweg* arrows all the way to Gstaad.

Walk #3

Wispile Top Station to Gsteig
Walking Easy Time: 3½ to 4½ hours
Rating: Comfortable to more challenging

This popular hike begins at the top station of the Wispile Lift. The trail continues comfortably along the ridge of the Höhe Wispile to Chrinepass (Krinnenpass), where you have the option of descending three different ways. The views from the ridge trail are sensational—high-mountain peaks in all directions. *NOTE: Try to take this hike during dry weather—these trails can be muddy and slippery when wet.*

Directions: Take a morning bus marked GSTEIG from the bus *bahnhof*. Exit after a few minutes' ride at the Wispile Lift Station. Remain in the gondola to the top station at 6267 ft. (1910 m.).

Start: Follow signs KRINNENPASS—1HR., 20 MIN., (this may take *Easy Walkers* somewhat longer). You are now walking on the Meteopfad, or Weather Trail, which rises to 6365 ft. (1940 m.) at the peak, where a group of photogenic llamas greet you. This

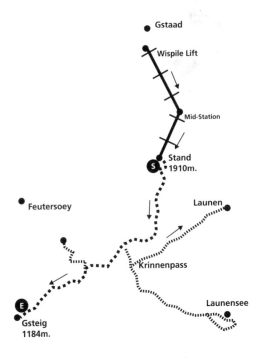

is the high point of today's hike. Continue ahead, following the *wanderweg* and Krinnenpass signs.

The Meteopfad turns around to the left as you descend ahead. You eventually arrive at a narrow entry with a descent to the right, signed to Gsteig, or a descent on the left trail to Krinnenpass, Lauenen, and the Lauenensee. This is where three options become available:

1. Follow the descending left trail to Krinnenpass, where the trail splits again. You can either hike down to Lauenen, a somewhat steep trail, with a bus return to Gstaad or take Option #2.

2. Follow signs for a steep descent down to the Krinnenpass (Chrinepass). From the pass you climb about 330 ft. (100 m.) to reach a path that slopes gently down to the Lauenensee nature reserve. At Lauenensee, take the bus to Gstaad.

3. The forest trail descending to Gsteig is our option today, because we visited the Lauenensee in Walk #2.

With Option #3, descend through the forest in the direction of Gsteig until you arrive at signs to Gsteig and Feutersoey. Walk through the gate, following the trail marked GSTEIG, continuing to descend through the meadow to a small farm with a sign on the other side of the barn. The sign points down to the right, along a wagon path, to the road below. Follow the yellow arrows on the road and the *wanderweg* signs, which shorten the descent by using forest trails cutting off the mountain road. In Gsteig, take the bus to return to Gstaad.

Walk #4

Eggli Top Station to Vorder Eggli to Saanen
Walking Easy Time: 3 hours
Rating: Comfortable

Today's walk combines an interesting visit to a working dairy farm, run by a friendly Swiss couple, with views of the rolling alps of Saanenland. At the farm you have the opportunity of tasting fresh milk and cheese made the old-fashioned way.

Directions: Walk, or take the bus stopping at the Eggli Lift Station. Buy a one-way ticket to the top.

Start: From Eggli Station, at 5118 ft. (1560 m.), follow signs to Vorder Eggli, a rise of 330 ft. (100 m.) along a wagon path. Visit the friendly couple at the rustic dairy and cheese-making cabin. They also serve fresh mountain products, so don't forget to taste the cheese. At the dairy at Vorder Eggli, you have several options:

1. Continue ahead, with the wagon road becoming a descending, narrow, mountain auto road with little traffic. You'll walk through Chalberhoni (Kalberoni) all the way to Saanen, where you can take the train back to Gstaad or pick up the river trail for an hour's stroll into Gstaad along the Menuhin Path.

2. Retrace your steps back toward Eggli Top Station where you can take the path down to Saanen (shorter than Option #1). In Saanen, take the train to Gstaad. As you descend the hill to Saanen, there is an option to walk directly back to Gstaad—just follow the signs.

Walk #5

Zweisimmen/Rinderberg Top Station to Parwengen to Horneggli
Walking Easy Time: 2½ hours
Rating: Comfortable

Reserve the better part of a beautiful day for one of the most scenic walks in the Bernese Oberland. You'll take the train from Gstaad to Zweisimmen, ascend by gondola to Rinderberg, at 6575 ft. (2004 m.), and hike up to an exciting viewpoint. The hike continues on a comfortable trail along the spine of the mountain, ending at the Horneggli Chairlift for a descent to Schönried and a train back to Gstaad.

Directions: Take a morning train to Zweisimmen and exit the train station, following signs to the Rinderberg Gondelbahn. Buy a one-way ticket to Top Station Rinderberg.

Start: Follow the large sign HOHENWEG NACH HORNEGGLI. Walk up to the *gipfel* (peak), at 6821 ft. (2079 m.), and check out the incredible panorama of the Bernese Oberland mountains. The trail continues—with minor ascents and descents, many of which are stepped for comfort—along Gandlouenengrat ridge to Parwengen, at 6024 ft. (1836 m.). Here follow directions to Hornberg and the Horneggli Lift. After passing two mountain restaurants at Hornberg, follow HORNEGGLI CHAIRLIFT—20 MIN. Walk through the meadow and down a mountain *bergweg* to the chairlift (buying your ticket at the bottom), and follow signs to the Schönried *bahnhof* for the next train or bus to Gstaad.

Walk #6

Château-d'Oex/La Braye Top Station to Château-d'Oex (Excursion to Château-d'Oex)

Walking Easy Time: 2 hours

Rating: Comfortable

The French-speaking village of Château-d'Oex (pronounced "chateau day") is in the Vaud canton, near the Bernese Oberland border. After walking in the lovely rolling countryside surrounding the village—where the famous l'Etivaz cheese is still produced in some 150 chalet dairies—visit the Musée du Vieux Pays d'Enhaut (Traditional Museum), located on three floors of an old chalet. At the end of town is the eighteenth-century Etambeau Chalet (also part of the museum).

Directions: Take the train from Gstaad to Château-d'Oex, about a fifteen-minute ride in the direction of Montreux. In the village follow signs for the five-minute walk to La Braye cable car. Exit at Mid-Station Pra-Perron, at 4003 ft. (1220 m.), and enter the covered chairlift for the ride to the top station, at 5414 ft. (1650 m.)

Start: Exit and follow signs to the right reading PRA-PERRON—50 MIN. and CHATEAU D'OEX 1 STD., 40 MIN. The descent from the top is on a gentle wagon path with lovely views of the surrounding countryside, eventually turning into a small, paved, rarely used mountain road. After about fifty minutes, a sign on a barn points through the meadows to the Pra-Perron Mid-Station and the cable down to the village. Or continue walking into Château-d'Oex. With either option, pay a visit to the museum before returning by train to Gstaad.

Walk #7

Arnensee to Feutersoey
Walking Easy Time: 2 hours
Rating: Comfortable

Directions: Take the only morning (10:00 A.M.) bus from Gstaad *bahnhof* to Arnensee, at 5059 ft. (1542 m.). Check current bus schedules.

Start: On exiting at the Arnensee, there are two options to return to Feutersoey. One is on an ascending, more challenging mountain *bergweg*; the other is on a descending *wanderweg* along the Tscharzisbach (river) via Linders Vorschess into Feutersoey, at 3708 ft. (1130 m.), where you take the bus back to Gstaad.

Walk #8

Saanen to Unterbort to Rougemont
Walking Easy Time: 2 hours
Rating: Comfortable

Today's walk brings beautiful views of the surrounding Alpes Vaudoises, ending in a tiny village, home to a tenth-century church nestled under a huge, sloping roof. The inside of the church is typically early Romanesque, but the adjoining sixteenth-century chateau was rebuilt in 1973. The church, ancient castle, and traditional chalets all contribute to Rougemont's unique historical charm.

Directions: Take the train from Gstaad to Saanen.

Start: At the Saanen train station, cross the main road, walk past the church, at 3317 ft. (1011 m.), and follow the street toward Unterbort. A well-kept path now leads to Point de la Scie, at 3599 ft. (1097 m.); La Sausse, at 3717 ft. (1133 m.); and finally Rougemont, at 3304 ft. (1007 m.). In Rougemont stop for a few minutes at the church before taking the train for the ten-minute ride to Gstaad.

VALAIS

SAAS-FEE

(SAAS VALLEY)

Saas-Fee is a picturesque, traffic-free village of 1,300 residents located high on a glacial ridge, at 5906 ft. (1800 m.), in the southern Valais Region of Switzerland. One end of this alpine village narrows gently into serene pastures, ending abruptly as mountains and glaciers rise almost vertically, appearing to encircle and swallow the tiny enclave. Saas-Fee, the "Pearl of the Alps," sits beneath a giant, frozen wave of ice and snow.

This charming resort attracts walkers of all ages, anxious to sample trails through woods filled with the aroma of pine needles, around gorges surging with cascading streams, and over rocks and ridges surrounded by breathtaking panoramas. Saas-Fee is ringed by more than a dozen mountains over 13,000 ft. (3962 m.), including the Dom, at 14,941 ft. (4554 m.), the highest mountain entirely in Switzerland; and in the distance, the imposing Monte Rosa, at 15,204 ft. (4634 m.), the tallest mountain in Switzerland, with its south face in Italy. The long, narrow Saastal, or Saas Valley, lies below the village of Saas-Fee, offering remarkable hiking options.

Saas-Fee is dotted with centuries-old feed barns called *mazots*, cornered on four to six round, flat, chiseled stones that serve as elevated foundations so that feed for livestock can be stored safe from rodents during cold winter months. These remarkable landmark buildings serve as a reminder of earlier days, proudly standing along the streets and meadows of Saas-Fee.

Modern-day Saas-Fee has evolved from an ancient mule path into chic walking and shopping streets, a center for several international music festivals with almost 174 miles (280 km.) of well-signed trails beckoning *Easy Walkers*.

Transportation

By Train and Bus - Take the train to Brig and change for the bus to Saas-Fee, located outside the train station. The PTT bus is the only form of public transportation into Saas-Fee.

By Car - At Visp, head south to Stalden, where the road splits—take the left fork to Saas Grund, following signs and ascending the mountain into car-free Saas-Fee. Park in the covered or open-air car park at the entrance to the village and call your hotel for pickup in its electric cart. A discount on parking fees is available with your guest card and should be validated in the Tourist Office.

Favorite *Walking Easy* Hotel

Hotel Etoile

Three-Star; Owners—Rolf and Daniela Bumann-Williner

CH-3906 Saas-Fee; **Tel:** 27 958 15 50; **Fax:** 27 958 15 55

Internet: http://www.saas-fee.ch/etoile

E-mail: hotel.etoile@saas-fee.ch

The Etoile is located in a quiet area of Saas-Fee, with balcony rooms overlooking the glaciers. The cuisine is regional Valais-style, and a typical Swiss buffet breakfast is served by a friendly staff. This family-operated hotel has twenty-two cozy rooms with modern bath facilities, TV, and minibar. The garden area with comfortable lounges provides a quiet place to relax after a day of hiking. Because Saas-Fee is a car-free village, call the hotel on arrival to be picked up. Rolf Bumann is an expert hiker and climber and can help you enjoy the trails in the Saas-Fee area. Evenings may feature a cookout in the spacious garden featuring fun and games inspired by Rolf's musical talent on the accordion. *Easy Walkers* will enjoy the homelike ambience at the Etoile, made possible by Rolf, Daniela, and their two children.

Excursions

The Saas-Fee Tourist Office is located across the street from the bus terminal.

Internet Saas-Fee: www.saas-fee.ch
E-mail Saas-Fee: to@saas-fee.ch
Internet Saas Valley: www.saastal.ch

Walking Easy trail

From mid-June to mid-October, the **Seven-Day Saas Valley Hiking Pass**, available at cable stations, can be used for unrestricted use of all lifts in the Saas Valley, the PTT bus from Saas-Balen to Saas-Fee to the Mattmark Reservoir, and free entry to the Ice Pavilion at Mittelallalin and the Saas Museum. One passport-size photograph is necessary.

1. **Saas-Fee** - The **Saas Museum,** located near the church, displays its collections on four floors of a typical Saas house, dating from 1732. Visit the world's largest **Ice Pavilion** on the Mittelallalin, at 11,484 ft. (3500 m.). (See Walk #3.)

   Music Festivals - Saas-Fee has added an international flavor, hosting major music festivals for summer visitors.

2. **Zermatt** - Zermatt is a tourist and hiking mecca in the valley next to Saas-Fee. Its surrounding mountains and glaciers encompass superb scenery, including the mighty Matterhorn. (See Zermatt section.)

   Directions: Take an early morning bus from Saas-Fee, arriving in Stalden in time to change for the connecting train to Zermatt (about a seventy-five-minute trip).

Saas-Fee Walks

Recommended Maps:
   ❖ Hiking Map of the Saas Valley
   ❖ Panoramakarte Saas-Fee

Walk #1

Introductory Walk—Hannig to Hohnegg to Saas-Fee
Walking Easy Time: 2 hours
Rating: Gentle

Today's walk serves as a fine introduction to the village of Saas-Fee and its alpine surroundings, and it can be enjoyed your first afternoon in Saas-Fee. At the Hannig sun terrace, look to the Fee glacier, dominating the panorama. Other cable lifts are visible—Plattjen directly across the valley; another to Spielboden and Längfluh, going directly up the center of the Fee glacier. A third lift, the Alpin Express, rises to Felskinn.

Directions: Follow signs in the village to Panoramabahn Hannig. Purchase a one-way ticket to Hannig, at 7710 ft. (2350 m.).

Start: Directional signs outside the lift station highlight the myriad walks available from this location. Today, however, follow the sign SAAS-FEE—1 HR. 20 MIN., walking to the right when facing the sign. The wide path descends easily, zigzagging down the mountain. Take the occasional footpaths serving as shortcuts to the main path, and follow signs to Saas-Fee. The trail leads you to a main path, where you turn right to signs HOHNEGG— 5 MIN. and SAAS-FEE—25 MIN. Tiny Hohnegg consists of a few picturesque restaurants and chalets. The path continues to descend, now running parallel to Saas-Fee, eventually bringing you to the outskirts of town. Your time is now free to explore the colorful streets of Saas-Fee.

Walk #2

Spielboden Lift Station to Saas-Fee (Excursion to Längfluh)
Walking Easy Time: 2½ to 4 hours
Rating: Comfortable

The glacier formations on either side of Spielboden and Längfluh look like giant waves of ice. A narrow finger of land juts up as the foundation for these two lift stations, and on this small area, surrounded on three sides by glaciers, are much-traveled hiking trails.

Directions: Walk down Saas-Fee's main street past the church toward the Fee glacier, following signs to the Längfluh–Spielboden Luftseilbahnen. Purchase a one-way ticket to Spielboden.

Start: Your walk begins at the Spielboden stop, at 8039 ft. (2450 m.), above the tree line on a tongue of land surrounded by the Fee glacier. *Easy Walkers* can first ascend to Längfluh, at 9417 ft. (2870 m.), on a cable car or walk up on the trail marked LÄNGFLUH—1 HR. (However, plan on a ninety-minute ascent.) Otherwise, meet and greet the marmots at Spielboden, waiting patiently for your arrival. A walk to either side of this lift station brings you into view of the powerful Fee glacier, dominating the panorama around tiny Saas-Fee.

The trail down from Spielboden begins with a sign to Saas-Fee. This is a gradual descent, and even though there are little spin-off trails, stay on the main trail. As you continue toward Saas-Fee, marmot families may come out to greet you, their burrows visible everywhere.

Winding down the trail, note a fork in the trail next to a small stone house. Take the path to the left for a close-up view of the glacier—a scene worth a detour. After glacier-gazing, return to the main path to Saas-Fee. Another sign directs walkers to Saas-Fee to the right, or to Saas-Fee and Cafe Gletschergarten to the left. Take the left fork to the restaurant, where you buttonhook to the right, following the trail into Saas-Fee.

Walk #3

Glacier Walk—Felskinn to Brittaniahütte to Felskinn (Excursion to Mittelallalin and Ice Grotto)
Walking Easy Time: 2 to 3 hours
Rating: More challenging

This glacier walk, at almost 10,000 ft. (3000 m.), emphasizes the grandeur and scope of the walking trails surrounding Saas-Fee. You'll travel by cable car to Felskinn, walk across the Fee and Chessjen glaciers to the Brittaniahütte, then walk back to Felskinn.

The excursion part of today's walk, a ride on the Metro-Alpin, the world's highest underground funicular, will bring you into the center of a glacial wilderness. Ride up for the unforgettable view and a visit to the Mittelallalin Ice Pavilion.

Directions: The high-capacity Alpin Express is found by walking to the bus station and following lift signs. Buy a round-trip ticket to Mittelallalin. The ride up to Felskinn deposits *Easy Walkers* at 9843 ft. (3000 m.), ready to begin an ex-

Hint: Check at the ticket office for the day's glacier walking conditions before taking this hike. Use caution and be deliberate. At any given time, depending on weather conditions, the trail can be slippery, slushy, rocky, or muddy. Stay on the well-marked path, and use all guide ropes provided.

Mittelallalin 3500m.

Glacier walk

Brittaniahütte 3030m.

Felskinn 3000m.

S E

Alpin Express

Saas-Fee 1800m.

citing glacier adventure. At Felskinn you have the option of continuing up to Mittelallalin, at 11,484 ft. (3500 m.), immediately, but we suggest saving this experience for after your walk.

Start: Leaving the Felskinn Lift Station, follow the signs to the Brittaniahütte, walking over a snowfield and on to the glacier. Enjoy the scenery and the fact that you're actually walking on a glacier. After about a half hour you'll come upon a tiny ski lift at the Egginerjoch, with the Fee glacier behind you and the Chessjen glacier ahead. The walk becomes more challenging after this point, so use your discretion to continue or turn back. To return to Felskinn, just retrace your steps back across the glacier, although many *Easy Walkers* decide to "glacier walk" as far as the ski lift at the Egginer and enjoy their picnic lunch on this rocky outpost before returning to Felskinn.

Exercising either option, at the Felskinn Lift Station take the Metro-Alpin up to Mittelallalin. The subway train cuts through the mountain, covering a distance of almost 1641 ft. (500 m.) in only three minutes, and passengers disembark at a height of 11,342 ft. (3457 m.) at the top station. This subway has made an exciting area of summer skiing and snowboarding available in the midst of a majestic mountain chain. The revolving restaurant is the highest in the world, rotating once an hour. A cafeteria is also on the site, with an exceptionally large terrace. You can step off the Metro-Alpin directly into the Mittelallalin Ice Pavilion—a walk into the ice of the Fee glacier—the world's largest and highest ice grotto. Return to Saas-Fee via the Metro-Alpin and the Alpin Express.

Saas-Fee

Walk #4

Saas-Fee to Saas-Grund to Saas-Almagell (Excursion to Kreuzboden/Hohsaas)
Walking Easy Time: 4 to 5 hours
Rating: Comfortable

Plan a full day for today's valley walk and high-mountain excursion. The hike includes the Kappellenweg, or chapel path, to Saas-Grund. Fifteen tiny chapels—built from 1687 to 1709—representing the fifteen secrets of the rosary, were originally used as a pilgrimage route from Saas-Fee into the valley between Saas-Grund and Saas-Almagell. This is a splendid way for *Easy Walkers* to familiarize themselves with some of the Saas Valley villages. After walking down to Saas-Grund, you'll take the lift to Kreuzboden and Hohsaas, at 10,165 ft. (3098 m.). After returning to Saas-Grund, the walk continues through the valley to Saas-Almagell, where you catch a bus for the return to Saas-Fee.

Start: Walk to the bus station. The path to Saas-Grund begins behind the station and is marked KAPPELLENWEG. The fifteen chapels along this route contain groups of carved and painted religious figures, and a small church still holds services. The valley, ravine, and river are on the right, and Saas-Fee is above on the left. In some areas the path descends on stone steps. Walk carefully, making sure your hiking boots are laced tightly.

The descent is about 600 ft. (185 m.), and before the hour is over, the end of the trail appears. A sign points to the right to Saas-Almagell, but turn left on the path and follow it along the river, past a campground. Cross the river on the first bridge, turning immediately left, and walk toward Saas-Grund. Follow lift signs to KREUZBODEN–HOHSAAS. Buy a round-trip ticket to Hohsaas, changing at Kreuzboden for the trip to the top station. As you look left toward Saas-Almagell and Mattmark, there are five high glaciers. After viewing the panorama, return to Kreuzboden Station, with its restaurant and sun terrace. If you've brought a picnic lunch, head for one of the most beautiful spots in the Swiss Alps. Walk around the restaurant to a miniature alpine lake with a tiny waterfall, breathtaking views of the Saastal, and a rock-strewn pasture that can serve as your outdoor dining room.

When ready to leave Kreuzboden, take the lift down to Saas-Grund to begin the valley walk to Saas-Almagell. Retrace your steps to the end of the Kappellenweg—to the sign you saw earlier marked SAAS-ALMAGELL—and follow the path ahead. This lovely path bisects the dozen houses of Unter den Bodmen and wends its way along the riverbanks, going inland a few times through meadow and forest to Saas-Almagell. The bus stop is on the outskirts of town. Check the posted schedule before exploring the town or settling in for a snack at the terrace restaurant conveniently situated by the bus stop. Take the bus back to Saas-Grund, changing for the bus to Saas-Fee. For those who want to continue walking to Saas-Fee on a comfortable ascending path, follow the BODME, SAAS-FEE sign on the main road—another hour's walk.

Walk #5

Saas-Fee to Bideralp to Stafelalp to Saas-Fee
Walking Easy Time: 5 hours
Rating: More challenging

Today's trails lead into the heights overlooking the Saas Valley, offering many types of alpine walking—waterfall and stream crossings, rocky trails, pine-needled paths, and an altitude change of more than 1000 ft. (305 m.). At the beginning of the hike the path is gentle. In about one hour the ascent steepens and the trail becomes rocky. After the Biderbruche crossing, the trail rises, swings to the left, and meets the high-altitude trail from Grächen. It then descends by way of Bärenfalle into the outskirts of Saas-Fee.

CAUTION: Because of an interruption in the trail after it rises to Stafelalp and meets the trail from Grächen, the return to Saas-Fee from Stafelalp would have to be on the same trail you came on. *Plans have been made to return this trail to normal. Check with the Tourist Office before taking this hike. This is a great walk and should be taken in any case.*

Start: Remember to pack a picnic lunch and extra water—this is one of the few trail areas without restaurants. Walk past the Hotel Etoile, away from the village. Passing the Alpen Hitte restaurant, follow signs to the right, to Stafelalp, Bideralp, and Sengg, in the direction of the Hotel Fletschhorn. After about fifteen minutes, walk through the Hotel Fletschhorn's sun terrace and pick up the trail, which continues on the other side with signs marked STAFELALP, BIDERALP, and SENGG. Follow this path but ignore the fact that it is marked STAFELALP—1 HR., 15 MIN.—it may take some *Easy Walkers* closer to two hours.

After passing the Fletschhorn, the path becomes a rocky, mountain *bergweg*. Passing through the hamlet of Sengg, enjoy the photographic possibilities in this area—it appears as though time and modern civilization have bypassed Sengg and its surrounding meadows. Walking through Sengg, follow directions to Stafelalp. The trail begins to climb in the direction of Bideralp, at 6296 ft. (1919 m), and Stafelalp, at 7028 ft. (2142 m.), crossing some swiftly running streams. As you ascend, follow signs to Bideralp. You'll cross the fast-running Biderbruche on a small wooden bridge to Bideralp, with many scenic opportunities for a picnic on its hillside. After Bideralp, be prepared to ascend 732 ft. (223 m.). Walking past some wooden cabins, the trail buttonhooks to the left around Stafelalp to meet the high path coming down from Grächen. *Note the trail caution above.* At the Grächen sign you are at the highest point of this walk, and from then on it's downhill into Saas-Fee, crossing streams and waterfalls as you descend from a rocky mountain trail to a pine-needled forest path leading into Bärenfalle and Saas-Fee.

If you leave your hotel by 10:00 A.M., you should be back before 5:00 P.M. after an exhilarating day of hiking.

Walk #6

Around the Mattmark Reservoir (Optional Hike to Tälliboden)
Walking Easy Time: 2½ to 4 hours
Rating: Comfortable

Today you'll take the bus to Mattmark, at 7244 ft. (2208 m.), and walk around Europe's largest reservoir on a comfortable trail with the option, at the end of the lake, to rise 800 ft. (244 m.) on a mountain *bergweg* to Tälliboden.

Directions: Take a morning bus directly to Mattmark (check current schedules).

Start: After exiting the bus at the Mattmark Restaurant, follow the sign SEERUNDGANG—2¼ HRS. Take the right-hand path around the reservoir, staying on the lower path. After an hour you'll reach Distelalp, at 7139 ft. (2224 m.), and the end of the lake, with signs to the Monte Moro Pass and Tälliboden. Here you have a few options:

1. You can take the mountain trail to Tälliboden, a rise of some 800 ft. (244 m.). Some hikers continue up to Monte Moro Pass, at 9220 ft. (2810 m.), for the trek into Italy. Other hikers will take the high route from Tälliboden and descend on the Offental Trail to the end of the reservoir. *Easy Walkers* will return down the same trail to Distelalp and continue along the opposite side of the reservoir, toward the dam and bus stop.

2. Stay level and continue around the lake to the dam and the bus stop.

   With either option, after about ten minutes, as you proceed along the opposite side of the reservoir, you have two more choices:

3. Take the middle route to the end of the reservoir by turning up on the higher Seerundgang Trail, eventually returning down to the reservoir for the walk across the dam and down to the bus stop.

4. Continue on the lower Seerundgang path to the dam and bus stop.

Walk #7

Saas-Fee to Bodme to Saas-Almagell to Saas-Grund to Saas-Balen
Walking Easy Time: 2 to 4 hours
Rating: Gentle

This walk begins at the Saas-Fee bus station, where you follow signs to Saas-Almagell and the restaurant at Bodme. The path descends gently through the forest to Saas-Almagell, passing the restaurant along the way.

In Saas-Almagell you can take the bus back to Saas-Grund, transferring to the Saas-Fee bus. Or walk back along the river in the valley to Saas-Grund or even Saas-Balen, with bus stops a short distance from the path on the main road.

ZERMATT

Zermatt, an all-season sports resort, nestles among alpine meadows and pine forests at 5315 ft. (1620 m.), encircled by many of Switzerland's tallest and most famous mountains. This *Walking Easy* base village is a hiker's paradise, with more than 250 miles (400 km.) of marked paths, encompassing some of the world's most superb scenery and appealing walking trails. This sophisticated town in the Valais Region of Switzerland encompasses two contrasting areas. One section includes the main tourist street from the railroad station past the church—filled with day-trippers, skiers, and hikers enjoying the crowded shops, bustling restaurants, and old-world hotels. The second area reaches into the countryside, in the shadow of the Matterhorn, with typical Valaisian chalets, *mazots* (preserved landmark barns), and a network of trails filling the needs of both occasional ramblers and experienced mountain climbers.

The Täsch railroad station car park in the valley below holds the cars of the thousands who visit Zermatt and wander through its quaint streets with only electric minitaxis and flower-bedecked horse-drawn carriages for local transportation.

Zermatt has become synonymous with the majestic Matterhorn; its silhouette and history are unique and instantly recognizable. *Easy Walkers* will enjoy Zermatt, boasting one of the finest networks of alpine trails in the Swiss Alps.

Transportation

By Train - Take the train to Brig or Visp and always change to the Brig-Visp-Zermatt Railway, located outside the station. To be picked up, use the bank of telephones inside the station, which are directly connected to local hotels.

The **Glacier Express**, sometimes called the "slowest express train in the world," traverses the miles between Zermatt and St. Moritz, with no change of train. This train is a panorama trip through the alpine heartland of Switzerland and departs from Zermatt twice each morning, arriving in St. Moritz seven and a half hours later. Seat reservations are mandatory except for the Zermatt to Brig portion.

By Car - Drive to Visp and head south to Täsch. Park and board the train for the last part of your trip to car-free Zermatt. Wheel your luggage cart directly onto the train. Call your hotel for electric cart pickup.

Favorite *Walking Easy* Hotel

Hotel Antares

Four-Star; Owners—Familie Schnidrig und Holenstein
CH-3920 Zermatt; **Tel:** 27 967 36 64; **Fax:** 27 967 52 36
Internet: www.hotelantareszermatt.com
E-mail: antares@zermatt.ch

The quiet location of the Antares is ideal. This contemporary chalet-style hotel features paneled guest rooms with modern conveniences, handsome public areas, spacious dining rooms, and an outdoor terrace; most rooms have a view of the Matterhorn. Buffet breakfasts are sumptuous, and half-board dining is particularly rewarding. Cheerful Monica is always available, while Gerry, master chef and Monica's husband, is a presentation-perfectionist, creating some of the most interesting and delicious dining experiences in Switzerland. We found ourselves wondering during afternoon hikes what's for dinner. When writing or faxing for reservations, ask for Monica.

Excursions

The Zermatt Tourist Office is located next to the railroad station.
Internet: www.zermatt.ch
E-mail: zermatt@wallis.ch

1. Zermatt

❖ Check the **Alpine Museum's** collection of documents verifying the first ascents of the mountains around Zermatt.

❖ **Alpine Cemetery** - This beautiful cemetery is located across from the church. It contains the graves of those killed while attempting to climb the Matterhorn.

❖ **Marmots' Fountain** - A sculpture by Swiss artist Edouard Marcel Sandoz stands in the center of Zermatt, across from the church.

2. Saas-Fee - Saas-Fee is a small, charming, car-free resort in the valley next to Zermatt. (See the Saas-Fee section.)

Directions: Take the train from Zermatt to Stalden and board the PTT bus to Saas-Fee outside the station, a total ride of about two hours.

Zermatt Walks

Recommended Maps:
- ❖ Wanderkarte—Zermatt–Cervina–Täsch
- ❖ Zermatt—Matterhorn Panorama Aerial Map

Walk #1

Schwarzsee to Stafel to Furi to Zermatt (Excursion to the Klein Matterhorn)

Walking Easy Time: 3 to 4 hours

Rating: Comfortable

Today's trip includes an exciting adventure to the Klein Matterhorn Top Station, at 12,533 ft. (3829 m.), and an optional glacial, snowfield walk with close-up views of climbers ascending the Breithorn. Enjoy the spectacular view from the top—this world of snow, ice, and rock has not changed much since the glaciers of the Ice Age destroyed everything in their paths.

> **Hint:** *Today's journey should be taken on your first clear day in Zermatt. Sunglasses, sunscreen, and warm outerwear are necessary. Be prepared to spend the better part of the day on this excursion and hike.*

You will return to Furi by cable car and change for the lifts to Schwarzsee. Schwarzsee is at the foot of the Matterhorn, an alpine lake below its northeast ridge.

You'll leave Schwarzsee, at 8472 ft. (2582 m.), descending comfortably to the Stafelalp mountain restaurant and sun terrace, at 7215 ft. (2199 m.). After taking in the views and outstanding *käseschnitte* (eggs, cheese, and bread casserole) at the restaurant, continue on a forest path—with views of the tiny mountain hamlet of Zmutt across the valley—to Furi, where you can walk or take the gondola down to Zermatt.

Directions: The Klein Matterhorn cable car is just past the Hotel Antares; follow signs from Zermatt. Buy a lift ticket to Klein Matterhorn, with a return to Schwarzsee. Furi is the first stop.

Start: After disembarking at the Klein Matterhorn Station, move ahead through a long tunnel. On the left is a small tunnel leading to an elevator that will take you to the *gipfel* or peak. Here you'll encounter a

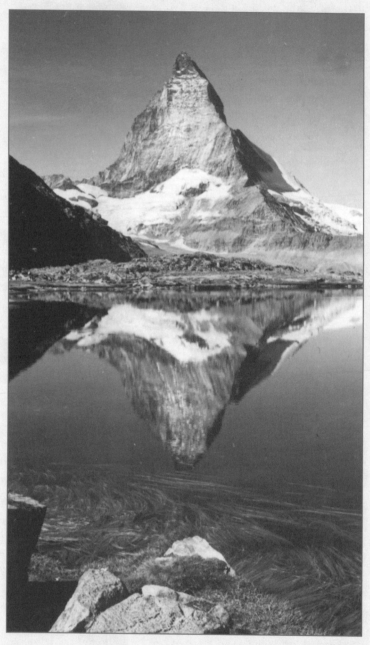

The Matterhorn

never-to-be-forgotten panorama: face to face with the Matterhorn!

When ready to leave, descend by elevator and continue through the tunnel to the glacial snowfield. Step out onto the snowfield if you wish and walk as far as you feel comfortable, returning to the cable car station when ready. *NOTE: Any extended hike in this area should be in the company of an experienced guide.*

To arrive at Schwarzsee, reverse the cable car procedure and return to Furi, where you take the lift to Schwarzsee, via Furgg. At Schwarzsee, follow the sign to Stafelalp at the side of the sun terrace of the Hotel Schwarzsee. After a while you'll come to an unsigned trail off to the right. Take it. This typical *bergweg* leads to Stafelalp and descends directly to the Stafelalp Restaurant, at 7215 ft. (2199 m.). This part of the walk from Schwarzsee takes about an hour.

After taking your fill of the Matterhorn view, walk behind the sun terrace, following signs to Furi. The path moves to the left down to the road, and after a few minutes' walking, the road forks. Take the right fork to Furi on the wagon path into the forest rather than staying on the road, although both meet eventually. Continue ahead, following signs to Furi. At the Furi Lift Station, follow the signed path ZERMATT—1 HR. Or climb aboard the Furi gondola for the quick descent to Zermatt.

Walk #2

Zermatt to Zmutt to Furi to Zermatt
Walking Easy Time: 3 to 4 hours
Rating: Comfortable

Today's hike is one of the most popular in the Zermatt area and will take you on a trail comfortably ascending 1037 ft. (316 m.), to a hamlet on the outskirts of town. Zmutt, at 6352 ft. (1936 m.), is a small cluster of buildings with typical Valaisian slate roofs, set among hilly pastures. From Zmutt you will cross the river and walk to Furi, where you continue to Zermatt.

Start: At the village church and Marmots' Fountain, head up the main street toward the Matterhorn. After passing a newspaper stand on your right, note a sign indicating ZMUTT—1 HR. There are several ways to approach Zmutt—we prefer following this well-trodden path, although it may take *Easy Walkers* closer to ninety minutes. As you ascend on the trail, the river is on the left with the Matterhorn ahead. You'll pass wooden *mazots*, barns from the early years of Zermatt. Soon the asphalt ends and the path

The Matterhorn from Stockhorn

ascends through woods and meadows.

After ascending for an hour, a sign indicates you have walked almost 1.9 miles (3 km.) from Zermatt. Buttonhook up the trail and continue by walking through the terrace of a restaurant. Zmutt is now only a five-minute walk through the meadows, its miniature whitewashed church, some old barns, and houses in view. The pasture is covered with wildflowers from June through August and is an idyllic place to enjoy a picnic lunch. From a vantage point in the high meadow, gaze down on the old slate roofs of Zmutt, the valley, and the peak of the Matterhorn. Legends say that these Zmutt meadows gave their name to the Matterhorn, which means "meadowhorn" in local dialect.

When ready, take the path into the center of Zmutt and follow a sign down the hill toward Furi and Stafelalp, walking through a pasture toward the hydroelectric plant, with the gorge on the left. Cross the bridge, walk up the hill to the road, and turn left toward Furi. Stay on this road and in another half hour the cable station at Furi can be seen. At Furi, you have two options:

1. Continue the hike, following the sign ZERMATT—1 HR.

2. Take the cable car from Furi down to Zermatt.

Walk #3

Riffelberg and/or Riffelalp to Zermatt (Excursion to Gornergrat and Stockhorn)

Walking Easy Time: 1½ to 2½ hours
Rating: Comfortable

Although today's walk begins in Riffelberg or Riffelalp and ends in Zermatt, we first include an excursion to Gornergrat and the Stockhorn: The unfolding mountain and glacier panorama is awesome, and the trip should be taken on a clear day.

From Gornergrat Station in Zermatt, the train winds its way up the mountain; sit on the right side of the train for the best views. The view from Gornergrat encompasses a spectacular panorama of twenty-seven peaks higher than 12,000 ft. (3660 m.). Looming over this frozen sea is Switzerland's highest mountain, the Monte Rosa, at 15,203 ft. (4643 m.). From Gornergrat, a cable car brings you over Hohtälligrat, at 10,781 ft. (3286 m.), and then to the Stockhorn, at 11,178 ft. (3407 m.), and an even closer view of the Monte Rosa and its surrounding glacial wilderness. You'll return to the Gornergrat railway, taking it down to Riffelalp for the hike to Zermatt. *NOTE: This hike can be extended by getting off the train at the high plateau of Riffelberg, at 8472 ft. (2582 m.). You can then pick up the trail, descending 1181 ft. (360 m.) to Riffelalp, another hour of walking time.*

Directions: Walk to the Gornergratbahn, across from the Zermatt train station. Buy a ticket, Zermatt to Stockhorn, with a return to Riffelberg/Riffelalp. The train makes four stops before arriving at Gornergrat, where you follow signs to board the Stockhorn cable car. Take the cable car back to Gornergrat and its famous Kulm Hotel. When ready, reboard the train at Gornergrat and disembark at the Riffelalp station, the stop after Riffelberg (unless

Stockhorn
3407m.

Gornergrat
3130m.

Riffelberg
2582m.

S

Riffelalp
2211m.

Gornergratbahn

E

Zermatt
1620m.

The Matterhorn from Riffelalp

you've decided to walk the extra hour from Riffelberg to Riffelalp).

Start: At the Riffelalp station, walk to the right, toward Zermatt and the Riffelalp Hotel. Within a few minutes a sign points to Zermatt. Do not take this path on the right; instead, continue walking ahead on the main forest path. Within five minutes the newly renovated, five-star Hotel Riffelalp, with an unobstructed view of the Matterhorn, comes into view.

Passing the hotel, follow signs pointing right toward Zermatt and Winkelmatten. This trail descends over 1975 ft. (602 m.). The path divides at a restaurant—follow signs toward Zermatt and Winkelmatten until you reach a paved mountain bike path and road. Turn right to Zermatt. This road winds through the woods to the hamlets of Moos and Winkelmatten. In Winkelmatten, walk ahead, continuing along the river into Zermatt.

Walk #4

Sunnegga to Tuftern to Reid to Winkelmatten to Zermatt (Excursion to Blauherd and Unterrothorn)

Walking Easy Time: 3 hours
Rating: Comfortable

Today's walk is on one of the many trails leading from the Sunnegga plateau—primarily a forest path with a comfortable 2231 ft. (680 m.) descent—and spectacular views of the Matterhorn. The underground Alpen-Metro funicular brings you to Sunnegga. You can continue on the cable car to Blauherd and Unterrothern for more extensive views.

Directions: Follow signs to Sunnegga, and purchase a one-way ticket to Sunnegga for the underground funicular (or to Unterrothorn if continuing to the top). At Sunnegga take the cable car to Blauherd and Unterrothorn for incredible views (if you have not already taken this excursion), but return to Sunnegga to begin today's hike.

Start: At Sunnegga walk down to a plateau with a large cross, and follow the sign TUFTERN to the right. After a few minutes, another sign directs you again to the right (TUFTERN—30 MIN.). Remain on the main, wide jeep road (not descending on the grassy path).

The hamlet of Tuftern, at 7267 ft. (2215 m.), consists of a small group of picturesque old barns, houses, and a restaurant with a fabulous view of the Matterhorn. Ignoring the high trail to the right (the Europaweg) to Grächen or Täsch, and the steep descent to Zermatt on the left, continue ahead to Reid. This path, a ski trail in winter, buttonhooks through the forest and alpine meadows, passing Othmar's Hütte, a restaurant. In about twenty-five minutes (some of the time spent is on an auto road), follow the sign left indicating WINKELMATTEN—½ HR., taking you up, then winding evenly on a gentle *bergweg*. This path bypasses Zermatt and leads comfortably to the church in Winkelmatten. At the church walk halfway around, following a sign to Zermatt. This road leads down to the Klein Matterhorn cable station, where you turn right to your hotel.

Walk #5

Riffelalp to Grünsee to Findeln to Sunnegga
Walking Easy Time: 4 hours
Rating: More challenging

Today's hike will take *Easy Walkers* on the Gornergrat Railway to Riffelalp for the walk to Grünsee, a tiny glacial lake. From there you'll walk down through the forest, then up to the hamlet of Findeln, with its old wooden barns and houses. The walk continues on an ascending path from Findeln to the Leisee and eventually up to Sunnegga, with a return to Zermatt via the underground funicular. Although the walk to Grünsee is gentle, the last half of this walk requires some uphill hiking.

Directions: Walk to the Gornergratbahn, across from the Zermatt train station. Buy a one-way ticket to Riffelalp and exit at the Riffelalp station.

Start: Walk across the railroad tracks at the pedestrian crossing and follow the trail signed GRÜNSEE—1 HR. This path is wide and well marked, winding around the mountain and offering superb views of the towns in the valley below. You are at 6500 ft. (1981 m.) and slowly approaching the tree line. Note the Findelngletscher to the east and, up on the left, your destination at Sunnegga and the Blauherd–Unterrothorn Lifts. Continuing, take the right trail fork up the hill to the lake. The Findeln Glacier and its surrounding peaks are now in front of you. Passing over a brook, follow signs to Grünsee.

After enjoying the panorama, return on the same trail, walking past the restaurant to the sign FINDELN—¾ HR., on a right fork in the path. At this point you have two options:

1. Take the left fork back to the Riffelalp station, the same way you walked to Grünsee, and return to Zermatt by train.

2. Follow the trail to Findeln, winding through the forest, descending to the Findeln River. Reaching the gorge and the Findeln River, cross the bridge and walk up the steep path to Findeln, at 6788 ft. (2069 m.), perched on the side of the gorge.

Continue on the ascending path, walking above the village to a junction. Turn left for a short, aggressive, uphill walk to the Leisee, noticing the Sunnegga Lift Station above, at 7546 ft. (2300 m.). From the lake, take either path leading to the top and the funicular subway. Buy a one-way Sunnegga-to-Zermatt ticket.

Walk #6

Zermatt to Täsch

Walking Easy Time: 1½ hours

Rating: Comfortable

If it's drizzling, clouds are hanging low over Zermatt, and you can't see the Matterhorn, you might want to take a low-level hike. You can follow the *wanderweg* trail from Zermatt to the village of Täsch. Or, if you prefer walking up rather than down, the hike can be taken in reverse, from Täsch to Zermatt. In either case, the altitude change is not significant.

The Matterhorn

The walk is on a mountain trail, never far from the train tracks and the rapidly flowing river. You can take the train in either direction or walk the trail both ways. The following directions will take you from Zermatt to Täsch.

Start: Walk toward the Zermatt train station, past the *bahnhof* on a paved road to the TÄSCH sign. Turn left and walk up a concrete ramp, making a right turn on the unsigned but clearly defined trail toward Täsch. The trail rolls comfortably but can be a bit rocky in places as it parallels the train tracks through the valley. Do *not* be tempted by occasional trail offshoots. Stay on the main, signed trail to Täsch. You might want to take the train back from the Täsch station or return to Zermatt on the same *wanderweg* trail, depending on the weather.

Walk #7

Schwarzsee to Hermettji to Furi to Zermatt
Walking Easy Time: 3½ to 4½ hours
Rating: Comfortable

Today's walk begins in Schwarzsee, after taking the lifts to Furi and Furgg. You'll visit the little lake and its chapel. The hike is all downhill, offering enchanting views of Zermatt and the surrounding high peaks.

Directions: The lift to Schwarzsee is just past the Hotel Antares. Buy a ticket from Zermatt to Schwarzsee, then board the gondolas to Furi, where you change for the lifts to Furgg and Schwarzsee.

Start: Pick up the descending trail to Furi, following signs HERMETTJI and ZERMATT, by the sun terrace of the Hotel Schwarzsee. There are other ways to descend, but today we recommend staying on this trail—it's clearly marked, rocky but wide. At the first fork, take a left, following signs into Hermettji. At Hermettji follow signs to Furi. At the cable station in Furi, the following options are available:

1. Take the cable car from Furi to Zermatt.

2. Continue the walk down to Zermatt by following the sign ZERMATT—
   1 HR.

VERBIER

The sports village of Verbier, at 4920 ft. (1500 m.), is located in south-western Switzerland in the Valais, near the French and Italian borders, on a large, sunny plateau under the towering Mont-Fort and its 10,925-ft. (3330 m.) glacier. The language of Verbier, the cuisine, the mode, the atti-tude—are all *très Français*. It is difficult to believe that this chic winter and summer mountain area has developed from its pastureland heritage (mostly in the last quarter century) into a year-round resort offering visitors a full range of modern services, including a cybercafe for Web surfers. Access to Verbier is quite different from other alpine villages; you can take a gondola from the rail station in Le Châble directly to Verbier. You can also use more traditional methods by either driving up the scenic mountain road or taking the postbus from the train station.

While Verbier is most famous in winter for its 250 miles (400 km.) of ski runs and dozens of lifts, summer in Verbier offers miles of paths for hikers of all capabilities. In addition to the higher, more challenging hiking trails, miles of comfortable, crisscrossing paths cut back and forth along wide mountain ski slopes, all serviced by an operating network of summer lifts and free village bus service. The breathtaking views from the peaks at Mont-Fort, Attelas, Savaleyres, and Pierre d'Avoi, over to the Grand Combin and Mont Blanc massifs are worth this trip up the mountain to the village at almost 5000 ft. (1524 m.). In addition to all that spectacular alpine scenery, Verbier is also home to an eighteen-hole, par 70 golf course located above the village and is called the "Mecca of Paragliding" because of its exceptional flying sites.

If you enjoy a village with French atmosphere, lots of sports action, great hotels, and good summer *Walking Easy* in an exhilarating setting—try Verbier.

Transportion

By Train - Take the train to Martigny and change for the Martigny-Le Châble line. Sit in the car marked Le Châble. In Le Châble, change to a postbus or take the Le Châble-Verbier Cableway up to the village.

By Car - Drive to Martigny and take the Great-St-Bernard main road to Sembrancher. Turn left and drive into the Bagnes Valley all the way to Le Châble and the ascending road to Verbier.

Favorite *Walking Easy* Hotel

Golf Hotel
Three-Star; Owner—Familie Bessard
CH-1936 Verbier; **Tel:** 27 771 65 15; **Fax:** 27 771 14 88
Internet: www.golfhotelverbier.ch
E-mail: golfhotel@axiom.ch

This "three-star-plus" hotel is in a quiet location, a few minutes from the center of the village and across from the bus stop to the lifts. Jacques Bessard has created a comfortable chalet-hotel in a lovely garden setting. The atmosphere is relaxed, with spacious lounges, bar, sauna, and steam room. Attractive rooms, many with balconies, feature private facilities, telephone, radio, cable TV, and safe. Breakfast is continental, and dinners can be the highlight of your *Walking Easy* trip to Verbier—exquisite preparation and presentation; *demi-pension* (half-board with dinner) is recommended. Ask for Jacques Bessard when making reservations.

Excursions

The Verbier/Val de Bagnes Tourist Office is located in the center of the village, on the main pedestrian and shopping street.

> **Fax:** 27 775 38 89
> **Internet:** www.verbier.ch
> **E-mail:** verbiertourism@verbier.ch

1. **Verbier** - A highlight of the Swiss summer cultural season, the acclaimed **Verbier Festival and Academy,** featuring internationally famous soloists and orchestras, is held every year in July. An eighteen-hole, par 70 **Golf Course** has been built at an altitude of 5250 ft. (1600 m.).

2. **Montreux** - See Gstaad section, Excursion #2.
   Directions: Take the bus or gondola from Verbier to Le Châble and the train to Sembrancher. Change for the train to Montreux. A bus to Chillon can be picked up outside the train station.

3. **Martigny** - Recognized worldwide for exhibits of such famous artists as Gauguin, Manet, Degas and Modigliani, visit the **Pierre Gianadda Foundation**. This museum also houses a collection of works by the masters, a sculpture park, a car museum, and a Gaul-Roman museum.
   Directions: Take the bus or cable car to Le Châble and take the train to Sembrancher. Change for the train to Martigny.

4. Aigle - Dating from the thirteenth century, **Aigle Castle** is home to the Wine and Salt Museums. Opposite the castle is the **Maison de la Dime**, which includes the International Museum of Labels, the "Pinte du Paradis," and the Cellar of Chablais, where you can sample wines of the region.

Directions: Take the bus or cable car to Le Châble and board the train for Sembrancher. Change for the train toward Montreux, getting off in Aigle.

Verbier Walks

Recommended Map:

❖ Val de Bagnes, Verbier—Carte de randonnées pédestres

The following hikes are just a few of those available in the Verbier area. *Easy Walkers* can wander about the many trails along the mountain side.

Walk #1

Les Ruinettes to La Chaux, Excursion to Mont-Fort, Lifts to La Chaux, Walk to Cabane du Mont-Fort to Les Ruinettes

Walking Easy Time: 3 hours

Rating: Comfortable

Today's hike and excursion to Mont-Fort includes a short walk from Les Ruinettes, at 7195 ft. (2193 m.), to La Chaux, at 7218 ft. (2200 m.), and the beginning of a fascinating cable car system. You will see summer skiers and snowboarders on the glacier at Gentianes Mid-Station before continuing up to Mont-Fort, at 10,854 ft. (3308 m.), for unparalleled panoramic views. You will then descend back to the mid-station by cable car, where there is an additional lift system continuing to Tortin, Siviez, and farther, if you wish. Today, however, you will descend by cable to La Chaux for the hike up to the Cabane du Mont-Fort and the return to Les Ruinettes via a descending mountain path.

Directions: Walk or take the free shuttle bus to the Medran cable car. Take the lift to Les Ruinettes.

Start: After exiting the lift turn down to your right to the group of signs indicating LA CHAUX, where there are two options:

Tortin 2045m.

Verbier 1500m.

Les Ruinettes 2193m.

Glacier de Tortin

La Chaux 2200m.

Mont Fort 3308m.

1. Walk along the wide mountain road to La Chaux.

2. Descend a bit to the mountain bergweg just under the road toward La Chaux (*Bisse du Levron* on your map). If you've chosen the bergweg, follow signs up to La Chaux for a forty-minute walk.

At La Chaux, take the large cable car (capacity 150) to Mont-Fort, with a change at Gentiane at the base of the glacier. After taking in the views and noting the summer skiers on the glacier, descend to the mid-station, at 9495 ft. (2894 m.). While it is possible to take another series of cable cars and lifts up to Tortin and Siviez, you might reserve that for another day.

Return by cable down to La Chaux, passing the Cabane du Mont-Fort on your right. At La Chaux, follow the signed trail for an hour hike up to the cabane. After rest and refreshments, you have some options:

1. Walk down the mountain directly to La Chaux for the walk back to Ruinettes and the lift down to Verbier.

2. Take the mountain trail just under the Cabane du Mont-Fort that descends directly to Les Ruinettes and the cable car return to Verbier.

Walk #2

Savoleyres to Croix de Coeur to Les Ruinettes, Excursion to Attelas, Walk Les Ruinettes to Verbier

Walking Easy Time: 1¾ to 3½ hours

Rating: Comfortable

Today's walk gives *Easy Walkers* the opportunity to view the entire Verbier walking area—you'll see all the trails that cross the giant ski pistes around and above Verbier.

Directions: Take the bus to the Savoleyres Lift and ascend on the gondola to the top station, rising from 5217 to 7724 ft. (1590 to 2354 m.).

Start: At Savoleyres, follow the sign down to Croix de Coeur, at 7133 ft. (2174 m.). There, turn

onto the wide path to Les Ruinettes, at 7195 ft. (2193 m.). At Croix de Coeur, it is also possible to take other trails—make sure you take the wide path signed LES RUINETTES. Descend gently above the tree line, with fantastic views of Verbier and the Val des Bagnes. As you proceed, most of Verbier's hiking paths are visible. *NOTE: This path is also used by mountain bikers, so it's a good idea to stay to the right as you walk.*

About halfway, the path enters a short mountain tunnel; you'll then pass other trails rising up to Col des Mines and Attelas and down to Les Planards. Continue walking to the lift at Les Ruinettes. There, if the weather is clear, you might wish to continue by gondola to Les Attelas, at 8859 ft. (2700 m.), for panoramic views. We were considering the hike on the Tour du Val des Bagnes to the Cabane du Mont-Fort, but July snow covered much of the trail. Instead, we returned to Les Ruinettes by gondola and walked along the road down to Verbier. You can also take the Ruinettes Lift down to Verbier.

Walk #3

Savoleyres to Pierre d'Avoi to Savoleyres to Les Planards to Les Esserts to Verbier

Walking Easy Time: 3 to 5 hours

Rating: Comfortable

Today's hike, beginning at the top of the Savoleyres Lift, offers views down to the other side of the Val des Bagnes to Mayens de Riddes, with additional views of the mountains of the Grand Combin. You'll walk to the jut-ting peak of Pierre d'Avoi and ascend it if you desire, returning through Savoleyres to Croix de Coeur, to the restaurant at Les Planards, and then down through the meadows to the golf course at Les Esserts and Verbier.

Directions: Take the Verbier shuttle bus to the Savoleyres Lift Station and take the gondola to the top.

Start: After exiting the lift, take the mountain trail around the back of the lift station in the direction of Pierre d'Avoi. After about ten minutes, the trail crosses the wide road. Continue ahead on the trail, *not* walking up to the right on the wide road. This comfortable trail leads directly to the base of Pierre d'Avoi in thirty minutes. You now have two options:

1. Hike up to Pierre d'Avoi, a steep ascent with railing help toward the top—then hike back down on the same trail.

2. Admire the peak from its base.

With either option, return on the same trail to Savoleyres, walking on to Croix de Coeur, at 7133 ft. (2174 m.). At Croix de Coeur, follow the sign down to the restaurant at Les Planards, visible below. From the restaurant parking area, follow Chemin de Pedestre, a narrow mountain trail de-scending steeply through Le Clou to the golf course at Les Esserts. Here you can walk or take the free shuttle bus back to Verbier.

Walk #4

Les Ruinettes to Les Planards to Chute du Bisse to Verbier
Walking Easy Time: 4 to 4½ hours
Rating: Comfortable

The walk from Les Ruinettes to Chute du Bisse is mostly along the Bisse de Levron, through Les Planards. The *bisse* is a system of controlling and di-recting the mountain water for agricultural use, similar to the *waalwege* in Merano, Italy. (See *Walking Easy Italian and French Alps.*) From Chute du Bisse you'll return to Verbier through St. Christophe and Patier.

Directions: Take the gondola from Medran and exit at the Les Ru-inettes Station.

Start: Walk down to the right and follow signs to Les Planards and Chute du Bisse on the Bisse de Levron Trail. In Les Planards, continue on the mountain trail along the *bisse* to Chute du Bisse. From Chute du Bisse, descend to Patier on the outskirts of Verbier—through the viewpoint at St. Christophe. At Patier you can either take the shuttle bus into Verbier or walk fifteen minutes into the village.

NOTE: The following walks can be taken when the weather is not co-operating and you wish to stay low. These walks also give you an opportunity to discover the little villages down in the valley below Verbier, the Val des Bagnes.

Walk #5

Val des Bagnes Walk—Le Châble to Charançon to Cries to Cotterg to Le Châble
Walking Easy Time: 3 hours
Rating: Comfortable

Directions: Take the Verbier/Medran gondola down to Le Châble.

Start: Walk around to the back of the lift station and cross the river on the little bridge. Turn right on the road and left at the *boulangerie*. Make your first right turn into the village square with its town hall. Follow the sign to the path toward Charançon and then Cries, continuing back toward Le Châble by way of Cotterg.

Walk #6

Le Châble to Champsec
Walking Easy Time: 1½ to 3 hours
Rating: Comfortable

Follow directions in Walk #5 to arrive at the center of Le Châble. Follow the sign to Champsec. There are two ways to walk to Champsec—the higher trail through Bruson or the lower trail (Promenade de la Dranse) through Prarriyer. We stayed on the lower trail because of the rain and caught the bus from Champsecback back to Le Châble, where you can take a bus or gondola to Verbier. If the weather remains okay, continue the circle—walk back to Le Châble by picking up the path from Champsec.

GRISONS

AROSA

The Rhätische Bahn, or Rhaetian Railway, transports *Easy Walkers* from 2461 to 5742 ft. (750 to 1750 m.) via mountain ridges and sky-high trestles through dense pine forests, across alpine meadows, and near tiny mountain villages to the all-season resort of Arosa. The village lies in a sheltered hollow in the Grisons (Graubunden) canton, or state. This eastern region of Switzerland, home to the famous St. Moritz, Davos, and Klosters ski centers, is the largest and least developed of the Swiss cantons—sparsely populated, mountainous, thickly forested, and with over 140 square miles (363 square km.) of glaciers.

The main part of Arosa is built on the heights around two small lakes, the Untersee and the Obersee. Although parts of the village date from the fourteenth century, the predominantly modern architecture does not have that typical "Swiss chalet" feeling. However, Arosa does offer visitors a multitude of summer activities and an abundance of exciting day walks, with over 125 miles (200 km.) of trails and free bus service provided to all lifts and trails in the area.

Arosa's magnificent mountain scenery and excellent hiking attract an interesting mix of visitors. We hope more American walkers will sample Arosa's clear, invigorating air and its exciting summer hiking trails.

Transportation

By Train - To reach Arosa, always change trains in Chur to the narrow-gauge Rhätische Bahn, located outside the main station, at the sign NACH AROSA (a one-hour trip).

By Car - Follow the 19-mile (31 km.) winding road from Chur to Arosa.

Favorite *Walking Easy* Hotel

Hotel Alpina

Three-Star; Owner—Hans Eberhard

CH-7050 Arosa; **Tel:** 81 377 16 58; **Fax:** 81 377 37 52

Internet: www.arosa.ch/hotels/alpina/index

E-mail: alpina.arosa@bluewin.ch

Created, cherished, and lovingly tended by Hans Eberhard, the Hotel Alpina is centrally located in this cool, high-altitude mountain resort. With chalet-style buildings connected by a walkway filled with Swiss memorabilia, the Alpina has comfortable rooms and apartments, most with balconies offering views of Arosa's two lakes and surrounding mountains. The kitchen is just one of the reasons Alpina guests keep returning. Quality of service is warmly personal, and the cooking is *haus gemacht*. After-dinner drinks and coffee are served in a small, congenial bar area. The Alpina is exceptional when it comes to caring.

Excursions

The Arosa Tourist Office is located on the main street, across from the casino. Discount hiking passes are available for lifts and trains.

Fax: 81 378 70 21

Internet: www.arosa.ch

E-mail: arosa@arosa.ch

1. **Chur** - Chur is the oldest town in Switzerland, with archeological excavations dating back to 3000 B.C. Although this city of 30,000 inhabitants is now a large trade center, explore its colorful Old Town. The Tourist Information Office (follow the **i** signs outside the train station) provides walking maps of the Old Town area, its narrow, cobblestoned streets bordered by ancient houses, towers, and squares decorated with fountains, flowers, and flags.

Directions: *Trains leave hourly for the one-hour ride to Chur.*

Arosa Walks

Recommended Maps:

❖ Arosa Sommer-Wanderkarte

❖ Arosa und Umgebung Wanderkarte

Walk #1

Introductory Walk—Arosa to Maran to Prätschli to LAW Mittelstation to Tschuggenhütte to Arosa

Walking Easy Time: 2 hours

Rating: Comfortable

This walk is a pleasant introduction to the Arosa area. You'll take the Eichörnliweg, a gently ascending forest path to Maran, walking on to Prätschli, then the LAW Middle Station of the Weisshorn cable car. The path descends to Arosa past the Tschuggenhütte, with views of Innerarosa, the Weisshorn, and the Carmennahütte.

Start: Walk past the Hotel Alpina and up the road to the path signed EICHÖRNLIWEG NACH MARAN. Turn right and follow this pleasant path through the forest. This path, the "Squirrel Way," lives up to its reputation, as tame squirrels greet you and beg for food. After a half hour you emerge at the Hof Maran Hotel and tennis courts. Turn left on the Prätschliweg, ascending for fifteen minutes on a meadow path. At Prätschli, turn right and follow signs indicating LAW MITTELSTATION—35 MIN. At the Weisshorn Mittelstation, at 6611 ft. (2015 m.), walk to the back following the sign WANDERWEG—5 MIN. This path leads to the Tschuggenhütte, at 6533 ft. (1991 m.), and the sign 15 MIN. TO AROSA, the path descending to Arosa's main street.

Walk #2

Hörnlihütte Top Station to Alplisee to Schwellisee to Innerarosa to Arosa

Walking Easy Time: 3 hours

Rating: Comfortable

Today you'll take the Hörnli Express Lift from Innerarosa to the Hörnlihütte, at 8245 ft. (2513 m.). As you begin your descent to the Alplisee, at 7189 ft. (2191 m.), look at the rocks to the right—marmots play and dart in and out of their burrows. From Alplisee, the descent continues through Aroser Alp, past the Schwellisee, at 6342 ft. (1933 m.), with views up to the Weisshorn, Innerarosa, and the trail to Arosa.

Directions: Take the bus to the Hörnli Express and buy a one-way ticket to the top station.

Start: After leaving the lift station, proceed down the mountain to the left, in the direction of Alplisee. After about an hour, the trail forks. Take the left fork and make an immediate right turn when the trail splits again. The Schwellisee is down on the left, and Alplisee is off to the right. Follow the left trail until you come to another intersection. Turn left again, following signs to Schwellisee and Innerarosa.

Stay on the left side of the lake, on a path carved into the lower part of the mountain, descending gradually to the heights above Innerarosa, then to the Alpenblick Restaurant. Walk around the back of the restaurant and continue on the path marked INNERAROSA. In a few minutes the path splits. Stay on the right

A *Walking Easy* trail

path to Innerarosa. Walk ahead until you come to a fenced road and walk sharply down to the right, past private homes as you proceed toward the five-star Arosa Kulm Hotel in the heart of Innerarosa. You can catch the free Arosa bus from here, or walk fifteen minutes down the road, back to Arosa.

Walk #3

Hörnlihütte Top Station to Tschiertschen (Optional Excursion to Chur)
Walking Easy Time: 3 hours
Rating: Comfortable

The hike to Tschiertschen from the top of the Hörnli is a downhill, comfortable trek on the back side of Aroser Alp, the Weisshorn, and Ochsenalp. You will pass the Urdensee, at 7376 ft. (2248 m.), after descending about

920 ft. (280 m.) from the top of Hörnli Station. Continue walking on a descending trail through Inner Urden, at 6477 ft. (1974 m.), and Oberwald into Clus, ending in Tschiertschen, at 4430 ft. (1350 m.). Buses leave Tschiertschen for a thirty-minute ride and afternoon sight-seeing visit to the ancient city of Chur.

Directions: There are no restaurants on today's walk, although there are several in the quaint village of Tschiertschen, so be sure you've packed a picnic lunch and bottled water. Take the bus to the Hörnli Express Lift Station and purchase a one-way ticket to the top.

Start: Signs outside the station reading TSCHIERTSCHEN—2¼ HRS. direct you down and to the left. However, this hike will probably take *Easy Walkers* closer to three hours. As you walk down the hill, take the right fork, following signs to Urdensee–Tschiertschen. The path is blazed white and red throughout the entire hike. You're above the tree line as you approach Urdensee, an aqua lake down on the right. This path leads around to the left of the lake and bypasses it, dropping 1000 ft. (305 m.). Follow TSCHIERTSCHEN—2 HRS., as the path continues downhill to the right. It then swings around the mountain and turns into a wide, gravel path leading toward the farm at Inner Urden. As you descend, another group of signs points to Tschiertschen. Be sure you take the lower path on your right in the direction of the dairy farm. As you approach the farm, step over a small wire fence in order to continue (the fence is not for hikers but for cows). Walk around the right side of the barn, picking up the trail as you pass through a gate on the back side of the farm.

After reaching the farm at Inner Urden, a few more minutes brings you to a weathered, deserted barn. Follow a sign directing you to stay on the main path ahead, now marked CLUS–TSCHIERTSCHEN. As you reach the tree line, the landscape softens, the path is less rocky, and, looking over the deep ravine on your right, you will see the alps that are Switzerland's trademark. Note a sign that reads CLUS–TSCHIERTSCHEN straight ahead and FARWEG–TSCHIERTSCHEN to the right. Although both lead to the same destination, we recommend the mountain path through the forest—a typical descending, rocky *bergweg,* blazed in red and white.

When you reach a paved road, the *bergweg* meets the *farweg,* a different trail. This paved path becomes a road, leading into Clus, where a sign directs you to Tschiertschen. Within fifteen minutes you'll enter this picturesque mountain village. Walk ahead to the church—to the right is the post office and bus stop, where you take the bus to Chur; the schedule is posted. If it's still early, pay the old city of Chur a visit. With either option, take the Arosa train, outside and in front of the railroad station, signed NACH AROSA.

Walk #4

Prätschli to Rot Tritt to Ochsenalp to Scheidegg to Prätschli
Walking Easy Time: 3½ hours
Rating: Comfortable

A short bus ride will take you to Prätschli, where the walk begins, ascending from 6234 to 6726 ft. (1900 to 2050 m.). The return hike leads up and over an alp and eventually down to Prätschli, where you catch the bus back to Arosa.

Directions: Take the bus to Prätschli, the last stop.

Start: Signs direct you toward Rot Tritt on a wide, paved path, ascending at the rear of the circular bus stop. As you ascend, the path narrows, continuing toward Rot Tritt. Cows are grazing, farmers are haying, and you are surrounded by a tranquil, bucolic scene. Stay on the white-and-red blazed main trail to Rot Tritt.

Before the hour is up, you'll have turned around the mountain to reach Rot Tritt, a viewpoint at 6582 ft. (2006 m.). Following the sign OCHSENALP—35 MIN., you will soon be on a shady path descending gently to Ochsenalp, at 6352 ft. (1936 m.). Within forty-five minutes a sign indicates an abrupt change of direction. Walk up the hill to the left in the direction of Scheidegg. Within fifteen to twenty minutes you will have ascended this grassy peak, on your way to the signed intersection MARAN, AROSA—1 HR. Walk through the gate, continuing in the direction of Maran and Arosa. From this point, it's downhill all the way. Be sure to follow the white-and-red blazing, as there are branch trails going off in several directions. Cross a small gravel field, descending toward the main path back to Maran and Prätschli. The path is a bit rocky here before you meet the paved path you walked up earlier this morning. Turn right, descending gradually to the bus stop at Prätschli.

Walk #5

Hörnlihütte Top Station to Carmennahütte to Weisshorn Mid-Station to Prätschli to Innerarosa to Arosa
Walking Easy Time: 3 hours
Rating: Comfortable

Our hike begins after taking the lift up to the Hörnlihütte. You will descend to the Carmennahütte, continuing through the meadows to the Weisshorn Mid-Station, then to Prätschli for a forest walk above Arosa to Innerarosa, where you continue into town.

Directions: Catch a bus to the Hörnli Lift Station, and buy a one-way ticket to the top.

Start: Leaving the top station, follow the signs CARMENNAHÜTTE—40 MIN. and LAW MITTELSTATION—1¼ HRS. Within an hour you'll arrive at the Carmennahütte, with a sun terrace and restaurant. Continue walking down the path to the middle station of the Weisshorn cable car. At the middle station, follow the sign PRÄTSCHLI—30 MIN. by making a half-right turn on a white-and-red blazed path winding down through the meadow, rather than staying on the road. After entering a forest area, the trail narrows. At a fork in the path, turn right and walk down through the meadow, following the trail under the Weisshorn lift lines to a gravel path. Turn right, where signs direct you to Arosa. Turn right again to the Oberwald Promenade, ascending through the forest, over and around Arosa, to Innerarosa, and back to your hotel.

Walk #6

Weisshorn Mittelstation along the Arlenwaldweg to Prätschli to Rot Tritt through the Schafwald to Arosa (Excursion to the Weisshorn)
Walking Easy Time: 2½ to 3 hours
Rating: Comfortable

You might wish to reserve the better part of the day for this hike and excursion to the Weisshorn, Arosa's highest lift, at 8705 ft. (2653 m.). Walking from the Weisshorn Top Station might be a little tough on *Easy Walker* knees, so we'll bring you by return cable car to the mid-station for the start of today's walk.

From the Mittelstation you'll walk to Rot Tritt on a comfortable path. You visited Rot Tritt if you took Walk #4, but today, instead of walking up

to Ochsenalp and Schei-
degg, you will descend
from Rot Tritt, through
meadow and forest, to
Arosa.

Directions: Walk to
the Weisshorn Aerial Ca-
bleway, near the train station. If visibility is very
good, purchase a ticket to
the top station, with a return to the mid-station,
where the walk begins. If
visibility is questionable,
buy a one-way ticket to
the mid-station only.

Start: After taking in
the spectacular panorama
from the *gipfel*, return
by cable car to the LAW

Mittelstation, at 6611 ft. (2015 m.), and exit, following signs to the right
to Rot Tritt. After a twenty-minute descent on a comfortable path, signs
indicate Maran and Prätschli below, but follow the sign to Rot Tritt ahead,
a comfortable ascent from 6260 to 6582 ft. (1908 to 2006 m.). If you've
taken Walk #4, Rot Tritt will be familiar, but instead of continuing to
Ochsenalp and Scheidegg, descend from this point on the red-and-white
blazed trail next to the picnic table. This descent through the meadow lasts
for only ten minutes, until the trail empties onto a wagon road. Turn right,
toward Arosa. Along the way, a sign indicates LANGWIESSER AUSSICHT. Take this
five-minute detour to a scenic viewpoint of the villages in the valley below.
After about ten minutes, another sign directs you on a wagon path to your
right, leaving the road, through the forest to Arosa (a fifty-minute walk).
This comfortable *forest strasse* brings you directly to the Obersee in central
Arosa for the walk back to your hotel.

Walk #7

Arosa to Stausee to Furggalp to Arosa (Optional Walk to Medergen and Längwies)

Walking Easy Time: 3½ to 6 hours
Rating: Comfortable

Today's walk begins in Arosa and descends to the Untersee, continuing to the Stausee. A walk along the Stausee brings you to the mountain trail up to Furggalp, at 5578 ft. (1700 m.). At this point, you can continue the ascent to Medergen by way of Tieja. Or you can walk to the Grünsee and return to Arosa on the opposite side of the Stausee. If you choose to walk on to Medergen, a more challenging hike because of the time and steeper ascents and descents involved, you will ascend from 5250 to 6562 ft. (1600 to 2000 m.), then descend to 4518 ft. (1377 m.) at the train station at Längwies.

Start: Walk up the main street of Arosa, past the *kursaal* (casino), to where the street forks at a boutique. Follow a sign with a symbol of a swimmer directing you down and to the left. Walk down the paved road and follow it around to your left, passing the Central Hotel. Shortly a sign reading ZUM UNTERSEE points you to the right, into the forest. At a fork in the road, turn right at the sign TANNEWEG, passing the Robinson Club. Follow another sign left to Stausee. Eventually the path turns left around a private home and leads past some stables. The path joins an auto road; walk ahead to Stausee-Furggalp and the foot of the lake. Continue, with the lake on your right. A sign indicates FURGGALP—25 MIN. and GRÜNSEE—50 MIN.

At the end of the lake, signs point ahead to Litziruti and Längwies; however, turn up the hill in the direction of Furggalp and Grünsee. Do not follow the *lauf,* or running trail, a small path leading into the woods. Stay on the main trail up the hill to the left, ascending from 5250 to 5578 ft. (1600 to 1700 m.) at Furggalp, where additional signs direct you to Grünsee, Medergen, and Davos. You now have the following options:

1. Continue walking ahead to the intersection and turn right, following signs to Grünsee. At Grünsee, stay to your right, walking down to Stausee, this time along the opposite side of the lake, and joining the path to Arosa you walked on earlier today.

2. If the weather is clear and you are a strong walker, continue hiking for another ninety minutes from Furggalp up the mountain to 6562 ft. (2000 m.) and the incredible Medergen view. Continue the hike from Medergen by walking down the mountain for at least another

hour, dropping to Längwies, at 4518 ft. (1377 m.), and returning to Arosa by train. *NOTE: Think carefully about the timing for this route.*

SAMEDAN/ST. MORITZ

(Engadine)

Simplicity, understated elegance, and a feeling of antiquity characterize Samedan, a quiet Engadine village situated between its more famous sisters, St. Moritz and Pontresina. Samedan, our *Walking Easy* base village, is situated at 5643 ft. (1720 m.), with excellent rail and bus service, a small airport (the highest in Europe), and the oldest eighteen-hole golf course in Europe.

The well-preserved village of Samedan, with its centuries-old houses, appears to be lifted from a colorful history book of Switzerland, and the Engadine, in southeastern Switzerland, is probably the most interesting cultural and architectural area in the country. The Upper Engadine includes the famous resort towns of St. Moritz, Pontresina, Samedan, and Zuoz, while the Lower Engadine is known for the mineral springs of Scuol and the wildlife preserve of the Swiss National Park. Visitors to the picturesque Engadine villages marvel at the distinctively ornamented *sgraffito* (two-tone designs in plaster) etched into the stately sixteenth- and seventeenth-century houses and the ancient Romansch language, which is still spoken by many residents. Frequent trains and buses take hikers throughout the Engadine, from the Swiss-Italian border villages of Soglio and Castasegna, all the way to the unique villages of Zernez and Scuol.

St. Moritz is the commercial and social hub of this remarkably beautiful valley and the center of dozens of hikes along pristine lakes, into deep glacial valleys, and on balcony trails, using the many lift systems to reach the area's snow-covered peaks.

Transportation

By Train - Take the train to Chur, and change for the scenic two-hour ride. Or pick up the *Glacier Express* on one of its stops between Zermatt and Samedan. (See Zermatt, Transportation, for information.)

By Car - Samedan is situated on Route 27, north of St. Moritz. From Chur, drive over the Julier Pass to Silvaplana, then north on 27. From southern Switzerland or northern Italy around Lake Como, drive through the Maloja Pass to St. Moritz and follow signs to Samedan.

Favorite *Walking Easy* Hotels

Hotel Bernina

Four-Star; Director—Th. Bonjour

CH-7503 Samedan; **Tel:** 81 852 12 12; **Fax:** 81 852 36 06

Internet: www.hotel-bernina.ch

E-mail: hotel-bernina@bluewin.ch

> The hotel traces its origins back to 1864. Of course this comfortable *grande dame* has been updated over the years, now featuring an elegant, chandeliered dining room with warm, attentive service from the staff and romantic evening dining, always accompanied by a salad buffet. A full Swiss breakfast buffet is served, with the flakiest croissants this side of the French border. Mr. Bonjour, the managing director, is particularly effective and efficient, running this landmark hotel with unusual personal attention. If you arrive in Samedan by train, call the hotel for complimentary pickup service.

Golf-Hotel des Alpes

Three-Star; Owners—Familie Tarnuzzer

CH-7503 Samedan; **Tel:** 81 851 03 00; **Fax:** 81 851 03 38

Internet: www.golf-hotel-des-alpes.ch

E-mail: hotel-des-alpes@bluewin.ch

> This cozy family hotel has been recently renovated and boasts an eighty-year tradition in Samedan. The hotel is located in a quiet section of town, near public transportation. The rooms are comfortable, equipped with radio and TV. South-facing rooms have balconies, and a fitness room, Turkish bath, Jacuzzi, and solarium are all available, as well as a garden and roof garden. In addition to a full Swiss breakfast buffet, a salad buffet is featured at dinner, with owner Arnold Tarnuzzer, the talented chef, preparing excellent regional cooking.

Excursions

The Samedan Tourist Information Office is located on the main street across from the Hotel Bernina.

Fax: 81 851 00 66;

Internet: www.samedan.ch

E-mail: info@samedan.ch

1. **Samedan** - Visit the old parish church, built in 1771, in the center of the village. The Planta House, also in the heart of town, is now a valued Romansch library.

2. **St. Moritz** - The resort of St. Moritz is a ten-minute train ride from Samedan. Situated at 6000 ft. (1829 m.) in a unique landscape of crystal-clear lakes, imposing glaciers, and majestic mountains, St. Moritz also boasts five lifts for summer hikers to use. The St. Moritz Tourist Information Office is located at via Maistra 12, in the main square.

   Directions: Trains and buses run frequently from Samedan to St. Moritz. A city bus runs between St. Moritz Bad, the spa area, and St. Moritz Dorf, the shopping and hotel area.

3. **Pontresina** - Near St. Moritz, at an altitude of 5821 ft. (1774 m.), Pontresina lies on a high, sunny terrace, surrounded by the Bernina mountains and imposing glaciers; three areas operate lift systems in summer. One is at **Diavolezza**, with summer skiing available at the glacier. The cable car rises to 9771 ft. (2978 m.) and a spectacular glacial panorama. Take the train from Samedan to Pontresina and change for the train to Poschiavo, exiting at the Bernina–Diavolezza station. Because cable car **Lagalb** is only a few minutes' train ride from Diavolezza, you might plan the day to visit both peaks.

4. **Zuoz** - Considered the best-preserved village in the Upper Engadine, Zuoz nestles at 5750 ft. (1753 m.) in lush meadows. (See Walk #6.)

   Directions: Trains leave Samedan hourly for Zuoz.

5. **Celerina** - Lying between St. Moritz and Samedan, at 5675 ft. (1862 m.), this small Engadine village is sometimes considered a suburb of glitzier St. Moritz. Celerina contains charming houses that are worth exploring on a walk from Samedan.

   Directions: Trains and buses run frequently between Samedan and Celerina. However, it is a short walk from one village to the other.

6. **Sils-Maria** and **Sils-Baselgia** - With a combined population of fewer than 500 persons, these quiet, charming resorts in the Upper Engadine are situated at the beginning of the Inn (En) Valley. From 1881 to 1889 Sils-Maria was summer home to the philosopher Nietzsche, who wrote *Thus Spake Zarathustra* there, and his museum is located to the right of the main bus station. A Pferde Omnibus (horse and carriage) leaves every day from the post office in Sils-Maria for trips into the beautiful Fex Valley. Reservations are necessary. (See Walk #2.)

   Directions: Take a morning train, arriving in St. Moritz to connect with the bus to Sils-Maria at the St. Moritz train station (a total trip of about an hour).

7. **Scuol, Tarasp, Vulpera** - These tiny towns are enchanting, with their cobblestoned streets and *sgraffito*-decorated houses. A bus from Scuol or Tarasp takes you to Schloss Tarasp, a restored castle still in use. *Directions: Trains leave Samedan regularly for the seventy-five-minute ride to Scuol.*

8. **Poschiavo** - This small, Italian-speaking Swiss village offers a different style of architecture and surroundings from its Engadine neighbors, mixing German and Italian styles into its transalpine surroundings. From July 1 through September 1, an open-air market is held every Wednesday in the town square. *Directions: Take the train from Samedan to Pontresina, then change for the Bernina Express to Tirano, stopping in Poschiavo.*

9. **Swiss National Park** - In this protected alpine sanctuary, plants and animals are allowed to develop without human interference. The National Park House is in Zernez, and we recommend a stop before entering the park. *Directions: A midmorning train arrives in Zernez from Samedan in about forty-five minutes. Check with the tourist office—they offer trips into the park.*

Samedan Walks

Recommended Maps:
- ❖ Wanderkarte—Oberengadin, Bergell, Nationalpark
- ❖ Kümmerly+Frey Wanderkarte—Oberengadin, Bergell-Puschlav
- ❖ Kleiner Wanderführer der Engadiner Bergbahnen

Walk #1
Muottas Muragl Top Station to Alp Languard Top Station
Walking Easy Time: 3 hours
Rating: Comfortable

Today you will take the short train ride from Samedan to Punt Muragl and the funicular to Muottas Muragl, at 8048 ft. (2453 m.). The path *Easy Walkers* will take is a midlevel balcony trail at a comfortable 6600 ft. (2000 m.) toward Pontresina and the Alp Languard Chairlift, under the famous Segantinihütte, at 8960 ft. (2731 m.).

> **Hint:** *The views from this trail into the Val Roseg and its glacier, St. Moritz and its lakes, and the surrounding high peaks of the Engadine are so compelling that we caution Easy Walkers to admire the views while taking a "scenery break" rather than risking an accident while walking.*

Directions: Take a train toward Pontresina, one-stop to Punt Muragl. Buy a round-trip ticket—up to Muottas Muragl on the funicular and down on the Alp Languard Chairlift.

Start: On leaving the funicular, walk ahead through the turnstile and follow the sign ALP LANGUARD—2¾ HRS. This scenic hike speaks for itself—just continue to follow signs to Alp Languard, ignoring the side trails to Samedan and Pontresina.

After taking the chairlift down to Pontresina, follow signs for the fifteen-minute walk to the train station.

Walk #2

Furtschellas Top Station to Marmorè to Curtins/Fex Valley to Sils-Maria
Walking Easy Time: 3¼ hours
Rating: Comfortable

Today's beautiful hike begins in Sils-Maria with the lift up to Furtschellas, at 7586 ft. (2312 m.). You'll hike to Marmorè, which offers exceptional views over the lakes and through the valley to St. Moritz. The hike continues on a mountain *bergweg* to the village of Curtins in the Fex Valley, for the gentle walk back through Crasta and into the *schlucht* (gorge) to Sils-Maria and the bus.

Directions: Take a train from Samedan to St. Moritz, then pick up the bus to Sils-Maria outside the train station. In Sils, follow signs to the Furtschellas Lift Station and buy a one-way ticket to the top station.

Start: On exiting, follow the path around the sun terrace signed MAR-MORÈ–VAL FEX—1 HR. Climb the hill for a few minutes until you reach a second sign directing you down the hill on a rocky path, eventually leveling, until you reach the viewpoint at Marmorè.

After taking in the outstanding views, follow signs to Curtins on the lower path. The trail can be steep and sometimes slippery, so use caution while descending. The village of Curtins, at the foot of the glacier, can be seen during your descent.

The *bergweg* ends at the road, where you have two options:

1. Return to Sils via horse-drawn carriage.
2. Take the short walk along the road to Crasta and visit the famous Fex church with its ancient murals. Then follow Schluchtweg, Sils-Maria through the village of Fex-Platta and the gorge.

In Sils-Maria, continue ahead for a few minutes to the bus stop. Exit the bus at the Schulhaus Platz stop in St. Moritz and change for the bus to Samedan.

Walk #3

Pontresina to Val Roseg (Optional Walk back to Pontresina)
Walking Easy Time: 2 to 4 hours
Rating: Gentle

This lovely valley walk will take *Easy Walkers* on a gently ascending forest trail from Pontresina to the foot of the Val Roseg Glacier—one of the most popular walks in the area. The path ascends comfortably from 5922 to 6562 ft. (1805 to 2000 m.), and in two hours you'll reach the Restaurant Roseggletscher, with a buffet served on its sun terrace. You can return by Pferde Omnibus or walk back on the same trail. Make reservations for the wagon ride in advance at your hotel.

Directions: Take a train from Samedan, and in ten minutes you'll be at the *bahnhof* in Pontresina.

Start: After leaving the station, turn right, and within a few feet note the standing area for the Pferde Omnibus. Follow the sign FUSSWEG–VAL ROSEG 150 M., and note VAL ROSEG FUSSWEG on your right, in front of a parking area. The path begins in back and to the right, ascending gradually into the forest.

The path ascends easily and meets the road. Take the trail to the left to avoid the bikers and horses and walk through the forest to the hotel.

Check out the dessert buffet—the choices are up to you (and your wallet).

After lunch, a walk around the restaurant will disclose signs to various destinations. Take the path toward the glacier on the restaurant side of the river and walk as long as you feel comfortable. Before taking any additional walks, make your decision as to whether to take that horse-and-wagon ride back to Pontresina or return on the same path you came on. The wagon ride takes about fifty minutes, while the return walk will take less than two hours.

Walk #4

Sils-Baselgia to Grevasalvas to Sils-Maria (Excursion to St. Moritz or Optional Walk to Maloja)

Walking Easy Time: 3 to 4½ hours
Rating: Comfortable

Today's walk leads to the alpine hamlet where the 1960 remake of *Heidi* was filmed. *Easy Walkers* will take the train to St. Moritz and change for the bus to Sils-Baselgia, where the trail begins. After a steady ascent from 5900 to 6560 ft. (1798 to 2000 m.), you'll reach the heights overlooking Grevasalvas. We're not sure Grandfather is around anymore, but this wondrous little hamlet is still situated below a grassy alp, surrounded by grazing cows and craggy peaks. After conjuring up images of blond braids, dirndl skirts, and gentle, pipe-smoking grandpas, you will return on the same path, proceeding down the mountain toward Sils-Baselgia and Sils-Maria. Or continue ahead on the same path to Maloja, where you can take a bus to St. Moritz and Samedan.

Directions: Catch a morning train to St. Moritz, in time to take a connecting bus to Sils-Baselgia, located outside the front of the station and to the left.

Start: When you get off the bus in Sils-Baselgia, walk ahead through the small village toward the mountains. After crossing the road, follow the sign left, up toward Grevasalvas. This stone-strewn trail is shaded by pine forests, and it gradually ascends 650 ft. (200 m.). Following the sign GREVASALVAS—½ HR., you'll see waterfalls rush over rocky promontories on the right, as you step over streams, ascending on a narrow, rocky trail. Reaching the high point of 6562 ft. (2000 m.), you'll spy the hamlet of Grevasalvas below and to the left. You can walk down a steep path to this cluster of houses if you're going to continue on to Maloja, or remain on the hillside and enjoy lunch on a green-carpeted alp.

An alpine trail in Grevasalvas

There are options for your return:

1. Continue ahead and follow signs to Maloja, bringing you down from 6562 to 5955 ft. (2000 to 1815 m.) in about ninety minutes. Buses leave regularly from Maloja to St. Moritz, where you change at Schulhaus Platz for the bus to Samedan.

2. Retrace your steps along the same trail, passing through Sils-Baselgia, visiting Sils-Maria, taking the bus to St. Moritz and then to Samedan.

If you decide on Option #2, this reverse walk should take about seventy-five minutes. At the base of the trail in Sils-Baselgia, cross the road and walk past a restaurant with a sun terrace and rest room facilities. Continue to walk up the main street into Sils-Maria, taking the bus to the St. Moritz Schulhaus Platz stop in the heart of the St. Moritz shopping area. This is a short block from the famous Hanselman's tearoom and pastry shop, tempting weary travelers with some of the most delectable desserts in town (except on Tuesday, when it's closed). Check the bus schedule back to Samedan from Schulhaus Platz before exploring St. Moritz.

Walk #5

Marguns Top Station to Alp Muntatsch via Alp Clavadasch to Samedan
Walking Easy Time: 3½ to 4 hours
Rating: More challenging

A quick train ride from Samedan will bring you to Celerina and the gondolas to Marguns. The hike is mostly comfortable, except for a more challenging ascent during the first forty-five minutes. *Easy Walkers* should be able to handle this, but proceed slowly. Reserve the better part of a clear day for this hike. There are no restaurants or rest room facilities along this trail.

Directions: Take a train one stop to Celerina. As you exit the train, turn right, then right again on a paved path to the lift station. Take the gondola to the top station at Marguns.

Start: Although it's possible to take a chairlift up to Corviglia and eventually up to Piz Nair, at 10,042 ft. (3057 m.), we suggest getting started on today's hike by turning left down the hill as you leave the Marguns Lift Station, following the ALP CLAVADASCH sign. Just past the sign, enter the unsigned, red-and-white blazed path rising through the meadow. After ascending about forty-five minutes on a mountain *bergweg*, you'll reach the high point of today's hike, at 7358 ft. (2240 m.). Stay on the lower right path to Celerina and Samedan. This trail rambles along Alp Clavadasch in the direction of Alp Muntatsch. We do *not* recommend taking the steep paths that head down the mountain toward Samedan or Celerina. Stay on the trail toward Alp Muntatsch, at 7181 ft. (2186 m.). After resting at the barn at Alp Muntatsch, follow the sign onto the jeep road, SAMEDAN TRAIN STATION—1¼ HRS.

Walk #6

Zuoz to Madulain to La Punt to Bever to Samedan (Excursion to Zuoz)
Walking Easy Time: 3 hours
Rating: Gentle

Zuoz nestles in lush green meadows at 5742 ft. (1750 m.), far from the hustle and bustle of St. Moritz, and is considered to be the best-preserved village in the Upper Engadine. Today's excursion and walk brings *Easy Walkers* to this enchanting town, leaving time for sight-seeing, photography, and lunch. The afternoon will be made up of a low-level walk through the valley from Zuoz through the small and photogenic villages of Madulain, La Punt, and Bever—largely through the meadows and close to the Inn River.

Directions: Take a train to Zuoz, a fifteen-minute ride from Samedan.

Start: Arriving in Zuoz, cross the tracks and walk up the hill to the town center. As you reach the main street, make a right turn, and within a few minutes you'll reach the town square. Take an hour or so to explore the cobblestoned streets and alleys and *sgrafitto*-decorated houses before beginning today's walk. The village has retained its original character, restoring its elegant sixteenth- and seventeenth-century houses. Most of its 1,200 inhabitants speak Romansch as well as Swiss-German. Visit Planta House, located on the main square of Zuoz, and the church with its heraldic symbol of the Planta family—a severed bear's paw. The church's modern stained-glass windows were designed by famed sculptor Augusto Giacometti.

Leave Zuoz by retracing your steps to the railroad station. At the station turn right, then walk through the long parking area to the end, picking up a path through a small tunnel underneath the tracks. Walk past a restaurant and down to the river. Turn right along the river path, following the sign to Madulain, a tiny, quiet, well-preserved Engadine village.

After twenty-five minutes, the path veers up a hill to the right, where you turn left on an unsigned path to Madulain. This is the Zuoz–Madulain Innweg, a promenade between the two villages along the Inn River. As you proceed, Madulain comes into full view, and in the distance to the left is the village of Chamuesch-ch. Walk ahead through Madulain on its main road.

As you leave Madulain, the path crosses a major auto road. Do not cross. Walk across the wooden bridge over the river on your left. Make a sharp right turn at the end of the bridge and walk down a flight of stairs, under the auto road, with the path spilling into the meadow on the other side. Continue to a four-way intersection and turn right to La Punt–Bever. At the Hotel Krone you have two options:

1. Turn right and follow signs to the *stazione* for the next train back to Samedan.

2. Cross the street behind the Hotel Krone and follow directions to Bever–Samedan–Pontresina. Cross a stream on a small wooden bridge to pick up a path alongside the river that leads directly into Bever, then Samedan.

Walk #7

Ospizio Bernina to Sassal Massone to Alp Grüm
Walking Easy Time: 2½ hours
Rating: More challenging

The Swiss area closest to the mountains separating Italy from Switzerland provides the setting for today's hike. You'll take the train to Ospizio Bernina, the Rhaetian Railway's highest station, and hike to Sassal Massone and its restaurant, at 7392 ft. (2253 m.). The walk will continue down the mountain to the 6860 ft. (2091 m.) railroad station at Alp Grüm, a wonderful spot to admire the view across to the Palü Glacier and Puschlav, as far as the Bergamo Alps, before the train ride back to Samedan.

The train from Samedan to Ospizio Bernina brings you into the Italian-influenced region of Switzerland, and the signs and names are now in Italian instead of German or Romansch. This change in atmosphere makes Switzerland even more appealing to visitors, as language, customs, cuisine, dress, and living styles change dramatically the closer you get to the Italian border: *See,* or lake, becomes *lago,* and *stunde,* or hour, is now *ora.*

Directions: We suggest a train leaving about 9:00 A.M. to Pontresina, changing for the train to Ospizio Bernina and Tirano waiting on an adjacent platform. Sit on the right side for the best views, and within forty minutes you'll arrive at your destination: Ospizio Bernina.

Start: At the end of the station, follow SASSAL MASSONE—1¼ HRS. Walk along the Lago Bianco reservoir and railroad tracks—below the Cambrena Glacier—on a white-and-red blazed path. At the end of the lake, the path forks. Take either path (they meet) for a short distance until you come to another fork in the road and a sign indicating SASSAL MASSONE to the right. Turn right, proceeding up the mountain, bringing you to the Sassal Massone restaurant, at 7392 ft. (2253m.), and a fabulous view of the glacier.

To return to Alp Grüm, walk to the rear of the terrace and proceed down a dirt path facing the glacier. This trail is a rocky, narrow mountain *bergweg,* but well marked, well defined, and well used. There are many side trails; stay on the main path, blazed white and red. The trail button-hooks and, instead of facing the glacier, turns toward the train station of Alp Grüm.

Within an hour you'll reach the bottom of the mountain. Turn right and walk up to the railroad tracks. Follow a sign pointing to a lower path along the tracks for the ten-minute walk to the Alp Grüm station and its restaurant, inviting sun terrace, and rest room facilities. Trains to Samedan (with a change in Pontresina) run hourly.

Walk #8

Signal Lift Station on the "via Engiadina" to Alp Suvretta to Orchas to Silvaplana

Walking Easy Time: 3½ hours

Rating: More challenging

As with all high-level walks in the Samedan/St. Moritz area, try to take this sensational hike on a clear, sunny day. You'll take the cable car from St. Moritz Bad to the signal station, where the hike begins. The first part is a delightful balcony walk along Alp Giop. At Alp Suvretta, the path becomes more of a mountain trail as it continues toward Silvaplana through Orchas, with some more challenging ascents. This "via Engiadina" trail is well signed and well traveled and can be taken all the way to Maloja on a path above Lake Silvaplana and Lej da Segl. Today, however, *Easy Walkers* will depart the via Engiadina and descend to the village of Silvaplana for the bus ride to St. Moritz.

Directions: Take the bus from Samedan to the St. Moritz Bad Signal lift stop. Buy a one-way ticket to Signal.

Start: At the Signal Lift Station, at 6989 ft. (2130 m.), follow signs left indicating ALP SU-VRETTA—45 MIN., picking up via Engiadina signs along the way. Within forty-five minutes to an hour you'll reach Alp Suvretta, at 7254 ft. (2211 m.). The path button-hooks and descends, signed VIA ENGIADINA, now on a typ-ical *bergweg*, occasion-ally blazed red and white. The trail crosses a wooden bridge to an un-signed fork in the trail.

Scenic *Walking Easy* trail

Stay on the lower left trail, still blazed red and white.

At a signed intersection, follow via Engiadina to the right, as the trail begins to ascend.

After about two hours, follow a large red-and-white unsigned arrow directing you sharply left for a short descent to a group of signs, leaving the via Engiadina, which continues on to the right. Passing a large sign announcing an artillery position from World War I, the red-and-white blazed path continues to descend. The trail eventually buttonhooks down and around to the left at a via Engiadina sign, with a clear view of the road ahead.

Follow an arrow down to the auto road. Cross the road, turn left, and walk on the road for about 100 yards to a sign indicating SILVAPLANA—15 MIN. Shortly, enter a wagon path, blazed red and white on a fence. It descends through the forest, reaching a paved, rarely used mountain road and eventually emptying into an auto road. Turn right on the auto road. Cross the road and turn left where a sign indicates SILVAPLANA BUS, entering the forest on a winding, red-and-white blazed trail signed TRUOCH PIGNIA. After a few minutes the trail empties into the village of Silvaplana. Wind down into the village, turn left on the main auto road, and walk to the PTT bus station on the right.

Walk #9

Soglio to Castasegna (Excursion to the Val Bregaglia over the Maloja Pass)
Walking Easy Time: 1 hour
Rating: Gentle

There are many opportunities for hiking in the Val Bregaglia or Bergell (the same place—just differences in Italian or German spelling), the smallest of the southern Engadine valleys of the Graubunden/Grisons canton. Today, however, you'll descend gently through Europe's largest chestnut forest on the "Romantic Trail" from Soglio, a historic mountain hamlet, to the village of Castasegna at the Swiss-Italian border. This walk is only an hour, but we bring you on a bus ride over the exhilarating (read, hair-raising) Maloja Pass so that you can experience the gradual architectural and cultural change from Engadine Swiss to Engadine Italian. You'll ride through tiny hamlets that seem untouched by modern culture—the picturesque and unspoiled villages of the Val Bregaglia.

Stone house near Soglio

Directions: Check bus and train schedules carefully. Take an early-morning train from Samedan to St. Moritz. Walk outside the station to the bus terminal and take the connecting bus to Chiavenna. This bus is non-stop to Soglio, after a thrilling ride over the Maloja Pass and through the quaint mountain towns of the Bergell.

Start: Take some time to explore this village where time stands still. The view from the church cemetery is breathtaking—glaciers and mountains in all directions—and the narrow streets are a photographer's paradise. When ready, walk back down the narrow road in the direction the bus came from. In about twenty minutes, turn into the forest on the right, following the sign CASTASEGNA ON THE HISTORIC PATH. In five minutes, arriving at a lovely waterfall, follow the path through the mountain and under the falls, and continue through meadows filled with old log cabins and surrounded by chestnut trees, following signs to Castasegna. After about an hour, and just before Castasegna, there's a tiny park with a picnic table.

Arriving at Castasegna's main street, turn left to La Posta and the bus, leaving hourly for Schulhaus Platz in St. Moritz, where you change for the bus to Samedan.

EASTERN SWITZERLAND

APPENZELL/APPENZELLERLAND

A first visit to Switzerland's Appenzellerland evokes a rush of excitement as the idyllic, rolling, velvety hills of the countryside embrace typical Appenzell farmhouses framed by the magnificent Alpstein mountain range—an ideal marriage for *Walking Easy* in an unforgettable landscape.

There are over 320 miles (515 km.) of marked hiking trails in this area, and *Easy Walkers* will enjoy passing through verdant meadows and alps, past farms with herds of grazing cows, their milk used in the making of world-renowned Appenzeller cheese. One meadow walk features a unique *barfussweg*, a grassy path so soft that you are asked to remove your hiking boots as you cross the rolling fields. Other hikes wind through Stone Age caves at Wildkirchli and lead to a visit to Seealpsee, a picturesque mountain lake. A thrilling cable car excursion to the Säntis peak takes you from 4436 to 8209 ft. (1352 to 2502 m.), with far-reaching views into Switzerland, Germany, Austria, and the Dolomites of Italy.

Historic Appenzell, with its brightly painted houses—now filled with busloads of day-trippers—is the political and economic center of Appenzellerland. Shops offer famous Appenzell lace, cheese, baked goods, chocolates, and primitive paintings by the area's artists. Choral and instrumental concerts featuring Appenzell string music and yodeling are frequent, as are folk festivals featuring traditional Appenzellerland costumes. Local bus and rail transportation brings hikers to and from the start of hikes, making sight-seeing excursions to charming nearby villages easily accessible.

Once you've discovered the Appenzell trails, you'll fall in love again—as we did.

Transportation

By Train - Take the train to Gossau or St. Gallen, then transfer to the local train to Appenzell.

By Car - Drive toward St. Gallen and follow signs to Appenzell.

Favorite *Walking Easy* Hotel

Romantik Hotel Säntis
Four-Star; Owner—Catriona and Stefan Heeb
CH-9050 Appenzell; **Tel:** 71 788 11 11; **Fax:** 71 788 11 10
Internet: www.romantikhotels.com/rhappen
E-mail: romantikhotelsaentis@bluewin.ch
The Romantik Hotel Säntis is situated on the historic Landsgemeinde-platz, a famous square in the village of Appenzell. The hotel features traditional Appenzell architecture and design. Its rooms are quaintly yet elegantly furnished and have all the modern amenities expected in a four-star hotel. A recent renovation added six suites, a bar, a sauna, and a solarium. There are several top-quality restaurants in the hotel serving excellent Swiss and Continental cuisine. Friday nights are reserved for a special Appenzeller buffet dinner featuring local music and entertain-ment. The Heeb family are always in attendance, creating that special family atmosphere *Easy Walkers* will appreciate.

Excursions

The Appenzell Tourist Office is located on the main street.
Fax: 71 788 96 49
Internet: www.myappenzellerland.ch
E-mail: infotourismus@ai.ch

1. **St. Gallen** - The largest city in northeast Switzerland, St. Gallen is the area's cultural and economic center and the highest city of its size in Europe. Also known for its embroidery and lace, its Old Town boasts medieval houses built in narrow, car-free alleys laid out during the Middle Ages.
Directions: The direct train from Appenzell arrives in St. Gallen in forty-five minutes.

2. **Stein** - This village is situated on a sunny hilltop and is famous for its Appenzell cheese. An Appenzell Showcase Cheese Dairy has been estab-lished here, and visitors can watch the production of this famous cheese—from the milk delivery to its ripening.
Directions: Check with the Tourist Office for a bus excursion to Stein.

3. **Zurich** - Switzerland's largest city, Zurich is located on Lake Zurich and bisected by the Limmat River. It is a center of international finance and its main street, Bahnhofstrasse, is lined with shops and banks. The Old

Town, however, boasts cobblestoned streets and ancient squares.

Directions: *Take a train from Appenzell to Zurich, changing in Herisau for the connecting train (a trip of about two hours).*

Appenzell Walks

Recommended Maps:

- ❖ Appenzell-Toggenburg-St. Gallen-Säntis
- ❖ Kümmerly+Frey–Säntis-Alpstein
- ❖ Wanderkarte—Obertoggenburg-Appenzell

Walk #1

Introductory Walk—Sammelplatz to Hütten to Höch Hirschberg to Gais (Optional Walk to Appenzell)
Walking Easy Time: 2 to 3 hours
Rating: Comfortable

Today's walk can serve as an introduction to the tranquil green alps of Appenzellerland. You'll take a six-minute train ride to Sammelplatz and hike from 3042 ft. (927 m.) to Hütten, at 3452 ft. (1052 m.), continuing up to Höch Hirschberg, at 3829 ft. (1167 m.), for views of the surrounding alps. You'll then descend to Gais, at 3061 ft. (933 m.), for the short train ride back to Appenzell. If it's early enough, you might want to return by walking to Appenzell.

Directions: Take the train toward Gais at the Appenzell *bahnhof.* *NOTE: Be sure that immediately after the train passes Hirschberg (where it may or may not stop), you press the halt button next to the train exit door, signaling the engineer to stop the train at Sammelplatz, an on-request-only stop station.*

Start: After exiting the train at Sammelplatz, cross the tracks, walk forward to the group of signs, and follow HÖCH HIRSCHBERG HOHENWEG—1¼ HRS. Walk up the paved path, past the Gais/Guggeloch intersection, following signs to the *hohenweg* (high trail). As you ascend through the meadow and arrive at an unmarked path to the right, proceed straight ahead, up the mountain on a beaten, grassy path to the paved road. Turn left and continue through the meadow to a house and barn. Turn left and walk past the barn. After about an hour of walking from Sammelplatz, you'll arrive at a four-way intersection at Hütten. Here, *Easy Walkers* have a few options:

1. Continue walking for another thirty minutes up to the country restaurant at Höch Hirschberg for rest and refreshment, then walk down to Gais via Schachen.
2. Turn left at Hütten for the forty-minute walk to Gais.
   At Gais you also have two options:
   1. Take the train back to Appenzell.
   2. Follow the *wanderweg* signs and walk from Gais to Sammelplatz to Guggerloch to Appenzell.

Walk #2

Ebenalp Top Station to Wildkirchli Caves to Ascher to Seealpsee to Wasserauen (Optional Walk to Schwendi, Weissbad, and Appenzell)
Walking Easy Time: 3 to 5 hours
Rating: Comfortable

After ascending by cable car from the village of Wasserauen to Ebenalp, at 5394 ft. (1644 m.), and viewing the soft green meadows of Appenzellerland framed by the Alpstein mountain range, you'll descend to Wildkirchli and walk through its prehistoric caves. Stone Age bones and tools once used in this area are displayed in the hermit's dwelling just outside the cave exit. The unusual altar-cave is evidence of the religion practiced by hermits who lived in the caves for several hundred years, beginning in 1658.

The path to Seealpsee is rocky and can be slippery. It descends rapidly, aided by natural steps, all the way to the lake, at 3744 ft. (1141 m.). Here walkers can amble about the lake or have lunch on the terrace of the Berggasthaus Forelle, overlooking this charming lake with the Säntis peak in the distance. You'll then descend to Wasserauen, where you return by train or continue to walk toward Appenzell.

Directions: Take a train from Appenzell to Wasserauen. Walk to the Ebenalp lift across the street and purchase a one-way ticket to the top.

Start: At the Ebenalp Top Station, follow signs to Wildkirchli and Ascher. After about ten minutes, walk through the Wildkirchli caves, originally inhabited by Stone Age bears. On exiting the caves, stop at the hermit's hut, then continue past the altar-cave to the remarkable 150-year-old Ascher Restaurant, built into the face of the sheer cliff. Walk through its sun-terrace, continuing down the rocky trail through the forest. The final ten-minute walk ascends to the right to Seealpsee. Turn left to the restaurant, where walkers can amble about the lake or eat lunch (we recommend the bratwurst and rösti).

When ready, return to the main trail toward Wasserauen. Here you have a few options:

1. Take the ten-minute train ride back to Appenzell.
2. Walk along pleasant meadow paths to Schwendi, Weissbad, Steinegg, and Appenzell. The walk from Wasserauen to Appenzell takes two hours, but you can board the train at any of the above stations.

Walk #3

Wasserauen to Seealpsee to Hütten to Hüttentobel to Wasserauen
Walking Easy Time: 3 to 5 hours
Rating: Comfortable

If you prefer not to hike down from Ebenalp as in Walk #2 but would like to visit the beautiful lake at Seealp, this is the hike for you. After taking the train to Wasserauen, hike up to the lake from 2848 to 3744 ft. (868 to 1141 m.) on a paved path, and return by walking along the lake for a short distance to Hutten, at 4072 ft. (1241 m.). You'll then hike down to Wasserauen on a mountain *bergweg*, more interesting and more demanding than the paved path you walked up on. At Wasserauen, take the train back to Appenzell or continue the hike by following signs to Schwendi and Weissbad, all the way to Appenzell, with the option of taking the train at any of those villages.

Directions: Take the train from Appenzell to Wasserauen.

Start: Exiting the train, follow signs to the left, walking up the path to Seealpsee. Turn left around the lake and left again at Resien, ascending up

All dressed up returning from the summer alps

to Hütten. At this point the trail descends, partially through the forest to Wasserauen. Be a bit cautious with this descent; it can be a little slippery and steep at times. If you're concerned about a steep descent after wet weather, return to Wasserauen on the same path you came up on.

At Wasserauen take the train back to Appenzell, or follow the trail for the two-hour hike from Wasserauen to Appenzell.

Walk #4
Gonten to Gontenbad to Appenzell on the Barefoot Trail (Excursion to Säntis)
Walking Easy Time: 1½ to 2½ hours (not including Säntis Excursion)
Rating: Comfortable

When skies are clear, plan an early start for today's excursion and hike. You'll take the train to Urnäsch and board a bus to Schwagalp, the location of the Säntis cable car. We recommend the fabulous views from the *gipfel* (peak), taking the lift up.

After descending by cable car to Schwagalp, you'll return by bus to Urnäsch to take the train to Gonten for the beginning of today's pleasant walk on the "Barefoot Trail." Most of this walk takes place on the soft, grassy meadows of Appenzellerland. Signs remind you to take off your hiking boots, inviting you to walk barefoot through the meadows to preserve the grassy paths. This scenic trail offers those special views of what Appenzellerland is all about—undulating, grassy alps filled with cows and dotted with the architectural details that make this area so distinctive.

Directions: Take a morning train to Urnäsch and transfer to the post-bus to Schwagalp. Purchase a round-trip lift ticket to Säntis. The cable car brings you from Schwagalp, at 4436 ft. (1352 m.), to Säntis, at 8209 ft. (2502 m.). The views are spectacular, encompassing the peaks of Austria and Italy as well as those of Switzerland.

When ready, descend by cable car to Schwagalp for the return bus ride to Urnäsch. Take the train to Gonten, where today's jaunt through the meadows begins.

Start: After leaving the Gonten train station, turn right, walking into the village and following the sign APPENZELL—1½ HRS. The next sign reads *wanderweg*, directing you left, then right, between two small houses. At last visit, there was some construction in this area. Watch for signs. Turn right, along the fence and up a little grassy hill. Ascend gently to the farm-house and note yellow arrows directing you past the left side of the house to a sign pointing to the right toward Gontenbad and Appenzell. Eventually you'll bear right at a fork in the road, **always** following the *wanderweg* signs and blazes. The path switches between grassy meadow and jeep trail, and after about forty minutes you'll reach Gontenbad, at 2937 ft. (895 m.), where it's possible to make a right turn and walk to the *bahnhof* to take a train to Appenzell, if necessary. To continue, there are additional options:

1. If you wish to stay on a fairly level path, walk ahead following the *wanderweg* and Appenzell signs.

2. Turn left and walk up a narrow, grassy, yellow-blazed *bergweg*, following signs to Himmelberg. The ascent to Himmelberg takes you to 3609 ft. (1100 m.), where you follow signs across the meadows into Appenzell.

Walk #5

Hoher Kasten Top Station to Brülisau via Plattenbödeli and Ruhsitz
Walking Easy Time: 3 hours
Rating: Comfortable

You'll leave Appenzell by train and arrive at Brülisau by bus, taking the lift up to Hoher Kasten, at 5889 ft. (1795 m.). There are several hikes from the top, but today you'll descend towards the Sämtisersee, cutting across the mountain to the restaurant at Ruhsitz and ending at Brülisau for the bus ride back to the train in Weissbad.

Directions: Take the train to Weissbad and change for the bus to Brülisau. At the lift station, buy a one-way ticket to the top.

Start: At Hoher Kasten visit the easily accessible viewpoint that will acquaint you with most of Appenzellerland—past Appenzell to the Alpstein massif and, if a clear day, to the mountains of Austria. Follow the signs SÄMTISERSEE—1¼ STD. and PLATTENBÖDELI—1¼ STD., the trail circling around the peak and descending in the direction of the lake. At Kastensattel, 5506 ft. (1678 m.), turn left toward Plattenbödeli and the lake. Eventually you will be able to see the lake in the distance. Continue to follow signs down the mountain, on a sometimes steep, rocky bergweg, to the road. Turn right on this road to Brülisau. Now you are walking away from the lake toward Brülisau through Ruhsitz, at 4200 ft. (1280 m.), and its mountain restaurant.

At Ruhsitz restaurant, you can either take the marked trail (perhaps a more interesting option) or remain on the road all the way to Brülisau. Take the bus to Weissbad and change for the train to Appenzell.

Walk #6

Hoher Kasten Top Station to Kamor-Rossberg to Brülisau
Walking Easy Time: 3 hours
Rating: Comfortable

Today's walk was suggested by Willy Raess, retired director of the Appenzell Tourist Office. Although we did not have the opportunity to complete this hike (Walk #5 also begins at the Hoher Kasten peak), it appears to be a comfortable downhill walk from the peak of Hoher Kasten, at 5889 ft. (1795 m.), via Kastensattel. The descent continues to Kamor, ending via Rossberg, in Brülisau, at 3025 ft. (922 m.).

Directions: Take the train to Weissbad and take the bus to Brülisau. Buy a one-way ticket to the top station at Hoher Kasten.

Start: After taking in the panorama, descend the mountain via Kastensattel to Kamor, at 4488 ft. (1678 m.), winding around through Rossberg all the way to Brülisau. Although it is possible to walk on the road before entering Brülisau, you might find it more interesting to stay on the mountain trails.

At Brülisau, take the bus to Weissbad, connecting with the train to Appenzell.

Walk #7

Kronberg Top Station to Scheidegg to Kaubad to Eichen to Appenzell
Walking Easy Time: 3 hours
Rating: Comfortable

For today's hike, you will take the train from Appenzell to Jakobsbad, where you take the Kronberg Lift to the top station. The views from the top are mesmirizing—the nearby Säntis towering above the tranquil Appenzell alps. This walk descends Mount Kronberg to Scheidegg along trails with country inns located along the way—continuing to Kaubad and Eichen before returning to Appenzell.

Directions: Take the train to Jakobsbad. *NOTE: Immediately after the train passes Gonten, press the halt button next to the train exit door, signaling the engineer to stop the train at Jakobsbad, an on-request-only station.* Walk across to the Kronberg Lift Station, and purchase a one-way ticket to the top.

Start: There are several options from the Kronberg Top Station. Today, follow the sign to Scheidegg, at 4351 ft. (1326 m.), passing the little chapel at St. Jakob. In Scheidegg follow the signs to Kaubad and Eichen. Pass the restaurant in Kaubad, at 3406 ft. (1038 m.), and follow the forest trail that cuts off to the right into Eichen. At Eichen follow signs into Appenzell.

CENTRAL SWITZERLAND

ENGELBERG
(LUCERNE)

The picturesque village of Engelberg, at 3281 ft. (1000 m.), is tucked between mountain ranges in a fertile valley south of Lucerne, along the Aa River. Sunny, terraced meadows reach from the valley floor to high, green alps, filled in summer with grazing cows and crisscrossed by some of the most exciting combinations of lifts and trails in the Swiss Alps.

Engelberg's name and history are connected to its famous Benedictine *kloster* (monastery), located on the edge of the village. According to local legend, the builder of the *kloster* heard voices of angels from the peak of a nearby mountain instructing him to build where the monastery is now located; thus began *Engel berg*—town of angels.

Towering above Engelberg is Mount Titlis, Central Switzerland (Zentralschweiz) canton's highest peak, at 10,500 ft. (3200 m.). It's reached by a series of lifts, including an innovative, rotating "Rotair" cable car, the first in the world. Imagine a rotating platform in a cable car, rising 2000 ft. (610 m.) to reach the top station.

Surrounded by high mountains, icy glaciers, and green alps, with a multitude of hiking trails for every level and only an hour by train to enchanting Lucerne, Engelberg is waiting to be discovered by *Easy Walkers*.

Transportation

By Train - From Zurich airport it's a two-and-a-half-hour train ride to Engelberg, with a change in Lucerne. From the Bernese Oberland area, take the train from Interlaken Ost to Lucerne, always changing in Hergiswil for the ride to Engelberg.

By Car - Take N2 south—the north/south Basel–Gotthard motorway—exiting at Stans-Süd for Engelberg.

Favorite *Walking Easy* Hotel

Hotel Schweizerhof

Three-Star; Owners—Familie Burch-Weibel

CH-6390 Engelberg; **Tel:** 41 637 11 05; **Fax:** 41 637 41 47

Internet: www.schweizerhof-enfelberg.ch

E-mail: schweizerhof.engelberg@bluewin.ch

The Schweizerhof is a recently renovated turn-of-the-century hotel located in central Engelberg. Rooms have been redecorated and are spacious, bright, and airy; a convenient, modern laundry facility is provided for guests' use. The hotel, which features a sauna and fitness room, is popular with tour groups from the United States and other countries. As a result, the Burch-Weibel family is aware of the needs of foreign tourists. They're also experienced Engelberg hikers. The dining room is tastefully appointed, serving a breakfast buffet and Swiss cuisine at dinnertime.

Excursions

The Engelberg Tourist Office is located in the Tourist Center, across from the Coop supermarket.

> **Internet:** www.engelberg.ch
>
> **E-mail:** tourist.center@engelberg.ch

1. **Engelberg** - The **Benedictine Monastery**, a must visit, was founded in 1120 and is still inhabited by monks of that order. The magnificent Baroque church, built in 1728, houses the largest pipe organ in Europe. Guided tours are given at 10:00 A.M. and 4:00 P.M., Monday through Saturday. (See Walk #1.)

2. **Lucerne** (Luzern) - Once a simple fishing village, Lucerne is now a fashion mecca for shoppers, and sightseers throng its narrow, cobblestoned streets lined with painted houses. (See Walk #5.)

   Directions: The direct train from Engelberg brings you to Lucerne in one hour.

3. **Mount Pilatus** - Nine miles south of Lucerne, at 6995 ft. (2132 m.), Pilatus is a landmark of the area, with its distinctive rock pyramid at the top. From Kriens (twelve minutes by bus from Lucerne), cable cars glide over meadows and forests to Fräkmüntegg, where an aerial cableway swings along the steep cliff, rising year-round to the peak. From May to November, the south side of the mountain at Alpnachstad boasts the steepest cogwheel railway in the world. At the peak are hotels and

restaurants with sun terraces for viewing the incredible panorama.

Directions: For a unique circle tour take the train to Hergiswil, changing for the local train to Alpnachstad, where you take the old cog railway to Pilatus Kulm. Return to Kriens via the cable car and catch a bus to Lucerne, taking the train back to Engelberg.

4. **Mount Rigi** - At 5896 ft. (1797 m.), Rigi is located 15 miles (24 km.) east of Lucerne. Pilatus boasts the panoramic vistas, but the view from Rigi is considered more beautiful and the hiking trails more gentle.

Directions: Take an early train from Engelberg to Lucerne. Just outside the bahnhof, catch the lake steamer to Vitznau, where you connect with the rack railway to Rigi Kulm, the oldest cog railway in Europe. Confirm all transport schedules before you leave for Rigi.

Engelberg Walks

Recommended Maps:

❖ Wanderkarte Engelberg, Central Switzerland
❖ Panoramakarte—Engelberg
❖ Wanderkarte Jochpass
❖ Wandern im Herzen der Schweiz—Engelberg–Jochpass–Engstlenalp–Melchsee–Frutt–Hasliberg–Meiringen

Walk #1

Introductory Walk—Engelberg to Horbis/End der Welt to Engelberg (Excursion to Monastery)
Walking Easy Time: 2 hours
Rating: Comfortable

Today's get-acquainted walk brings you to the impressive Benedictine *kloster* for an hour tour and a walk into the countryside to End der Welt, or "End of the World," the narrow, closed-in valley behind Horbis and its fifteenth-century country church. The return walk to Engelberg is through the meadows and past the monastery. Benedictine monks have resided in this *kloster* since it was founded in 1120, and the imposing buildings dominate the landscape at the eastern end of town, both architecturally and culturally. The beautiful Baroque monastery church, built in 1728, houses one of the largest organs in Europe.

Start: Walk through town on the main, traffic-free, cobblestoned shopping street to the *kloster*, at the end of the village. Tours are given

Monday through Saturday at 10:00 A.M. and 4:00 P.M.; time your arrival for the morning visit, or hike early afternoon and take the 4:00 P.M. tour.

The walk begins at hiking signs on a wall outside the monastery grounds. Follow the sign END DER WELT—55 MIN. Ascend the flight of steps next to the school, then turn right at another sign leading through a valley.

After about forty minutes, cross the road and follow signs to Horbis and End der Welt. The village of Horbis soon appears, with its country church, originally built in 1489. After visiting the church, continue into town to the Restaurant Horbis End der Welt.

To return, walk back on the same path, but instead of turning right over the bridge, follow the sign pointing ahead to Engelberg. The path continues past a grass-processing plant (*grastrocknungsanlage*). You will then arrive at a narrow lake and picnic area. Proceed toward Engelberg along the auto road. After passing the Eggliweg (a small road to the right), continue following the road over the river. At the gravel path, turn into the *kirchweg*, leading back to the monastery. This path splits; continue ahead on the upper path, which spills into the cemetery above the monastery and leads to the flight of steps you climbed earlier in the day.

Walk #2

Trübsee Lift Station to Untertrübsee to Engelberg (Excursion to Mount Titlis)
Walking Easy Time: 3 hours
Rating: Comfortable

Today you'll take the series of aerial cableways from Engelberg to Mount Titlis, the highest viewpoint in Central Switzerland, at 9935 ft. (3028 m.), with spectacular views of glaciers and icefalls. The last part of the cableway, from Stand to Klein Titlis, will be in a cable car whose platform revolves as it rises to the summit station. After visiting the peak, you'll descend to the Trübsee station for a walk around the lake, picking up the descending path to Engelberg.

Directions: Walk *through* the Engelberg train station and, passing the post office, follow the sign to the right to TITLIS ROTAIR. Purchase a ticket to the top station with a return to Trübsee. Take the cableway system to the top, staying in the gondola at Gerschnialp, changing in Trübsee and again in Stand for the cable car to the Titlis Top Station. After visiting the Glacier Grotto and the Panorama Restaurant, descend to Station Trübsee, at 5893 ft. (1796 m.), where the walk begins.

Start: Exit the Trübsee Lift Station and follow the path signed ZUM SEE, to the lovely glacial lake. Walk around the lake's left bank on a wide path, around the Alpstübli Restaurant, where you follow the sign to Huehütte, at 5758 ft. (1755 m.). At Huehütte, turn left and walk down the path marked UNTERTRÜBSEE—50 MIN. and ENGELBERG—1½ HR. This white-and-red blazed trail narrows and becomes a descending, rocky *bergweg*. When the trail changes to a wagon road, follow the lift station sign. At the lift station, your options are:

1. Take the gondola down to Untertrübsee and continue walking to Engelberg.

2. Follow the red arrow pointing to the red-and-white blazed trail leading sharply down to the left. If you decide to walk, the next fifteen minutes of descent is rocky and steep but manageable. This trail meets another path to Untertrübsee, becoming an open ski path. Turn right, through the meadow to the Untertrübsee Restaurant. With either option, turn right again, down the hill, on a little-used auto road to Engelberg. After rounding the first bend, take a *wanderweg* trail on the left through the meadow. Reaching a paved road, follow signs to Engelberg.

Walk #3

Gerschnialp Lift Station to Cafe Ritz (Vorder-Stafel) to Untertrübsee to Haltenhütte to Untertrübsee to Engelberg

Walking Easy Time: 3 hours

Rating: Comfortable

Today you'll take the Titlis gondola from Engelberg to the first stop at Gerschnialp, at 4141 ft. (1262 m.), and walk on a level trail to Cafe Ritz at Vorder-Stafel. The path continues through the Gerschnialp to the restaurant at Untertrübsee, then ascends gently through the meadows to Haltenhütte at the end of the valley. *Easy Walkers* will return to the Untertrübsee Restaurant along the same path for the final descent to Engelberg.

Directions: See Walk #2 and purchase a one-way ticket to Gerschnialp, first stop on the Titlis lift system.

Start: After exiting at Gerschnialp, turn left to Cafe Ritz, walking through forest and meadow—a short, fifteen-minute stroll. At the restaurant, walk around the terrace to the parking area and follow the sign UNTERTRÜBSEE on a *wanderweg*. This peaceful path, along a small mountain road, is through Gerschni Alp, a wide-open grassy meadow filled with farms, old barns, and herds of grazing cows. Leaving the road, follow signs to Untertrübsee, ascending gently on a beaten, grassy path, eventually reaching a paved road and the Untertrübsee Restaurant. Pass the restaurant and continue along this road through the meadow in the direction of Arnialp. After about forty-five minutes, you'll come to the end of the valley, the path turning right in the direction of Arnistalden. However, *Easy Walkers* will return on the same path to the Untertrübsee Restaurant, where you have two options:

1. Walk past the restaurant on the road and, after the bend, take the *wanderweg* trail on the left, cutting down through the meadow. After reaching a gravel path, turn right and follow the road up to a group of signs directing you left to ENGELBERG—30 MIN. This mountain auto road goes down to the bottom of Titlis Lift Station (about a forty-minute walk). It's possible to follow a *bergwanderweg* (mountain trail) sign cutting through the forest, but this trail can be steep and slippery in places; we recommend staying on the road until you reach Engelberg.

2. Retrace your steps to Cafe Ritz and take the Gerschnialp gondola down to Engelberg.

Walk #4

Engelberg to Alpenrösli to Engelberg (Optional Excursion to Fürenalp)
Walking Easy Time: 4 hours
Rating: Comfortable

The restaurant at Alpenrösli is your destination today, and the walk through the valley on the left side of the Aa River ascends 847 ft. (258 m.) quite gradually. While the views are exhilarating, the *rösti* and desserts at the Alpenrösli Restaurant are your final reward.

Start: Walk through the pedestrian shopping street of Engelberg to the monastery. Just before the gates, on the left, follow the sign ALPENRÖSLI—1 HR., 50 MIN. Walk up the steps and turn right at the Alpenrösli sign, leading through the cemetery and exiting on the other side onto a meadow path. The *kloster* is on your right as you walk. Cross the auto road, following signs to Alpenrösli. The path begins to ascend gently, and you soon pass by the Fürenalp Bottom Station, at 3557 ft. (1084 m.). (You can take the free Engelberg bus to this point if you wish.) If the weather is clear and sunny, take a ride to the top station and enjoy the views.

Return to the path toward Alpenrösli, which eventually splits, both paths going to the same destination. Stay to the left as you ascend to the restaurant, at 4128 ft. (1258 m.), famous for *rösti*, Switzerland's national dish. To return, head back to Engelberg in the direction of the Fürenalp Lift.

Walk #5
Trübsee Lift, Walk to Jochpass Lift, Walk to Engstlenalp and Return
Walking Easy Time: 3 to 3½ hours
Rating: Comfortable

This full-day Jochpass excursion and hike is an Engelberg favorite. You'll take the Titlis Lift to Trübsee, at 5896 ft. (1797 m.), and walk past the lake to the Jochpass Chairlift, at 5811 ft. (1771 m.), rising to the Jochpass, at 7241 ft. (2207 m.), with sensational views of the glaciers above. You'll then walk down past the Engstlensee to Engstlenalp, at 6021 ft. (1834 m.), your destination for today. The return is by chairlift up to the Jochpass, then down to Trübsee, walking back to the lift station for the descent to Engelberg.

Directions: See Walk #2. Buy a lift ticket to Trübsee and take the gondola to the second stop at Trübsee.

Start: Follow signs to the Jochpass, walking around the left side of the lake to the Jochpass triple chairlift. Buy a round-trip ticket and ride up to the Jochpass, at 7241 ft. (2207 m.). The hike down to Engstlenalp, at 6021 ft. (1835 m.), begins at the top of the chairlift station. There are two paths to Engstlenalp. Take the lower path to the left, marked #3A B on your hiking map, signed ENGSTLENALP—

1 HR., on a comfortable mountain *bergweg*. This trail descends to the lake, then to the restaurant at Engstlenalp. At Engstlenalp, you have a couple of options:

1. The longer way time-wise, but involving no hiking: Take the bus (2:15, 3:15, 4:15 P.M.), to the Meiringen *bahnhof,* then take the train in the direction of Lucerne, changing in Hergiswil for the Engelberg

train. Note: Check all bus and train timetables at the bus stop in En-gstlenalp before choosing this option.

2. The option we prefer: Return on the same path; however, when the path splits at the lake, instead of following the sign to the Jochpass, walk ahead to the *sessellift* (chairlift), about forty-five minutes from the restaurant. Take the double chairlift to the top (where your hike began), then change for the chairlift down to Trübsee. Walk back to Trübsee Lift Station and take the gondola down to Engelberg.

We left our hotel at 10:00 A.M. to begin this day's exhilarating hike—from the canton of Central Switzerland over the Jochpass into the Bernese Oberland. We returned to our hotel at 4:30 P.M.—a full day in the mountains of Switzerland and the best of *Walking Easy.*

Walk #6

Excursion to Lucerne and City Walk
Walking Easy Time: 2½ hours
Rating: Gentle

This charming city is situated on Lake Lucerne. Its covered wooden bridges are still preserved, as are remains of the town's ancient fortifications. Lucerne is now a fashion mecca for shoppers, and sightseers throng its narrow, cobblestoned streets lined with painted houses. Today's excursion features a two-and-a-half-hour walk around Lucerne's lakeside quays and old squares.

Hint: It's a good idea to take your backpack with you on a city walking tour like this. You can stow raingear and a picnic lunch, which you can enjoy on one of the many benches along the lake.

Directions: The train from Engelberg arrives in Lucerne in an hour.

Start: Exit the train station. From Bahnhofplatz on the south bank of the river (at the train station), walk across the **Seebrücke** (bridge) directly in front of the *bahnhof.* At the first yellow-striped pedestrian crossing, cross the busy street to your left. You are now on **Schwanenplatz (Swan Square)**.

Walk ahead into the small square of **Kappelplatz**, with its colorful fountain and statue of a Swiss Guard on top. **St. Peter's Church**, built in 1178 and the oldest church in Lucerne, is on your left. Continue ahead on Kappellgasse, passing the church and entering another square, the **Kornmarkt**, or **Grain Exchange**, the site of **Altes Rathaus (Old Town Hall)**, a Renaissance building dating from 1602. To the left of the Town Hall is a seventeenth-century building housing the **Picasso Sammlung (Picasso Museum)**. If you visit the museum, when you exit make a right turn and a quick right again on Badergässli. Turn left at the river, walking past the outdoor cafes. Next, turn right, entering the famous Lucerne landmark, the **Kappellbrücke (Chapel Bridge)**, a covered, wooden footbridge crossing the Reuss River—the symbol of Lucerne. The original bridge, built in 1333, unfortunately burnt down in 1993 but was rebuilt within the year. After crossing the Chapel Bridge, turn right immediately and walk along the river, paying a visit to the large, beautiful Baroque **Jesuitenkirche (Jesuit Church)** on your left.

Recross the river on the covered **Spreuerbrücke (Spreuer Bridge)**, built in 1407 and restored in the nineteenth century. After crossing this bridge, make a sharp right turn and walk around to **Mühlenplatz (Mills Square)**. Turn left and walk diagonally through Mühlenplatz, bearing right on Kramgasse, with a quick left into **Weinmarkt (Wine Market)**, a lovely square with an old fountain. Note the ancient dwellings on this square. After passing the fountain, bear left to **Hirschenplatz (Stag Square)**, another square bordered with old, restored buildings.

From Hirschenplatz, turn right onto Weggisgasse, to Hertensteinstrasse. Walk on Hertensteinstrasse to its end, and bear left into Löwenplatz. Cross the street at the yellow pedestrian stripes to the one-hundred-year-old circular building housing the **Bourbaki-Panorama**, a huge painting depicting the bloody retreat of the French army into Switzerland during the Franco-Prussian War. After exiting the Panorama, walk ahead up the narrow street, Denkmalstrasse, to the sign pointing to the right to **Gletschergarten** and **Löwendenkmal**. View one of the most famous statues in Switzerland, the **Löwendenkmal**, or **Lion Monument,** hewn out of natural rock and dedicated to the bravery of the Swiss Guards who died in Paris trying to save Marie Antoinette.

Walk back to Löwenplatz and head down Löwenstrasse toward the trees and lake. On the left, pay a visit to the **Collegiate Church of St. Leodegar,** with its twin towers, wrought-iron work, carvings, and famous pipe organ. Cross the road to the lake and enjoy a wonderful view—the Alps from Rigi to Pilatus. You can walk back to the *bahnhof* along the lake, take a relaxing boat ride, or turn back into the Old Town and visit some of the stores and cafes you passed earlier.

Walk #7

Ristis Lift Station to Schwand to Engelberg
Walking Easy Time: 2½ hours
Rating: Gentle

Use the Engelberg Panorama Wanderkarte for this walk. You'll take the Brunni cable car from Engelberg to Ristis, at 5269 ft. (1606 m.), and walk on the country road to the restaurant at Schwand (marked #21 on the Panorama Wanderkarte). This is a gently descending mountain road with views over Engelberg. From Schwand you will take #18 on the Wanderkarte, passing through the heights over the valley and, eventually, to Engelberg's pedestrian street.

Directions: Walk up the pedestrian street toward the *kloster*, turning left at the large BRUNNI sign. Purchase a one-way ticket to Ristis.

Start: At Ristis, follow the sign RESTAURANT SCHROND—1 HR., 30. MIN. left and eventually the sign ENGELBERG—2 HRS., 30 MIN. Walk past the chairlift rising to the Brunnihütte and continue on the rarely used mountain auto road all the way to Schwand. In ninety minutes you'll reach the restaurant at Schwand (Schroand), just after passing a tiny church. Turn left on the road below the restaurant, following the Engelberg sign. *Easy Walkers* now have two options:

A *Walking Easy* trail

1. If it hasn't been raining, you might wish to take the right fork just ahead, which goes through the meadow and forest, eventually joining the same auto road to Engelberg as in the second option.

2. Take the left fork, remaining on the road all the way to the outskirts of Engelberg and the Hotel Waldegg. Just past the hotel, a path called the Sonnenweg descends to the right, leading to the center of Engelberg.

From the Austrian National Tourist Office

Welcome to the Austrian Alps, where the walking is easy . . .

We Austrians take good care of our country; environmental awareness is virtually universal and goes deep. In a small country such as ours, land is a finite and cherished resource. Farmers are the guardians and caretakers of the land who work hard to ensure healthy turf, stable soil, erosion prevention, and good watersheds. Their labor extends into the high mountain regions where they maintain and preserve their summer pastures, the "Alps."

We will also take good care of you. Hospitality is an old and hallowed tradition in Austria. Get to know our comfortable hotels, cozy inns, typical restaurants, and unique mountain huts, and experience the Austrian gemütlichkeit firsthand. It is not difficult to get there; leave your car behind—board a train or a local bus—and take some easy walks in the footsteps of Chet and Carolee through the mountainous valleys of Austria.

—Erich Neuhold
Director, North America
Austrian National Tourist Office

AUSTRIA

Austria shares its border with eight other countries—Germany, Italy, Switzerland, Hungary, the Czech Republic, Slovakia, Liechtenstein, and Slovenia—and each has had a dramatic cultural impact on Austrian lifestyles. These different ethnic groups contribute richly to Austrian cuisine, and *Easy Walkers* should be sure to sample local food specialties. Austrians take their dining and coffee enjoyment seriously. In fact, the Viennese coffeehouse is truly an institution. It is not merely a place to savor coffee in venerable surroundings; it is also where one reads a newspaper, chats with friends, and, of course, enjoys mouthwatering Viennese pastries.

Over 70 percent of Austria's countryside is forestland in the shadow of dramatic snowcapped peaks, and the hiking trails are well signed and well maintained. Hiking maps are available in local tourist offices, conveniently located in every base village and designated by an **i** sign. *Walking Easy* hotels are charming and offer some of the best values in Europe. The warm and friendly Austrian welcome is almost as famous as their apple strudel. Try it once, and you'll come back for seconds—and thirds.

TYROL

ALPBACH

Alpbach is probably the most charming *Walking Easy* base village in Austria. This Tyrolean resort, nestled on a sunny mountainside at 3281 ft. (1000 m.), offers walkers a wide range of trails in the idyllic, picture-postcard landscape of the Alpbachtal (Alpbach Valley). Hikers have a choice of over 100 miles (160 km.) of well-marked trails. The Wiedersbergerhorn gondola rises to 5919 ft. (1804 m.) and is the starting point of hikes with panoramic views of the Ziller and Inn Valleys, the Stubai and Ziller glaciers, and the Karwendel mountain range.

The secret of Alpbach's charm is the standards established for restoration of old buildings and construction of new ones, making sure the village represents traditional Tyrolean architecture and atmosphere. Every balcony and window is adorned with colorful flowers, framing the old-style, wood-beamed construction. Considering there were no major roads into Alpbach until 1926, Alpbach has transformed itself from a sleepy farming community to a major Austrian tourist destination very quickly. It is interesting to note that many mountain farms in the countryside around Alpbach still exist and function as they have for centuries.

Much of the hills surrounding Alpbach are grassy meadows, where walkers can stroll for hours on signed paths, all within sight of Alpbach's beautiful church steeple. Walkers can also hike from village to village, taking advantage of bus service in the Alpbach Valley. The helpful Alpbach Tourist Information Office ministers to the needs of visitors from around the world, including the annual August meeting of the European Forum, where leaders in the fields of economics, politics, and science meet to discuss European and world issues.

Enjoy Alpbach—its hiking, its scenery, and its flower-bedecked homes—a favorite *Walking Easy* setting.

Transportation

By Train and Bus - Alpbach is reached by bus from Brixlegg, a local train stop. From the west, always change trains in Innsbruck for the local train to Brixlegg. From the east, always change in Wörgl for the local train to Brixlegg. The bus from Brixlegg to Alpbach is located across the street from the train station. There are two bus stops in Alpbach: Tell the driver where you will be staying for the most convenient drop-off point.

By Car - Drive on the A12 *autobahn* to Kramsach and pick up the local road to Brixlegg, Reith, then Alpbach.

Favorite *Walking Easy* Hotel

Haus Angelika (No credit cards)
Three-Star; Owners—Sepp and Erna Steinlechner
A-6236 Alpbach/Tirol; **Tel:** 53 36/53 39; **Fax:** 53 36/55 28

Haus Angelika is a lovely, flower-bedecked *pension*. Located on Alpbach's quiet main street, it offers fifteen comfortable rooms with balconies. The spacious front lawn provides a relaxing stop after a day of hiking. Buffet breakfast is personally attended to by Mrs. Steinlechner, and Mr. Steinlechner is an accomplished hiker—he can suggest outstanding walks in the Alpbachtal. Although dinner is not served at Haus Angelika, the Haus Elizabeth next door serves dinner in its Reblaus, located in front of the *pension*—an outstanding restaurant, specializing in local and Italian cuisine. When making reservations at Haus Angelika, ask for the special **Walking Easy Half-Board Package**, including dinner at Reblaus.

Excursions

The Alpbach Tourist Information Office is located in the new Congress Center.

Fax: 53 36 600 200
Internet: www.alpbach.at
E-mail: info@alpbach.at

1. **Alpbach** - The **Farmhouse Museum** is located in Inneralpbach, a hamlet near Alpbach. This mountain farmhouse was built in the early 1600s. (See Walk #3.)
2. **Innsbruck** - See A Trail of Three Cities—Innsbruck.
   Directions: Take a morning bus from Alpbach to Brixlegg and the local train west to Innsbruck.

Tyrol decor

3. Rattenberg - The best-preserved medieval community in the Tyrol is noted for its historic squares, narrow alleyways, frescoed houses, and the etching and cutting of fine crystal. A must on your visit is the Augustinermuseum Rattenberg, with collections displaying Tyrolean art treasures.

Directions: Take the bus from Alpbach to Brixlegg and the train or bus to Rattenberg.

4. Kramsach - Located in the village of Kramsach, next to Rattenberg, the Museum Tiroler Bauernhöfe, or Farmhouse Museum, presents farms from different parts of the Tyrol, removed from their areas and rebuilt— an interesting way to see how people lived and worked in Old Tyrol.

Directions: See Rattenberg directions above.

5. Schwaz - In the fourteenth and fifteenth centuries, Schwaz was a copper- and silver-mining center, known as the "silver town of Europe." The silver mine is still open to visitors, and the mine railway takes sightseers through tunnels and stalactite formations.

Directions: Check for weekly excursions to Schwaz.

6. Wattens - The Swarovski factory and retail store is located in Wattens.

Directions: Take the morning bus to Brixlegg and transfer to the local train to Wattens. Check also for excursion buses.

7. Achensee - The largest mountain lake in Austria, Achensee is also considered the most beautiful mountain lake in the Tyrol. Take a steamer trip around the lake, or just relax and enjoy the beauty of the countryside.

Directions: The early-morning bus from Alpbach arrives in Brixlegg in time to take the local train to Jenbach, where you change to the Achenseebahn.

Alpbach Walks

Recommended Maps:
- ❖ Mayr Wanderkarte #40—Alpbachtal
- ❖ Ortsplan—Street Map

Walk #1

Introductory Walk—Alpbach to Rossalm to Trat to Alpbach
Walking Easy Time: 1½ to 2 hours
Rating: Comfortable

Today's walk can be taken on the afternoon of arrival in Alpbach, introducing you to this picturesque village, its flowered chalets, the Alpbach Valley, Inneralpbach, and the snow-covered Kitzbüheler Alps in the distance. After viewing Alpbach from its surrounding heights, you'll walk through the upper part of the village, returning to the village center by descending to a forest path, ending at Alpbach's main street.

Start: Walk out of town along the side of the Hotel Post, on the paved road marked A2 on your hiking map. Continue on this road, passing a sign indicating the end of Alpbach city limits. The charming homes maintain the original wooden Tyrolean chalet flavor, bedecked with flowers from every window and balcony. Follow the auto road up and around until you reach a signed intersection. Make a right turn in the direction of ROSSALM A2—30 MIN. The views across the valley are picture-postcard perfect.

Continue on the road, walking past Rossalm and the few houses that are Alsten. The paved road becomes a gravel wagon path, entering the forest for a few minutes. At the road, continue to the right, to the restaurant in Trat. Turn right and follow the descending path and road back to the Hotel Post. Turn left at the hotel and left again at the church. Follow the road around to the right, walking through the upper part of the village, passing the Hotel Bögler and the newly built Kongresshaus. After walking past the Alphof Hotel, turn right on the first paved street, signed ALPHOF RUNDGANG, with a red fire hydrant. Walk down toward the tennis courts. Continue past the courts, over the bridge, and make a right turn onto a forest path signed MÜHLBACH. Follow this trail along the stream until you arrive at a narrow road. Turn right, walk up the hill, and in a few minutes you'll be in the center of Alpbach.

Walk #2

Hornboden Top Station to Loderstein to Hechenblaikenalm to Kerschbaumer Sattel to Reitherkogel Top Lift Station
Walking Easy Time: 4¾ hours
Rating: More challenging

This hike is made up of almost every kind of trail; it's rated more challenging because of the rather lengthy downhill *bergweg* near the end of the walk. You'll travel to Wiedersbergerhornbahn Base Station for the gondola ride to Hornboden Top Station, at 5919 ft. (1804 m.). This is followed by a hike up to the *panoramaweg*, at 6202 ft. (1890 m.), partially around the mountain, picking up a spectacular trail along the spine of the mountain before descending through the forest to Hechenblaikenalm, at 4570 ft. (1393 m.). The trail rises again to the Reitherkogel Lift Station for the ride down to Reith. There are *no* restaurants between the Hornboden Station and the top station of the Reitherkogelbahn, so pack a picnic lunch and lots of water.

Directions: Take an early-morning bus (before 9:00 A.M.) from Alpbach to the Wiedersbergerhornbahn. If you prefer to walk to the base station, walk on the road out of town, past the Hotel Post, turning left on the road after Haus Barbara at the sign FUSSWEG WIEDERSBERGER-HORN. Take the A9 path down through the meadow, turning right on the main road to the lift base station. Purchase a round-trip ticket to Top Station Hornboden and return. This ticket allows you to use the lift at either

Reith or Alpbach in any direction. Exit at Top Station Hornboden.

Start: Follow the sign up to the *panoramaweg* (do *not* take the lower, signed path to the Reitherkogelbahn). At the *panoramaweg*, take the path to the right to walk around the peak. After an hour, a sign directs you to the Zillertal.

Hint: An early start is necessary for this hike. Before starting, confirm the closing time of the Reitherkogel gondola. If you miss it, you'll have to walk down the mountain to Reith.

However, take path R30 to the right along the ridge, with spectacular views on either side. The trail continues along the spine, ahead on R31 at a signed intersection. Bear left on R31, as you descend through the forest on a rocky *bergweg* from 6004 ft. (1830 m.) to Hechenblaikenalm, at 4570 ft. (1393 m.). The trail is well defined but can be steep and rocky in places.

At the Hechenblaikenalm road, turn left and left again at a signed intersection to R16, Reitherkogelbahn Bergstation. This path leaves the road and descends to Kerschbaumer Sattel, at 3645 ft. (1111 m.), at the road. Cross the road, following the R12 sign up to the *bergstation*. Bear right at the fork in the direction of the Nisslhof Gasthof and the *bergstation*. After the ride down, take the bus to Alpbach.

Walk #3

Alpbach to Thierberg to Zottahof to Rossmoos to Inneralpbach via the Oberer Höhenweg (Excursion to Farmhouse Museum)

Walking Easy Time: 4 hours

Rating: Comfortable

Reserve the day for this walk and excursion to the Farmhouse Museum in Inneralpbach (closed on Tuesday and Wednesday). You'll walk on the heights above Alpbach to visit the Zottahof, a country farmhouse restaurant (closed on Wednesday), famous for *kaiserschmarrn*, a large, pancake-style omelette made of eggs, milk, and flour; beaten and cooked in a large skillet until high, fluffy, and brown; then sprinkled with powdered sugar and served with homemade cranberry preserves. The walk to this restaurant takes about ninety minutes, followed by another two-and-a-half-hour walk to the Farmhouse Museum in Inneralpbach. The museum was originally a farmhouse, built in the early seventeenth century. After visiting the museum, you'll walk back to the main road for a short bus ride to Alpbach.

Start: Walk on Alpbach's upper town road with the church on the right, passing the Böglerhof on the left. Just past the hotel, turn left at the sign THIERBERG A3, LÄRCHENWEG. Ascend through the meadow, and at the top of the hill turn right, again in the direction of Thierberg and the Lärchenweg. Continue walking on the paved path, passing a large guesthouse on the left, soon entering a grassy carriage trail signed LÄRCHENWEG A3. This path rises gently through the meadow and enters the forest.

A sign soon indicates that Zottahof A3 is ahead, the first stop of the day. Turn right over the wooden bridge crossing the Hoslbach, following the path up to the auto road. Turn left and walk up the road to the Zottahof Restaurant, around the turn at the top of the hill. This uphill section of the walk from Alpbach will take *Easy Walkers* about ninety minutes. If it's a cool day, this cozy restaurant offers a warm place to rest and enjoy *kaiserschmarrn* or other house specialties.

Continue by walking back down the auto road and making a left at intersection A8, following signs to Rossmoos. Walk up the road, passing a little path to Alpbach on the right. Instead, continue in the direction of Rossmoos along the Oberer Höhenweg, past the Wurmhof Restaurant, continuing past the Putza farm, staying on the Oberer Höhenweg across the bridge to the Buben chapel. Turn right again on #721 on your map to the Restaurant Wiedersbergerhornhaus in Inneralpbach. Here you have an opportunity to visit the Bergbauern Museum before returning by bus to Alpbach. In the village, turn left on the main Inneralpbach road, walking past the bus stop and through the village to the Farmhouse Museum. When ready, walk back to the bus stop for the short ride to Alpbach.

Walk #4

Alpbach to Pinzgerhof to Reith (Excursion to Reith)
Walking Easy Time: 3 hours
Rating: Comfortable

Today's excursion to Reith is along a fairly level trail that darts in and out of the forest on pine needle–covered *bergwege* and wagon paths, all on signed path R20. After rising from 3281 to 3773 ft. (1000 to 1150 m.), you will walk west on the Alpbachtaler Höhenweg to the Pinzgerhof Restaurant, with a terrace overlooking Reith and Brixlegg. From the Pinzgerhof it's only a forty-five-minute descent along the road to the Reith church square and the return bus to Alpbach.

Start: Walk on the auto road alongside the Hotel Post, away from the village, on A2. After ascending about thirty minutes, follow a group of signs indicating #R20 HÖHENWEG REITH to the left.

At an intersection where a paved road goes up to the right, watch carefully and take the little forest path signed R20 NACH REITH, as it rises gently under tall pine trees. After a while, turn left on the wagon road to Höhenweg Reith R20. The path dips into the forest again, in the direction of Reith and Pinzgerhof R20. After about eighty minutes of walking, the forest ends and you enter an open area, still following the signs for R20. Arriving at an intersection, take the path up the hill. After walking between two wooden houses, take the road to the right marked FOREST STRASSE, and in a minute, a sign confirms your direction toward the Pinzgerhof Restaurant (closed on Tuesday). After crossing the brook, look for the Pinzgerhof sign and follow the rocky path down the mountain toward Reith. Coming out of the forest on the road, a view of Reith is on the left, the Pinzgerhof Restaurant on the right.

When ready, follow the zigzagging auto road down the mountain. At a signed intersection, continue to the right on the country road, following signs all the way into Reith. The bus stop to Alpbach is 50 yards past the church and Tourist Office—a forty-five-minute walk from the Pinzgerhof.

Walk #5

Alpbach along the Mittlerer Höhenweg to Inneralpbach into the Greiter Graben to Bögl to Wiedersbergerhorn Base Station

Walking Easy Time: 4½ hours

Rating: Comfortable

Begin today by walking to Inneralpbach on the Mittlerer Höhenweg, the trail ascending gently into the Greiter Graben as far as Greitereck. You'll return to Alpbach along the lower heights of the Wiedersbergerhorn to the Kolberhof Gasthof and the Wiedersbergerhornbahn bus stop. You have the option of visiting the Farmhouse Museum in Inneralpbach, if you have not already done so. This walk can also be extended by walking deeper into the Greiter Graben before walking back to Alpbach.

Start: Walk along the main street of Alpbach, passing the Tourist Office and the Hotel Alpbacherhof. Cross a bridge and turn right along the road to Mühlbachweg and the Oberer Höhenweg. As you turn down the road, bear right, do *not* take the Oberer Höhenweg paths to the left. The stream will be below you on your right. At the intersection, turn left and walk up and around through Feilmoos, following the Mittlerer Höhenweg

all the way to Inneralpbach. As you descend past the school, follow an unsigned path to your left that cuts through the meadow, down and around
into Inneralpbach. Passing the last bus stop, follow the sign to Greiter
Graben and walk along the narrow, gently rising auto road—being careful
not to take a signed cutoff back to Alpbach. The Greiterbach (Greiter River)
is on your left. Shortly after passing the Leitner Gasthof, turn right at a
four-way intersection on A12, back in the direction of Inneralpbach, eventually walking under the closed Böglalm ski lifts. The road descends on a
mountain trail to paved road #A11. Turn left, again in the direction of Alpbach, remaining on the A11 auto road to the Kolberhof, including a short
climb through the forest at Dornegg. However, at Oberhaus, you have a
couple of options:

1. You can cut the trip short by descending at the signed intersection A9
   FUSSWEG ALPBACH—40 MIN., turning left at the road, and picking up the
   bus at the Lagerhaus stop.
2. Continue walking another twenty minutes to the Kolberhof, just
   under the Wiedersbergerhorn Lift. A short walk down the path to
   the base station also brings you to a bus stop.

Walk #6

**Inneralpbach through the Lueger Graben to Faulbaumgartenalm to Steinberg-
alm to Inneralpbach**

Walking Easy Time: 5 to 6 hours
Rating: Comfortable

Because of the length of today's walk, take an early-morning bus from Alpbach to Inneralpbach, where the walk begins. You will enter the Lueger
Graben, at 3445 ft. (1050 m.), and gradually ascend along a comfortable
jeep road to Faulbaumgartenalm, at 4895 ft. (1492 m.). There you continue along the same jeep road to Steinbergalm, at 5617 ft. (1712 m.). This
walk is along the Alpbacher Acher (River) until you reach the cabin at Steinbergalm for refreshments. You'll descend into Inneralpbach along the same
path, with fabulous views of the sun-drenched, rolling green *alms*.

The walk up to Steinbergalm from Inneralpbach will take you from
two and a half to three hours.

Directions: Take the bus leaving before 9:00 A.M. from Alpbach to Inneralpbach, getting off at the last Inneralpbach stop.

Start: Walk past the Wiedersbergerhornhaus Restaurant on its left side, following signs to Faulbaumgartenalm and Steinbergalm. The first part of this walk is along a little-used auto road. Cross the river past Bubenkappelle and turn right, walking along the left side of the river as you continue into the Lueger Graben (valley), following signs to Faulbaumgartenalm and Steinbergalm.

At Faulbaumgartenalm you have the option of walking another forty-five to sixty minutes up to the cabin at Steinbergalm, at 5617 ft. (1712 m.), or returning to Inneralpbach. With either option, the walk back is along the same path, with picturesque views into the Alpbachtal. The bus to Alpbach leaves from the same bus stop as earlier.

Additional Walks

Walk #7

Hornboden Top Station to Panoramaweg around the Wiedersberger Horn, Mid-Station Almhof to Alpbach
Walking Easy Time: 4 hours
Rating: Comfortable

Take the Wiedersbergerhorn gondola to the Hornboden Top Station, at 5919 ft. (1804 m.), for a popular two-hour *panoramaweg* walk around the peak. Descend by gondola to the Almhof Mid-Station, at 4416 ft. (1346 m.), for a gentle walk down to the base station along a zigzagging mountain road. The return bus to Alpbach stops at the base station.

Walk #8

Alpbach around the Graflspitz and Return to Alpbach
Walking Easy Time: 6 hours
Rating: More challenging

Although it's possible to hike up to the peak of the Graflspitz, at 6217 ft. (1895 m.), it will probably be out of the comfort level of most *Easy Walkers*. We therefore suggest you walk around the back of the Graflspitz, mostly on a more comfortable jeep road. Leave Alpbach by way of the Lärchenweg to Hösljoch, an ascent of 3281 to 4872 ft. (1000 to 1485 m.), turning left on A20 via Kaiserbrünni to Hölzalmhaus. Turn left on A18 to the Hauser Alm, at 4544 ft. (1385 m.), leaving the road on A18 down to Bischoferalm, then down the zigzagging road to Rossalm and Bischofen. Turn right, then left again, descending on the road to Alpbach.

KITZBÜHEL

Kitzbühel, the internationally famous ski resort, attracts summer hikers with dozens of well-marked trails, rustic mountain restaurants, and scenic viewpoints, all supported by cableways. *Easy Walkers* can take valley walks to Schwarzsee, a resort lake only thirty minutes from Kitzbühel; to the nearby village of Kirchberg and its imposing church; to the tiny chapel in Oberaurach; and on the rolling forest and meadow Bichlach paths. High-level treks on the Hahnenkamm and Kitzbüheler Horn mountains can be enjoyed by recreational walkers of all ages. Nearby valleys extend from the quaint village of St. Johann to Pass Thurn, adding a multitude of additional walks to the Kitzbühel experience.

The Kitzbühel Tourist Bureau offers a variety of daily activities, and the town's walking streets are lined with an eclectic collection of shops, hotels, and restaurants—all housed in colorful Tyrolean-style buildings. Because of its location along an ancient trading route between Venice and Bavaria, Kitzbühel achieved importance in the thirteenth century as a mining and merchant center. However, the Duke of Windsor's "discovery" of Kitzbühel in the 1920s brought European wealth and royalty to the area, turning it into a fashionable year-round resort. *Easy Walkers* will enjoy Kitzbühel's Tyrolean hospitality—its cool forests, sunny meadows, high mountains, and exciting hiking trails.

Transportation

By Train - Always change in Wörgl for the local train to the Kitzbühel/Hahnenkamm station (closest to most of the hotels and shops) or to the main Kitzbühel station, away from town center.

By Car - Take the A12 *autobahn*, exiting at Wörgl Ost. Drive in the direction of St. Johann and then follow signs to Kitzbühel.

Favorite *Walking Easy* Hotel

Hotel Maria Theresia
Four-Star; Owners—Familie Harisch
A-6370 Kitzbühel; **Tel:** 53 56 647 11; **Fax:** 53 56 744 40
Internet: www.tirol.com/hotel-mtheresia
E-mail: hotel.mtheresia@tirol.com
This large full-service hotel is conveniently located in central Kitzbühel.

We usually recommend smaller, family-operated hotels, but considering Kitzbühel's offerings and chic surroundings, the Maria Theresia might add an upscale touch to a hiking vacation. The full buffet breakfast is a highlight, and dinner features Austrian and Continental cuisine, although you might wish to book with breakfast only and sample some of Kitzbühel's variety of restaurants. When writing or faxing for reservations, ask for one of the quiet, spacious rooms in the back.

Excursions

The Kitzbühel Tourist Office is on Hinterstadt, one block from Vorderstadt, the main pedestrian and shopping street.

Fax: 53 56 23 07

Internet: www.kitzbuehel.com

E-mail: info@kitzbuehel.com

Consider purchasing a **Summer Holiday Pass** for free use of all area lifts, the Bichlalm bus, and the indoor swimming pool. A *stadtbus* operates around the environs of the town, with posted schedules.

1. **Kitzbühel** - Every Tuesday and Friday in July and August, open-air concerts are presented by the Kitzbühel Town Band; local bands perform on Thursday.

   a. **Churches** - The **Pfarrkirche (Parish Church)**, built in 1435, was renovated in the Baroque style in the late 1700s and restored in 1951. The thirteenth-century **Liebfrauenkirche (Church of our Lady)** was renovated in the eighteenth century. Between these two churches stands the **Ölberkapelle (Ölberg Chapel)**, containing a Death Lantern from 1450 and frescoes dating from the late sixteenth century. **Katharinenkirche (St. Catherine's Church)** was consecrated in 1365 and restored in 1950, with a *glockenspiel* at the tower's top. The **Kapuzinerkloster (Capucine Monastery)** and its church were built outside Kitzbühel about 1700.

   b. **Museums** - The **Heimatmuseum,** located at Hinterstadt 34, features a chronicle of the town and its mining history. The **Cable Car Museum** at the top station of the Hahnenkamm lift provides a pictorial insight into the development of the cable car and the surrounding ski slopes.

   c. **Schwarzsee** - This pretty lake outside Kitzbühel offers swimming, boating, sunning, dining, and just relaxing. (See Walk #3.)

2. **Aurach Wildlife Park** - Located 5 miles from Kitzbühel in Oberaurach, the park features 200 animals living at 3609 ft. (1100 m.) in the largest open-air enclosure in the Tyrol.
Directions: Take a local bus to Aurach.

3. **Höhe Tauern (National Park) and Grossglockner Road** - There are 120 peaks over 9843 ft. (3000 m.), 169 glaciers, and thousands of waterfalls in Austria's National Park. (See Kaprun/Zell am See, Walk #7.)
Directions: Take an early-morning local train at the Kitzbühel/Hahnenkamm station for the hour ride to Zell am See. From the train station, walk across the street and take the next bus, which should get you to Kaiser-Franz-Josef-Höhe in the late morning.

4. **Innsbruck** - See A Trail of Three Cities—Innsbruck.
Directions: Take the train to Wörgl and change for a connecting train to Innsbruck (the ride takes ninety minutes).

5. **Krimml Waterfall (Krimmler Wasserfälle)** - Located near Mittersill, these shimmering falls are the highest in Europe, with a drop of 1250 ft. (381 m.). The second stage of the falls is a fifteen-minute walk from the lower level, with another five-minute walk to the third stage and trails leading even higher to the fourth and fifth stages. The sixth and seventh viewing areas overlook the middle part of the falls, but the most spectacular view is another twenty-minute walk from the seventh stage, at Bergerblick. Pack rain gear.
Directions: Check bus schedules carefully—there is limited service to the waterfall. If the Tourist Office sponsors a trip to the falls, it's the easiest way to go.

Kitzbühel Walks

Recommended Maps:
- ❖ Mayr Wander Karte #55—Kitzbühel
- ❖ Mayr Wander Karte—St. Johann in Tyrol
- ❖ Kitzbühel Wanderwege—Plan

Walk #1

Hahnenkamm Top Station to St. Bernhard's Chapel to Hochbrunn, Streitegg Chairlift to Steinbergkogel, Return Walk to Hahnenkamm
Walking Easy Time: 2 to 4 hours
Rating: Comfortable

This popular hike is one of many offering remarkable panoramas of this charming alpine town. The new Hahnenkamm gondolas ascend to 5473 ft. (1668 m.), gliding over cool forests and soft green meadows dotted with grazing cows. The top station offers new restaurants along with spectacular views. You'll walk from Hahnenkamm Top Station to the small Chapel of St. Bernhard on the *panoramaweg*. Here, you'll continue around the mountain and take the Streitegg Chairlift to the Steinbergkogelhaus, at 5467 ft. (1971 m.), the high point of today's walk, where *Easy Walkers* have several options to return to the Hahnenkamm Lift Station. This walk should be taken when the weather is clear to take advantage of the outstanding views across the valley.

Directions: Walk to the Hahnenkamm cable station, near the Kitzbühel/Hahnenkamm local railroad station, and purchase a round-trip ticket to the top.

Start: After exiting the cable car, savor the spectacular scenery, especially the Kitzbüheler Horn, at 6549 ft. (1996 m.). Take the signed *panoramaweg*, off to the right, leading to the whitewashed Chapel of St. Bernhard. At the chapel, follow signs to Hochbrunn, Streitegg, and Pengelstein, the path winding around the mountain with the Fleckalm Lift Station above you on the right.

Just before the Hochbrunn Restaurant, turn left to the Streitegg Chairlift and take it up to the high point of today's walk, the Steinbergkogelhaus, with its restaurant and facilities. From here you have the following options:

1. Return on the Streitegg Chairlift to the bottom station and walk back to Hahnenkamm on the same trail.

2. From Steinbergkogel, follow the trail down toward Pengelstein, but turn right at the fork in the road to Hochbrunn, returning to Hahnenkamm on the same trail you came on.

With either option, if you wish, at St. Bernhard's Chapel do *not* follow the *panoramaweg*, but stay on the main path directly to the lift station. At the Hahnenkamm Top Station, take the gondolas down to Kitzbühel.

Walk #2

St. Johann/Harschbichl Top Station to Stanglalm to Steinbergalm to Haslach to Kitzbühel via the Römerweg (Bauernmuseum Visit)
Walking Easy Time: 3½ hours
Rating: Comfortable

(Use the St. Johann hiking map.) Today's hike begins at the charming village of St. Johann, reached by a short train ride from Kitzbühel. You'll take the lift to Harschbichl, at 5263 ft. (1604 m.), then descend in the shadow of the Kitzbüheler Horn on a well-marked jeep road all the way to Haslach. Just below Haslach you'll return to Kitzbühel along the Römerweg, a peaceful, mid-level forest and meadow path, visiting the Bauernmuseum along the way.

Directions: Take the train or bus from Kitzbühel to St. Johann, and from the train/bus station, walk in a southwesterly direction on Speck-bacherstrasse, the main shopping street anchored by the church. Cross the railroad tracks and turn left on the Hornweg, walking to a large blue-and-white parking sign indicating the St. Johann Bergbahn. Buy a one-way ticket to Top Station Harschbichl.

Start: At the top, turn left at signed #1 STANGLALM. Stay on the wide path as it descends around the mountain, avoiding the temptation to climb up to the Kitzbüheler Horn peak, a steep rise of 1286 ft. (392 m.). Continue in the direction of Stanglalm. Turn left at the intersection to visit the friendly, family-owned Stanglalm Restaurant, with its sun terrace, stunning views of the valley, and delicious apple strudel. Continue down the zigzagging road, passing Steinbergalm, at 3957 ft. (1206 m.). Turn left at the intersection, on #34 on your map, to Haslach. At the church in Haslach, turn left again on #9, bearing right down the hill to Hintersteinerbach, at the intersection with the Römerweg, #2 on the map. Turn left, back in the direction of Kitzbühel, all the way to the Bauernmuseum (Farmhouse Museum), for a must visit. This authentic farmhouse, dating from 1559, is open in summer only from 1:00 to 6:00 P.M. Continue on the Römerweg, following signs into Kitzbühel.

Walk #3

Kitzbühel to Schwarzsee to Münichau to Gieringer Weiher to Steuerberg to Kitzbühel
Walking Easy Time: 3½ hours
Rating: Comfortable

Today's midlevel walk from Kitzbühel rolls gently on a trail through the Bichlach, a lovely forest and meadow area. There are many walking paths in the region north of Kitzbühel, and this hike can be a full day's excursion, past Schwarzsee, over the meadows to Münichau, around the small lake at Gieringer, to Steuerberg, then returning to Kitzbühel.

Start: The first part of this walk begins similarly to Walk #5. Begin at the church square, just outside the central Kitzbühel shopping area. Just before the church, walk down the steps to the left, past the *bäckerei* (bakery). Follow the blue Schwarzsee sign to the right, picking up a path next to the church signed SCHWARZSEE #14. Turn right on the main auto road, toward Schwarzsee. At a fork in the road, cross the road and bear right on the Steuerberg road. After a few hundred yards, turn left onto meadow path #12, all the way to the Alpen Hotel and the lake.

When ready, walk to the back of the parking area and turn left on #12, the Seepromenade around Schwarzsee, walking around the end of the lake. Turn right at the intersection on signed Bichlachweg #14 in the direction of Kirchberg and Reith. Walk past the campgrounds on the left and bear left on #14 and #39 to Münichau.

At the end of this path, just before the imposing Schloss Münichau Hotel, turn right in the direction of Gieringer. Continue to follow signs to Gieringer Weiher until you come to the restaurant on your right, which you walk through to get to the lake—a nice spot for a picnic.

When ready, walk past the restaurant, still on #14, to a dead end. Follow the sign right in the direction of Steuerberg through the forest, all the way to a major road just below the village of Steuerberg. Turn right, continuing on #14 again, to the Seebichl Hotel. Walk ahead, past the hotel, to meadow trail #12, which you walked on earlier in the day. Turn left here and follow the signs back to Kitzbühel.

Walk #4

Kitzbüheler Horn Top Station to Alpengarten to Alpenhaus to Adlerhütte Mid-Station

Walking Easy Time: 1 to 3½ hours

Rating: Comfortable

Today's hike takes you from the center of Kitzbühel to the Hornbahn. You'll take the gondola to Adlerhütte Mid-Station, continuing by cable car to the top. In twenty minutes you'll arrive at the top station with its exciting 360-degree panorama from the peak of the Kitzbüheler Horn. After visiting the Alpengarten and continuing to the Alpenhaus, at 5479 ft. (1670 m.), you have a number of options to return to Kitzbühel.

Directions: Walk on Vorderstadt toward the church. Turn right at the Hornbahn sign and walk down the steps and along the street until the road splits. Follow Hornbahn Fussweg to the right, to the Hornbahn. Purchase a ticket to the peak (the return trip is included).

Start: At the top station take the path to Alpenhaus via the Alpen-blumengarten (Alpine Garden). When leaving the garden, use the exit at the bottom level, entering the path to the Alpenhaus. Excluding your garden visit, plan on a leisurely forty-five-minute walk on a well-traveled, downhill path. You'll soon understand why Kitzbühel is a famous international ski resort—there are ski lifts in every direction. The Alpenhaus is at 5479 ft. (1670 m.), with a restaurant and large terrace. There are a couple of options from this point:

Trail signs in Kitzbühel

1. Continue walking down from the Alpenhaus to Mid-Station Adler-hütte, at 4154 ft. (1266 m.), then ride down to Kitzbühel. (The trail from the mid-station to Kitzbühel is quite steep.)
2. Take the gondola from the Alpenhaus to Mid-Station Adlerhütte and change for the gondola to Kitzbühel, riding down the entire way.

After arriving at the bottom, turn right and walk down the hill to Kitzbühel.

Walk #5

Kitzbühel to Schwarzsee to Kirchberg
Walking Easy Time: 2¾ hours
Rating: Gentle

You might wish to take this excursion and low-level walk on a cloudy day. A comfortable path brings you out of Kitzbühel to Schwarzsee, a lovely resort lake thirty minutes from the center of the village, offering visitors many options. The walk continues past the lake and a golf course framed by jagged mountains in the distance and on to Kirchberg, with its imposing hilltop church. Although it's possible to walk back along the same path, a train or bus is available from Kirchberg to Kitzbühel.

Start: Begin at the Kirchplatz or church square, found by walking on the main street of Vorderstadt toward the church spire. Just before the church, walk down the steps to the left past the *bäckerei*. At a fork in the road, follow the blue Schwarzsee sign to the right, picking up a path next to the church, marked with a walking sign to Schwarzsee. You are now on path #14 on your hiking map. After crossing the road at a signed split in the path, stay on the left, marked #12. Continue on #12, with the lake on your right. After walking through a parking area, take paths #10 and #39, next to the railroad tracks, to your first left—#10 Golfweg toward Kirchberg on the Kitzbühel Town Street Map. This path brings *Easy Walkers* alongside the golf course on the right.

The path narrows, leading to Kirchberg, with the towering steeple of its famous old church acting as a beacon. Pass through a tunnel and ascend steps to the left, which take you to the town center. After visiting the church, return by train or bus to Kitzbühel. A sign on the main street points to the *bahnhof* for the short train ride. The bus stop is on the right, before you reach the train station.

Walk #6

Kitzbühel to Aurach to Oberaurach to Bichln to Kitzbühel
Walking Easy Time: 3 to 4 hours
Rating: Comfortable

Today's low-level walk along the Ache River leads to Aurach and the charming village of Oberaurach. You will return along the hills and meadows overlooking Kitzbühel.

Start: Walk past the Hotel Maria Theresia. Bear right at the fork in the road at the Hotel Schwarzer Adler, walking on Ehrenbachgasse. Continue past private homes and through a small tunnel until you see Achenpromenade #1. Turn right, walking through a suburban area of Kitzbühel with Tyrolean-style chalets.

As you proceed, the promenade alternates between a gravel path and a small auto road, with the river on the left. After about 3 miles (5 km.), turn left and walk over a small bridge at Gasthof Auwirt. Cross the road and turn right. Just before the gas station turn left on a country path signed OBERAURACH AND WILDPARK. After a few minutes you'll reach an intersection. Turn right and follow the sign to Wildpark, walking through rolling farmland and pasture until you reach an auto road. Turn left on the road and walk up the hill to the onion-domed church, visible above the trees.

After visiting the beautifully restored church, continue to follow the ascending road for a few hundred feet. Cross over the brook on a small footbridge and follow a path across from the Alterscheim (residence for the elderly). In a minute you'll be at a chapel built in 1867, still in use today. The grounds around this quiet chapel are shaded, and its bench can provide a lovely spot for a picnic lunch.

When ready, return to the church and walk down the auto road to the first signed right turn to Unteraurach. Follow this path, but at the same intersection you passed through earlier in the day, do not turn left; instead walk straight ahead. This country road takes you to the tiny hamlet of Dorfmühle. Follow signs to Bichlalm and Kitzbühel through the hamlets of Eichenheim and Mauringhof (marked #6 on the hiking map) below the Bichlalm Sesselbahn. At Mauringhof you have several options:

1. Continue ascending on #6, following signs to Bichln and the lift station, and catch an hourly bus back to Kitzbühel.

2. At Mauringhof, continue through the forest following Kitzbühel signs along the side of the golf course. At the tennis stadium, turn left into town.

3. Before reaching Mauringhof, this walk can be shortened by retracing your steps to the Gasthof Auwirt and catching the bus to Kitzbühel on the main road.

NEUSTIFT

The Tyrolean village of Neustift fits snugly between high-mountain peaks, reached via the narrow Stubai Valley road, which winds through picturesque villages all the way to the impressive Stubai Glacier at Mutterberg. Here a series of lifts takes over, bringing hikers and summer skiers up to Eisgrat, at 9351 ft. (2850 m.) for a visit to the hub of all-season sporting activity, the Stubai Glacier, which features skiing and glacier-walking in summer.

Neustift's hiking is exceptional and improving every year. Eight mountain *hütte* (huts) encircle the Stubaital (Stubai Valley), with overnight facilities for hut-to-hut hikers. The Stubai Trail starts and finishes in Neustift, with 75 miles (120 km.) of high-level walking trails, most between 7218 and 8859 ft. (2200 and 2700 m.). But *Easy Walkers* should not be intimidated, as hut-to-hut walking is only one of Neustift's appeals.

A second feature, within the reach of most recreational walkers, is the trails to *alms,* or pastures, located well below the higher level huts but above the valley floor. *Alms* offer rustic restaurants featuring local culinary specialties—*kaiserschmarrn* (a fluffy omelette served with homemade preserves), soup with *knödl* (dumplings), *wurst* with sauerkraut, and freshly made *kuchen* (cake).

Finally, there's a network of low- and medium-level trails and paths, connecting *alms* with valley walks. Most of the paths in the Neustift area are well maintained and well signed, helping first-time walkers feel comfortable on the trails. It's interesting to note that every bus stop in the Stubaital is at the beginning and/or end of a hike.

Transportation

By Train and Bus - Neustift is served only by the Bus Stubaital line from Innsbruck (a fifty-minute ride). Arriving by train at the Innsbruck station, walk to the front of the *bahnhof*, turn left, then walk around to the *busbahnhof* (bus station). Look for the yellow-and-green Bus Stubaital sign closest to the main street.

By Car - Drive on the A12 *autobahn* east or west toward Innsbruck, then follow signs into the Stubaital and Neustift.

Favorite *Walking Easy* Hotel

Hotel Bellevue

Three-Star; Owners—Familie Hofer

A-6167 Neustift/Stubai; **Tel:** 52 26 26 36; **Fax:** 52 26 26 36 9

Internet: www.bellevue-tirol.at

E-mail: bellevue@neustift.netwing.at

Hans and Patti Hofer created their hotel in a quiet location outside the center of Neustift, perfect for views of the Stubai Valley yet close to shops, hiking trails, and bus stops. The Hotel Bellevue offers comfortable bedrooms with balconies, gardens and sun terrace, large public rooms, and, most important, traditional Tyrolean hospitality combined with personal service and good food. Hans Hofer is happy to share his hiking knowledge about the Stubai Valley. Patti, a former Pan Am flight attendant, literally bubbles with enthusiasm about the special qualities of the Stubaital. Full breakfast buffet is included, and traditional Austrian specialties are served at dinner. If you arrive in Innsbruck by train or bus, the Hofers will pick you up at the station with an advance call.

Excursions

The Tourist Information Office is located across from the church, with information about summer activities in the Stubaital.

Fax: 52 26 25 29

Internet: www.neustift.com

E-mail: tv.neustift@neustift.at

1. **Neustift** - The beautiful, Baroque Neustift church is the second-largest country church in the Tyrol region. Note the magnificent rococo side altar, contrasting with its Baroque interior. The church grounds, as is the custom in Austria, are devoted to an ornate cemetery, and most of the decorative ironwork headstones were crafted in nearby Fulpmes, a famous center for ornate metalwork.
2. **Innsbruck** - See A Trail of Three Cities—Innsbruck.
   Directions: Take the hourly bus from Neustift to Innsbrook.

Neustift Walks

Recommended Map:

❖ Kompass Wanderparadies—Stubaital

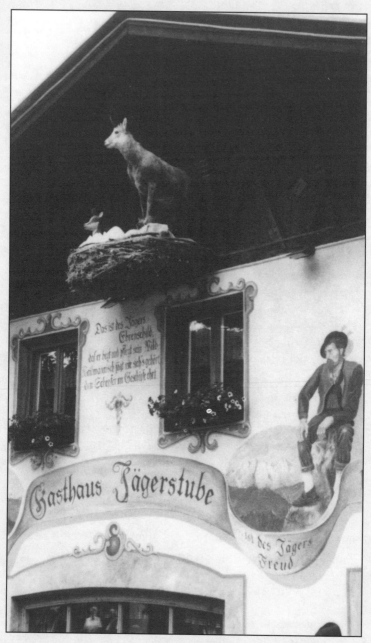

A charming Austrian restaurant

Walk #1

Elfer Top Station to Pinnisalm to Issenanger Alm to Neder to Neustift
Walking Easy Time: 3½ hours
Rating: Comfortable

The hike to Pinnisalm, returning through the Pinnistal (Pinnis Valley), is one of our favorites. You'll take the Elfer Chairlift to the top station, at 5886 ft. (1794 m.), for a superb view of the valley below. While there are a number of walks from this point, today you'll walk down the back side of the Elfer-spitze on a mountain trail to Pinnisalm, at 5118 ft. (1560 m.). This busy little oasis is the crossroad of several walks; after lunch you'll continue back through the valley, past Issenanger Alm, along the Pinnisbach (Pinnis River), descending all the way into Neustift.

Directions: At the Neustift church, walk down to the main road and turn left, walking to the ELFER LIFT sign, which points across the road to the right. Follow the path to the lift station and buy a one-way ticket to the top.

Start: At the top station, turn left and follow the sign to Pinnisalm on the carriage path, which soon becomes a narrow mountain trail. *NOTE: Be sure to follow the sign to Pinnisalm rather than continuing on the road down the mountain.* The Pinnisalm trail leaves the road and continues into the forest, and after seventy-five minutes, the restaurant in the Pinnisalm meadow appears. It's possible to lengthen this hike by walking deeper into the valley, ascending to the country restaurant at Karalm, at 5732 ft. (1747 m.). The route back to the restaurant at Pinnisalm is along the same path.

Either way, walk in the direction of Neustift on a wide, gravel jeep road. After forty-five minutes you'll arrive in Issenanger Alm, at 4528 ft. (1380 m.), and then Herzebenalm, at 4390 ft. (1338 m.), each with its own rustic restaurant. Be sure to stay on the main road toward Neustift, eventually reaching the sign OBERGASSE–NEUSTIFT. Turn left onto this midlevel panoramic trail with its views of the surrounding chalets and meadows. Descend into the village at the NEUSTIFT–DORF sign.

Walk #2

Elfer Top Station to Autenalm to Neustift (Optional Walks to Elferhütte and/or Klamperbergalm)
Walking Easy Time: 2½ to 4 hours
Rating: Comfortable

Today's walk begins in Neustift, using the Elfer Chairlift to the top station, at 5886 ft. (1794 m.), where the walk begins. You'll take a trail to Autenalm through the forest, with occasional glimpses of the valley below, descending from Autenalm to Neustift along a pleasant jeep road. The tiny mountain restaurant at Autenalm serves local specialties on a terrace overlooking the spectacular Stubaital.

A more challenging option is to first climb to the Elferhütte, at 6825 ft. (2080 m.)—a steep rise of 938 ft. (286 m.)—descending to Autenalm from there. Another option (taking three to three and a half hours round-trip) is to continue the hike from Autenalm to Klamperbergalm, at 5889 ft. (1795 m.), returning on the same path to Autenalm to begin the return hike to Neustift.

Directions: See Walk #1.

Start: At the Elfer Top Station, turn right and follow the AUTENALM sign, marked #5b on your map, into the forest and onto a pleasant balcony trail, descending comfortably to Autenalm, at 5440 ft. (1658 m.), in about an hour. As an option, strong walkers might wish to hike to Autenalm by first ascending for forty-five minutes to the Elferhütte, on a steep trail to the right of the chairlift station, then descending on trail #5 on your map, directly to Autenalm from the *hütte*.

After enjoying the spectacular views and refreshments at the Autenalm mountain cabin, it's possible to lengthen this hike by another three to three and a half hours round-trip by following the sign to Klamperbergalm, returning to Autenalm on the same trail.

At Autenalm, return to Neustift by following the jeep road, considerably less steep than the Fussweg Neustift mountain trail. Stay on this comfortable jeep road, following signs to Neustift. After crossing back and forth under the chairlift as you approach Neustift, turn onto the little path to the right marked NEUSTIFT–DORF, then follow signs into the village.

Walk #3

Nürnberger Hütte Bus Stop to Bsuchalm and Return, Walk Ranalt to Falbeson to Volderau to Krössbach (Optional Walk to Neustift)
Walking Easy Time: 3 to 5 hours
Rating: More challenging

After taking the bus from Neustift to the Nürnberger Hütte bus stop, you will climb along the Langanbach (Langan River) from 4298 to 5250 ft.

(1310 to 1600 m.), through the woods to Bsuchalm. This walk is the first part of the climb for hikers continuing on to the Nürnberger Hütte. *Easy Walkers* can end their hike at the rustic restaurant at Bsuchalm, although stronger walkers may wish to continue on to the *hütte*, a steep climb to 7481 ft. (2280 m.).

You'll return on the same route and take the bus to Ranalt, at 4275 ft. (1303 m.), to resume walking, switching from side to side of the river, going through Falbeson, Volderau, Gasteig, and finally Krössbach, at 3612 ft. (1101 m.). This part of the walk through the valley is gentle and can be shortened or lengthened at will, at bus stops marked with the yellow-and-green **H** signs. In fact, the walk can be continued on valley paths all the way into Neustift; there are restaurants, rest room facilities, and bus stops throughout the valley.

Directions: Take a bus toward Mutterberg and get off at the Nürnberger Hütte bus stop.

Start: After getting off the bus, cross the street and walk through the parking area and up to the right, on the trail marked BSUCHALM—40 MIN. (It may take *Easy Walkers* an hour for the walk to Bsuchalm, as the trail steepens.) Passing an impressive waterfall, continue on the ascending trail and note the sign BSUCHALM—15 MIN. The path levels off and veers to the right over a wooden bridge to the rustic restaurant.

You have walked up through the Langantal, where strong hikers can continue on to the *hütte*. It should be noted that each of the huts forming the Stubaital hiking infrastructure has an *alm*, or pasture, below it for hikers to enjoy. After lunch at the *alm*, retrace your steps down to the main road. Try to time your return to take the bus from the parking area to Ranalt. Exit the bus on the far side of Ranalt, then take the fork on the left side of the road toward the Wald Cafe. Cross the road and follow path #1, a gentle trail all the way to Volderau. The path recrosses the road, passing Gasteig and leading into Krössbach, at 3612 ft. (1101 m.). You can shorten or lengthen this walk toward Neustift by checking the bus schedules posted at each bus stop along the valley.

Walk #4

Stubai Glacier Walk (Optional Walk to Mutterberg)
Walking Easy Time: 2 to 3½ hours
Rating: More challenging

Glacier walks are always exciting, and today you'll travel through the narrowing Stubai Valley until the road ends at a giant winter sports arena encircled by stark, towering mountains and the Stubai Glacier. The bus leaves Neustift for a thirty-minute ride, taking you from 3258 ft. (993 m.) to the Gletscherbahn Base Station, at 5647 ft. (1721 m.). You'll take the gondola to the Fernau Mid-Station, at 7553 ft. (2302 m.), and continue on the same gondola over the barren, treeless landscape to Eisgrat, at 9351 ft. (2850 m.).

The one-hour (each way) hike from Eisgrat, at 9351 ft. (2850 m.), on the *gletscherpfad* (glacier trail) to 10,332 ft. (3149 m.) is well marked, well used, and roped. The walk is not difficult, but it should be taken when the weather is clear enough to enjoy the views from the top. After returning from the glacier, you'll proceed by gondola back to the mid-station to visit the Dresdner Hütte. From this point you can exercise the option of returning to the base station by gondola or taking the rocky, steep trail down the front of the mountain. Buses leave for Neustift from the parking area at Mutterberg.

Directions: Take a bus from Neustift to the Stubaier Gletscherbahn at Mutterberg, the last stop. Purchase a round-trip lift ticket to the top, staying in the same car as you glide by the mid-station to Eisgrat Top Station.

Start: Depending on summer snow conditions, begin at the marked glacier trail for the hour-long hike on the *gletscherpfad* to the kiosk, at 10,335 ft. (3150 m.). Your descent will be on the same glacier trail. Skiers and snowboarders will be schussing down the glacial slopes, while sunworshipers gather on the terrace of the Panorama Restaurant. When ready, take the gondola down to the mid-station, where you can pay a visit to the Dresdner Hütte—bratwurst and sauerkraut might hit the spot. At the mid-station you have the following options:

1. Hike down the steep, zigzagging rocky trail to the base station.
2. Take the gondola down. If it's wet, snowy, or slippery, or if you're a novice walker, we suggest that you continue on the gondola, using the balance of your lift ticket. If it's clear and dry and the view from the trail entices you, continue down by foot.

Walk #5

Neustift to Kartnall to Forchach to Bärenbad to Milders to Neustift
Walking Easy Time: 2½ hours
Rating: More challenging

We added this hike for those days when the weather is not conducive to high-level walking. Transportation is not necessary, as the hike starts and ends in Neustift. You'll walk from the valley floor in Neustift, at 3258 ft. (993 m.), to the heights above the valley and Kartnall, at 4265 ft. (1300 m.)—a climb of 984 ft. (300 m.). The hike continues up and around the mountain, then descends along a quiet road to Forchach. You'll continue down to Milders, at 3366 ft. (1026 m.), for the gentle valley return to Neustift.

Start: From the Hotel Bellevue, walk in the direction of the village. Turn left, following signs to Kartnall, Forchach, Starkenburger Hütte, and the *schwimbad* (swimming pool). Walk up the road until you reach the *schwimbad* parking area and turn left to Kartnall. Another sign directs you left again, up the gravel path toward Starkenburger Hütte and Kartnall. However, the Starkenburger trail branches off to the right as you walk ahead to the restaurant at Kartnall. After this climb, it might be time for a bowl of homemade *knödl* soup and some *apfel* strudel.

When ready, continue on the road, ascending to the high point at 4265 ft. (1300 m.). Descend past the restaurant at Forchach, meeting the road from Oberissalm. Turn left and walk down the road into Milders to the main auto road and bus stop. To walk back to Neustift (another half hour), turn left on the road, cross to the other side, then take the path through the fields to the church square in Neustift.

Walk #6

Kreuzjoch Top Station to Schlickeralm to Froneben Mid-Station to Vergör to Fulpmes to Gröbenhof to Rastbichl to Rain to Neustift

Walking Easy Time: 5 to 5½ hours

Rating: Comfortable

Today's walk begins at the Kreuzjoch Top Station, and you'll walk through Schlickeralm to the Froneben Mid-Station of the Kreuzjoch Lift, continuing through the forest on a pine needle–covered trail to the little hamlet of Vergör. After stunning views of the Stubaital, you'll return to the base station of the Kreuzjoch Lift for a low-level walk to Neustift.

In case of poor visibility this walk can be shortened by not taking the gondola to the Kreuzjoch Top Station. Instead, start the walk at the Froneben Mid-Station. It's also possible to begin the walk at the Kreuzjoch Base Station—not taking the lift at all.

Directions: Take the bus from Neustift to Fulpmes, a fifteen-minute ride. In Fulpmes center, the bus stops in front of the **i**, inside a corner sou-

Kreuzjoch 2100m.

S

Schlicker Alm
1643m.

Vergör

Mid-Station
Froneben 1316m.

Kreuzjoch Lift

Rain

E

Fulpmes 937m.

Neustift

Gröbenhof

venir store across the street from the bus stop. Walk up the hill in front of the **i** to the end of the street. Turn right and continue uphill to your left, passing in front of the firehouse. Continue on this *panoramaweg* to the base station of the Kreuzjoch Lift. Purchase a one-way ticket to the Kreuzjoch Top Station.

Start: At the top lift station, at 6890 ft. (2100 m.), follow directions to Schlicker Alm, at 5391 ft. (1643 m.), then Froneben Mid-Station, at 4318 ft. (1316 m.), on a wide, comfortable path. At Froneben, pass the outside of the snack bar and pick up the trail marked VERGÖR. This peaceful trail descends gently through the forest, eventually entering a sunny, open meadow with views throughout the Stubaital. At Vergör, just before an old barn, buttonhook left on a wide jeep road in the direction of Fulpmes and the base station of the Kreuzjoch Lift. At the base station you have a pair of options:

1. Walk to Fulpmes and take the bus to Neustift.
2. Walk to Neustift as follows: As you reach the Kreuzjoch Base Station, buttonhook sharply to the right on a path eventually signed NEUSTIFT. The trail descends gently as you walk through Gröbenhof, its meadows dotted with old barns. Passing the Rastbichl Gasthof on the left, walk ahead to a signed intersection before reaching the main auto road. Turn right to Neustift–Rain. This narrow trail takes you uphill through a working farm as it winds up and around to the left in the direction of Rain and Neustift. Reaching an unmarked intersection at Rain, take the ascending road to the right, staying on the heights above Neustift. Turn left at a fork in the road, descending gradually until you arrive at the church square.

Walk #7

Kreuzjoch Top Station to Starkenburger Hütte to Neustift
Walking Easy Time: 5 to 6 hours
Rating: More challenging

The hike to the Starkenburger Hütte begins with the lift from Fulpmes to Kreuzjoch Top Station, at 6890 ft. (2100 m.). It will take about three hours to hike to the Starkenburger Hütte, at 7340 ft. (2237 m.), along a narrow mountain trail that may be uncomfortable for those concerned about balance and footing. This is one of the most popular trails in the area, but there are some rocky sections. Strong walkers should have no problems completing the hike. The descent to Neustift is probably best taken along the jeep trail, down the mountain to beyond the Kartnallhof Restaurant, walking into the village from there.

Directions: Take an early-morning bus from Neustift to Fulpmes. See directions in Walk #6.

Start: At the Kreuzjoch Top Station take the trail to Sennjoch and the Starkenburger Hütte—the most traveled trail from the Kreuzjoch. The trail starts with a bit of a scramble and is marked #4 on your map all the way to Sennjoch. From Sennjoch, at 7185 ft. (2190 m.), take the easier, most direct trail, also marked #4 (*not* the dotted red line trail over the mountain), to the Starkenburger Hütte. There are no restaurants along the way, so be sure you've packed food and plenty of water. After about ninety minutes of walking, the trail proceeds around a rocky prominence and the Starkenburger Hütte is within grasp. Pick up the jeep road descending to Kaserstattalm, at 6201 ft. (1890 m.), buttonhooking right on #4 all the way to the Kartnallhof for the descent into Neustift on #3.

Additional Walks

Walk #8

The Besinnungsweg (Meditation Trail)
Walking Easy Time: 2½ hours (one way)
Rating: More challenging

The newest trail in the Neustift area is in the Pinnistal (Pinnis Valley). It begins at the jeep road above Neder and above the entry to the Obergasse Trail to Neustift, which you take in Walk #1. This new path ascends about 1000 ft. (300 m.), somewhat quickly. You can access the trail from Neustift by taking the Obergasse Weg, path #2 on your hiking map, to the road.

A *Walking Easy* trail

Turn right at the signed entry to this new trail (Besinnungssteig on your map). The entrance is on your left, and you climb rapidly with the aid of 300 steps, through the forest and up the mountain, reaching a height of 5250 ft. (1600 m.), passing original sculptures that give you an opportunity to rest and meditate. The trail then descends on a zigzag path to the terrace of the Issenangeralm Restaurant, at 4482 ft. (1366 m.). The walk to Neustift is back along the jeep road through the Pinnistal, as in Walk #1, but walk past the Obergasse Weg into Neder, where a left turn brings you past the Elfer Lift Station and Neustift.

SEEFELD

Seefeld, sitting on a sunny plateau at 3872 ft. (1180 m.), appears to have been created especially for *Easy Walkers*—it's cooled by mountain breezes and rimmed by rocky crests surrounding meadows dotted with walking trails. This is a cosmopolitan village of 2,900 inhabitants, with the Wetterstein and Karwendel mountain ranges forming an imposing backdrop and the unusual formation of the Höhe Munde towering above the village. A major resort in Austria, Seefeld attracts an international clientele of tourists and hikers, offering a championship golf course, casino, tennis center, concerts in the town park and Parish Church, cable lifts rising to mountain and ridge walks, and a car-free village.

Only 15 miles (24 km) northwest of Innsbruck, Seefeld is easily accessible by train, bus, and car. Easy-to-reach excursions to Innsbruck in Austria and Mittenwald, Munich, and Garmisch-Partinkirchen in Germany make Seefeld an enticing stop. Seefeld is a first-class walking and hiking center, with trails attracting all levels of walkers.

Transportation

By Train - Seefeld is a half hour from Innsbruck and two and a half hours from Munich by train, making it easily accessible from any area of Austria.

By Car - Driving from the east, take the A12 *autobahn* toward Innsbruck. Turn north before reaching Innsbruck, following signs to Seefeld. From the Salzburg area, take A12 past Innsbruck and drive north into Seefeld.

Favorite *Walking Easy* Hotel

Hotel Regina (No credit cards)
Three-Star; Owner—Monika Egger
A-6100 Seefeld/Tyrol; **Tel:** 52 12 20 70; **Fax:** 52 12 22 70 77
Internet: www.seefeld.at/hotel.regina
E-mail: regina.seefled@nextra.at

Supervised with the personal touch of Mrs. Egger and her pleasant staff, the Hotel Regina, located on a quiet side street, is a five-minute walk from the center of Seefeld. The large, comfortable rooms have balconies, and there is a traditionally furnished *stube* and lounge in which to enjoy an after-dinner drink. The garden is shady and relaxing, the site of a once-a-week dinner barbecue. This hotel is a favorite with the English, and under the watchful and caring eye of Monika Egger, this family-oriented establishment is a good choice for *Easy Walkers* because of its excellent location, pleasant rooms, good regional food, and caring staff.

Excursions

The Seefeld Tourist Office is located in the main square opposite the church.

Fax: 52 12 33 55

Internet: www.seefeld-tirol.com

E-mail: info@seefeld.tirol.at

Concerts in the church and band shell are held twice a week. A free shuttle bus is available to and from many Seefeld walking areas and lift stations. Pick up a map and schedule at the **i**.

1. **Innsbruck** - See A Trail of Three Cities—Innsbruck.

   Directions: The trip to Innsbruck takes thirty-five minutes by frequent train from Seefeld.

2. **Mittenwald, Germany** - Only 8.5 miles northeast of Seefeld and just over the German border in Bavaria, Mittenwald is noted for its uniquely painted buildings. (See Walk #4.)

   Directions: Train service is frequent for this half-hour trip. Remember to take your passport.

3. **Garmisch-Partenkirchen, Germany** - These twin Bavarian towns, lying at the foot of the Wetterstein range, are international resorts. At the Garmisch railroad station, the trains leave every hour to the Zugspitze, Germany's highest mountain.

   Directions: The train from Seefeld arrives in Garmisch in forty-five minutes. Remember to take your passport.

4. **Munich, Germany** - Stroll to the center of town and the famous Marienplatz to hear the renowned *glockenspiel*. Enjoy the Gothic **Church of Our Lady (Frauenkirche),** the city's most famous landmark, built in the 1400s. Meander through the shopping streets, but don't forget to have a wurst in the world-famous Hofbrauhaus—with a Munich beer, of course. Visit the **Old Pinakothek (Alte Pinakothek),** an immense building housing collections of paintings gathered over hundreds of years.

   Directions: The trip to Munich takes a little over two hours. Remember to take your passport.

Seefeld Walks

Recommended Map:

❖ Mayr Wanderkarte #15—Seefeld

Walk #1

Introductory Walk around Seefeld

Walking Easy Time: 1½ hours

Rating: Gentle

This walk can be taken on the day of arrival, to become acquainted with the Seefeld area. You'll walk along the main, car-free street, lined with cafes, shops, and hotels, and around the lake in the direction of Auland, returning to Seefeld along the opposite side of the lake.

Start: Walk south, past the church on the main street, until you reach the Wildsee. Walk around the lake on the road for a few minutes and turn right on a signed gravel path toward Auland and Reith. Turn right at the first intersection, through a boggy area around the tip of the lake and back toward Seefeld on the other side of the lake. Turn left on an intersecting road, #4a on your hiking map, back through the forest, following signs to the zoo and *kinderspiel* (children's playground) in the direction of Auland. Turn left toward Seefeld and the lake to meet the original path back into Seefeld.

Walk #2

Gschwandtkopf Top Station to Mösern to Lottenseehütte to Wildmoosalm to Seefeld

Walking Easy Time: 4 hours

Rating: Comfortable

Today's walk begins by taking the Gschwandtkopf Lift and hiking down the back side of the mountain to the village of Mösern. The hike to Mösern—about an hour of pleasant downhill walking—brings you into this village with its magnificent views of the Inn River. You'll leave for the Lottenseehütte through forest paths, passing the golf course and walking through Wildmoosalm.

Directions: Take the free Seefeld Dorf Bus to the Gschwandtkopf Lift. Or, at the church square, walk on Klosterstrasse, passing the back of the church. Make the first left turn, following signs to the Gschwandtkopf Lift, past the Sports Center. Purchase a one-way ticket to the top.

Start: Although the top station is at only 4905 ft. (1495 m.), the views are spectacular. Look for directions on the side of the panoramic map down from the lift station. Follow #85 on your hiking map to Mösern. The forest trail passes tiny Gschwandtkopf Lake. Soon the lookout on the right brings initial glimpses of the Inn River and the village of Telfs. Continue on this wide path and turn right at MÖSERN #4. At intersecting trails, turn left and take #96 to Mösern, ascending over the Möserer Höhe.

In the village of Mösern, turn left on the main street, crossing the road and passing the Tourist Office. After about 50 yards, turn right and walk up the hill in the direction of Gasthof Menthof. The view from the Menthof's terrace is one of the most spectacular panoramas in the area. Path #2, the Pirchsteig leading to the Lottenseehütte, can be seen from the Menthof sun terrace—not marked, but easily located—walk up the little trail behind the restaurant.

After entering onto the Pirchsteig, signs confirm your direction to the Lottensee. Remain on this path through the forest, the trail ascending gently to the Lottensee and the restaurant to the left. Walk back to the main road if you have detoured to the restaurant, following path #2A along the road, with the golf course on the left. Or you can take the unsigned, grassy path along the lake, which is full only periodically, continuing along the right side of the golf course and up to the golf club parking area. With either option, continue on the main road, which soon becomes a gravel path leading to Wildmoos and its lake, also full only periodically. At the intersection, turn right to Wildmoosalm and Seefeld along path #3. At Wildmoosalm you have the option of taking the bus to Seefeld or walking back. If you decide to walk, turn right on #2 to the outskirts of Seefeld.

Walk #3

Seefelder Joch Top Station to Seefelder Spitze and Return, Walk Rosshütte Mid-Station to Seefeld

Walking Easy Time: 4 hours

Rating: Comfortable

You'll take the Rosshütte funicular from 4049 to 5745 ft. (1234 to 1751 m.), changing for the cable car to the Seefelder Joch, at 6805 ft. (2074 m.). The first part of the walk is a hike up to the Seefelder Spitze, at 7287 ft. (2221 m.), along the spine of the mountain. You'll return to the Seefelder Joch along the same path. After you take the cable car back to the Rosshütte, continue your walk down the mountain to Seefeld.

Directions: Walk up Andreas Hofer Strasse to the Rosshütte Standseilbahn Base Station. Purchase a ticket to Seefelder Joch, with a return to Rosshütte, with its large terrace and picnic facilities. At the mid-station, follow signs to the Seefelder Jochbahn for the cable car ride to the top.

Start: At the Seefelder Joch, walk up the hill toward the large cross, following the ridge trail to 7287 ft. (2221 m.) and the Seefelder Spitze. Although this walk is listed as forty-five minutes, *Easy Walkers* may take an hour to reach their destination. (It's possible to hike ahead, eventually making a right turn down and around the mountain to the Rosshütte. This trail is rocky and can be steep in places.) If you return to the Seefeld Joch by walking down on the same trail you came up on, take the cable car back to the Rosshütte Station. Here, take a new trail called the Zirbenweg, a twenty-minute circle route to the mountain rescue cabin just above the Rosshütte. After returning to the mid-station you have the option for an additional excursion: Take the Härmelekopf cable car for a short ride across a deep gorge to the paragliding headquarters of Seefeld, returning to the mid-station in the same manner.

Follow the sign from the mid-station to Seefeld on a wide gravel path, ending at the base station.

Walk #4

Seefeld to Triendlsäge to Giessenbach to Scharnitz (Excursion to Mittenwald, Germany)

Walking Easy Time: 3½ hours

Rating: Comfortable

Today's low-level walk and excursion takes hikers from Seefeld to Triendlsäge, at 3691 ft. (1125 m.), into the Lehenwald (forest), past Bodenalm and through the valley to Giessenbach and Scharnitz. This walk takes about three and a half hours, and you should arrive in time to catch a train for the seven-minute ride crossing the German border to the scenic village of Mittenwald. Do not forget your passport.

Mittenwald is a very pretty Bavarian town, with ornately decorated church, shops, and homes. The village is famous for its violin museum and the crafting of handmade musical instruments.

Start: Walk on Seefeld's main street, Münchnerstrasse, past the Hotel Eden, turning left on Geigenbühelweg and following signs to the *panoramaweg*. You'll shortly pass the Panoramagolf Driving Range on the right. At the intersection, continue ahead on #65 to Triendlsäge and Bodenalm. At the next intersection, turn left at the sign TRIENDLSÄGE #1. Walk down the hill, following signs to Triendlsäge and Seefeld.

Walking down to the intersection in Triendlsäge, make a right turn on the carriage road marked #64 BODENALM. This level path is an easy walk through the Lehenwald, a tall pine forest in the Drahnbachtal (Drahnbach Valley). Follow signs to Bodenalm, walking past a small farm and restaurant on your right.

At the next intersection, continue following #65 on your map, in the direction of Giessenbach and Scharnitz, crossing the Drahnbach River on a bridge to your left. Continue to the right on #19, passing Giessenbach, all the way into Scharnitz, where you follow signs to the *bahnhof* on the other side of the highway. Trains to Mittenwald leave about forty-five minutes past each hour—check the train schedule.

Get off at Mittenwald and be prepared to convert some Austrian schillings to German marks, although many shops are prepared to deal in both currencies. Visit the church, built in the early 1700s, with its fine stuccos and murals. The Geigenbau-und-Heimatmuseum (Stringed Instrument Museum) on the street behind the church displays the different phases of violin-making. The brightly painted houses lining the streets of the Obermarkt are a pleasure to behold, and photographers will appreciate a few hours spent in this "living picturebook," as described by Goethe.

Trains returning to Seefeld depart Mittenwald frequently for the short ride. Buy your return ticket from the conductor on the train using Austrian currency—it's cheaper than buying the ticket at the Mittenwald train station, which accepts only German marks.

The Fludertal near Seefeld

Walk #5

Wildmoosalm to Weidachsee to Leutasch/Weidach
Walking Easy Time: 2½ hours
Rating: Comfortable

This pleasurable, mid- to low-level walk provides *Easy Walkers* with a mix of open meadow, mountain paths, and forest trails through the beautiful Fludertal (Fluder Valley). A bus runs from Seefeld to Wildmoosalm, at 4311 ft. (1314 m.), where the walk begins. The trail altitude does not vary more than 150 ft. (45 m.) over the length of a pretty forest path, the Wurzelsteig, bringing you down to the lake and restaurant at Weidach. After visiting the village of Weidach, you'll take the bus back to Seefeld. *NOTE: Afternoon buses run infrequently between Weidach and Seefeld. Check bus schedules before you leave on your hike.*

Directions: Take the bus (usually leaving every hour on the hour) to Wildmoosalm, from the parking area diagonally across from the Hotel Eden, next to the *apotheke* (drugstore) on Münchnerstrasse. Purchase a one-way ticket to Wildmoosalm.

Start: At Wildmoosalm walk past the restaurant and a lake on the right to the signed intersection LEUTASCH #3. Turn right and walk uphill on a carriage path for about twenty-five minutes. Additional signs at the intersection confirm your direction—ahead on #3. Within minutes you'll enter the Fludertal, with stunning views of the Wetterstein mountain range towering behind tall pines.

After about an hour, the path descends to the auto road. Turn left, carefully walking alongside the road, taking the narrow, beaten path along the left side of the auto road, then descending down to the road again. Turn left up into the forest on a path marked with a blue-and-white sign picturing a biker and hiker. You are now on Wurzelsteig #42, soon to be confirmed by signing. This narrow forest path is blazed in blue. This trail lifts gently out of the forest and crosses a meadow, with a small *spielpark* (amusement park) in full view down the hill. Be careful as you walk under a chairlift, and cross over a flume slide and go-cart path, part of the amusement park.

Entering the forest again, walk to the right immediately on an unsigned, blue-blazed path. This path soon crosses a jeep road. Walk ahead following #42. Reaching an intersection marked #3 WEIDACHSEE, turn right. The path widens and drops easily toward the lake at Weidach. At the next intersection, turn right on Seerundgang #3, walking to this lake with its trout farm and fishing piers.

Walk on the auto road past the restaurant, making a right on the sidewalk at a main road. Continue until you reach the heart of the village—all the way to the main street. Turn right—the bus stop is just below Gasthof Zum See. (The postbus schedule will read LEUTASCH/WEIDACH GH ZUM SEE.)

Walk #6

Seefeld to Möserersee to Auland to Seefeld
Walking Easy Time: 4½ hours
Rating: Comfortable

Today you'll leave Seefeld by way of Möserer Mähder #2 in the direction of Mösern, with a walk around the Möserersee, at 4213 ft. (1284 m.). The walk continues down to the village of Mösern, around the Gschwandtkopf on Möserer Steig #4, to the village of Auland. This portion of the walk offers fabulous views of the snowcapped peaks of the Austrian National Park. The hike ends with a short ascent to Seefeld, walking around the Wildsee.

Start: Walk past the Seefeld Tourist Office and the post office on the right, to the main auto road. Pass the Olympic Centre on the left and make a left turn in the direction of the See Kirche. This part of the walk is along the road, but it lasts only for a few minutes. Cross the road a few hundred yards after the Seekirchl to Mösern #2, making a right turn up the hill. At the top of the hill, turn left and continue on Mösern #2. The Tennis School

On the trail again

is on the left. Continue on this path in the direction of Mösern. Within a short time, bear right at the fork, again in the direction of Mösern.

Passing trail #96, proceed on the path signed #2 ZUM SEE and MÖSERN up to the right, shortly reaching the Hotel Olympia. Follow the path ahead, passing the Hubertushof, making a sharp right up the hill to the Mösersee. Always follow the ZUM SEE signs. At the lake you will find a restaurant, if you decide not to picnic, and a delightful walking path around the lake.

When ready, retrace your steps through the parking area. Cross the rocky intersection ahead. Turn right on the road and follow the sign to Mösern, again passing the Hubertushof and the Olympia. Just past the Hotel Olympia, follow the auto road down the hill to Mösern. Cross the highway and turn left on the sidewalk, walking for about 100 yards to enter the path into the forest on the right, marked #4 AULAND—1½ HRS. After a few minutes you'll reach a picturesque viewing point with a bench. Turn left up the hill in the direction of Gschwandtkopf, as the path now rises from 3937 to 4295 ft. (1200 to 1309 m.). Walk past the intersection of #85, the path from the Gschwandtkopf peak. Continue on Möserer Steig #4, always in the direction of Auland.

After about a seventy-five-minute walk from Mösern, the path descends onto an easy trail into Auland. Passing the Alpenkönig Hotel on the left, a small sign directs you left on the road to the Englhof Hotel, with a sun terrace and tantalizing assortment of desserts. Continue walking uphill toward Seefeld for a short ascent on #4. Cross the road at the top, walk straight ahead to the outskirts of Seefeld, then turn left on See Promenade #4 around Seefeld's resort lake, eventually turning right into town.

Walk #7

Salzbachbrücke to Gaistalalm to Tillfussalm to Salzbachbrücke
Walking Easy Time: 3 hours
Rating: Comfortable

This hike in the Gaistal was discovered by enthusiastic *Easy Walkers* Lynn and Jud Ford. They reported that this comfortable ascent along the river, with magnificent views of the Wettersteins on one side and Höhe Munde on the other, is one of the prettiest walks in the Seefeld area. You will enter the Gaistal (Gais Valley) by walking along the river on the Nordalpenweg, returning to Salzbachbrücke on the higher trail.

Directions: Bus service to Salzbachbrücke in the Leutasch is very limited, so check your bus schedule carefully. If you go by car, we recommend that you park in the *farthest* of the four parking areas, as the trail begins near there.

Start: Take path #7 to Gaistalalm, on a comfortable ascent along the Leutascher Ache (river). You'll pass the Höhe Munde and Niedere Munde on your left and the impressive Wetterstein range up on the right. In about fifteen minutes, reaching a fork in the trail, stay left, continuing along the river, all the way to Gaistalalm, where you have a couple of options:

1. Turn right up to the restaurant at Gaistalalm and walk back to the parking area along the Ganghofer Weg.
2. Continue ahead and around through Tillfussalm, passing the restaurant at Gaistalalm, then returning on the Ganghofer Weg.

ZELL AM ZILLER

(Mayrhofen)

The narrow-gauge, red-and-yellow regional train *zugs* its way deeply into the Zillertal (Ziller Valley) from the wide valley entrance at Jenbach to Zell am Ziller. This is the preferred Ziller Valley *Walking Easy* base village because of its quiet location on the banks of the Ziller River, proximity to local bus and railroad service, and outstanding resort hotel.

A mecca for European tourists and finally being discovered by Americans who are beginning to learn about the charm and easy accessibility of this valley, the Zillertal manages to strike a balance between meeting the needs of vacationers and preserving the dignity and strong sense of tradition inherent throughout this region. The warm, comfortable feeling of *gemütlichkeit* seems to emanate from everyone in Zell am Ziller, from the tourist office to the hotel owners.

Mayrhofen, near Zell am Ziller at the end of the Zillertal, is the gateway into picturesque volcanic valleys called *grunde*, open only in summer and autumn, sealed at their distant ends by peaks usually covered year-round with snow. These U-shaped valleys were formed during the Ice Ages, gouged out by glaciers. Today these steep inclines are covered by forests, towering above lush green valleys used for farming and grazing—a walker's paradise.

The Zillertal also serves as an entry to the Tuxertal (Tux Valley). Year-round skiers and summer hikers are attracted to Hintertux and its glaciers, which features a high-level, multisection lift system. Many Zillertal lifts operate during summer months, transporting walkers to mountain restaurants and miles of marked paths and trails, through tall pine forests and flower-filled meadows—all guaranteed to evoke an annual urge to return to Zell am Ziller.

Transportation

By Train - When traveling to Zell am Ziller by train, there is always a change of train in Jenbach to the Zillertalbahn, next to the Jenbach station; follow the Zillertal sign.

By Car - Turn off the A12 *autobahn* at the Zillertal exit and follow signs to Zell am Ziller.

Favorite *Walking Easy* Hotel

Sporthotel Theresa

Four-Star; Owners—Familie Egger

A-6280 Zell am Ziller; **Tel:** 52 82 22 86 0; **Fax:** 52 82 42 35

Internet: www.theresa.at

E-mail: info@theresa.at

A personal favorite, this wonderful four-star resort hotel (with five-star ambience) features an outstanding kitchen, caring staff, and excellent facilities. From the indoor swimming pool, solarium, fitness room, and extensive spa facilities, to the clay tennis courts with a teaching pro, to the parklike setting for four o'clock tea and snack time (the Sporthotel Theresa's exclusive "three-quarter board"), to the superlative cuisine— nothing escapes the caring eyes of Theresa and Siegfried Egger and their family. They have created a warm, guest-oriented atmosphere in a full-service resort catering to leisure seekers and hikers alike. The breakfast buffet is copious, and dinners created and supervised by chef- author-son Stefan are culinary delights. Because of its four-star amenities, we wouldn't think of going to Austria and the Zillertal unless we checked into the Sporthotel Theresa.

Excursions

The Zell am Ziller Tourist Office is in the center of town on Dorfplatz.

Fax: 52 82 22 81 80

Internet: www.tiscover.com/zell

E-mail: tourist.info.zell@netway.at

Pick up the booklet *Zillertaler Gästerzeitung* at the Tourist Office; all local bus and train timetables are listed in the back. The **Wanderticket,** or Z-Ticket, is a local six-day pass for use on Ziller Valley cableways and trans- portation. Proof of identity with a photo is required.

1. **Zell am Ziller** - The **Pfarrkirche,** or parish church, was constructed in the 1700s in an unusual octagonal design and is topped by a huge dome.

2. **Mayrhofen** - Only thirteen minutes by train from Zell am Ziller, Mayrhofen is at the end of the Ziller Valley.

   Directions: Trains and buses (conveniently listed on the same schedule) run frequently from the Zell am Ziller train station to Mayrhofen. A steam train operates on this narrow-gauge railway twice a day from

May 1 to October 15. Or you can walk on the Ziller promenade between Zell am Ziller and Mayrhofen. (See Walk #1.)

3. **Hintertux Glacier** - This paradise for year-round skiers is at the end of the Tuxertal, reached by bus from Mayrhofen. Gondolas rise to Sommerbergalm, at 6890 ft. (2100 m.), and Tuxer-Ferner-Haus, at 8728 ft. (2660 m.), the heart of the glacier regions of the Tuxer Alps.

   Directions: Take a bus or train from Zell am Ziller to the Mayrhofen bahnhof. Catch the bus to the Hintertux Gletscherbahn.

4. **Innsbruck** - See A Trail of Three Cities—Innsbruck.

   Directions: Take a train from Zell am Ziller to Jenbach and change for the train to Innsbruck.

5. **Krimml Waterfall (Krimmler Wasserfälle)** - Located west of Mittersill, these shimmering falls have a drop of 1250 ft. (381 m.), the highest in Europe. (See Kitzbühel, Excursion #5.)

   Directions: Check bus schedules on this route—changes are frequent, bus service is infrequent. If the Tourist Office in either Zell am Ziller or Mayrhofen runs an excursion to the waterfall, try this option.

6. **Schwaz** - In the fourteenth and fifteenth centuries, Schwaz was a copper- and silver-mining center, known as the "silver town of Europe." The silver mine is open, and the mine railway operates through tunnels and stalactite formations.

   Directions: Buses run from Zell am Ziller to Schwaz on the Innsbruck route.

7. **Rattenberg** - This old fortress town is noted for its historic squares, narrow alleyways, frescoed houses, and the etching and cutting of fine crystal. (See Alpbach, Excursion #3.)

   Directions: Take a bus or train to Jenbach and change for the train to Rattenberg/Kramsach.

Zell am Ziller Walks

Recommended Map:

   ❖ Mayr Wanderkarte #33—Zillertaler Alpen

Walk #1

Introductory Walk on the Ziller Promenade—Zell am Ziller to Mayrhofen
Walking Easy Time: 2 hours
Rating: Gentle

This introductory walk from Zell am Ziller to Mayrhofen is a pleasant first afternoon's outing. The walk begins in Zell am Ziller, on the Ziller Promenade, ending in Mayrhofen, a busy town at the end of the valley. After exploring Mayrhofen you can walk back to Zell am Ziller or return by bus or train. Mayrhofen is the largest town in the Zillertal and serves as entry point to the *grunde*, or summer valleys, and to Hintertux at the foot of the Tux Glacier.

Start: From the Tourist Office, walk toward the river on Dorfplatz, the main street. Turn left at the river onto the Ziller Promenade, with the river on your right, following signs to Mayrhofen. After checking out the *konditorei* (pastry shops), the Tourist Office, and the local church and shops, you can return to Zell am Ziller by bus or train or walk back along the Ziller Promenade.

Walk #2

Rosenalm Top Station to Kreuzjochhütte to Kreuzwiesenhütte to Wiesenalm Mid-Station
Walking Easy Time: 3½ hours
Rating: Comfortable

Today's high-level walk offers stunning views of the Zillertal, with the peaks of the Zillertaler Alps across the Gerlos Valley, and a visit to two mountain *hütte*. After a twenty-minute walk from Zell am Ziller to the Kreuzjoch Lift, you will ascend to 5722 ft. (1744 m.) in a two-stage gondola.

From Top Station Rosenalm, *Easy Walkers* will take a scenic path ascending to the Kreuzjochhütte, at 6267 ft. (1910 m.), walking from there to the Kreuzwiesenhütte, at 6300 ft. (1920 m.), with two options to return. You can walk back on the same path to Rosenalm and take the gondola, or continue down the mountain to Wiesenalm Mid-Station, at 4295 ft. (1309 m.).

Directions: In Zell, walk toward the **i**. Turn left on Rohrerstrasse between the **i** and the Zillertaler Bier Company. Continue on Rohrerstrasse, and after about fifteen minutes, walk over the bridge to the lift station. Purchase a one-way ticket to Top Station Rosenalm.

Start: After exiting at the top lift station, turn left and walk down the hill on a jeep path in the direction of the Kreuzjochhütte. Turn right and continue uphill on the dirt road, following signs to Kreuzwiesenalm and Kreuzjochhütte. After walking about thirty minutes (resisting the uphill meadow shortcut to Kreuzjochhütte), you'll come to a signed intersection, with Kreuzjochhütte to the left and Kreuzwiesenhütte straight ahead. Turn left for a thirty-minute ascent to the Kreuzjochhütte and its great views of the Zillertal.

When ready, descend on the same path and turn left at the intersection toward Kreuzwiesenhütte on path #11—you should reach the *hütte* in a little over an hour. The views across the valley are worth another refreshment stop on the restaurant's large terrace, usually filled with hikers and sun-worshipers. Here you have two options:

1. Follow signs to the Wiesenalm Mid-Station on a comfortable forest trail and take the gondola down to Zell.
2. Return on the same path to the lift at Rosenalm, where you take the gondola down to Zell.

Walk #3

Grüne Wand Hütte through the Stillupgrund to Gasthaus Wasserfälle
Walking Easy Time: 2½ hours
Rating: Gentle

Mayrhofen lies on the far end of the Ziller Valley, linked to other smaller valleys, open only in summer, and known as *grunde*. One of these valleys is the site of today's hike: the Stillupgrund. You'll visit a beautiful lake/reservoir that reaches across the narrow valley floor, offering hikers a scenic path to the head of this valley.

You'll leave Mayrhofen by private bus for a ride to the Grüne Wand Hütte, at 4712 ft. (1436 m.). The walk back descends gradually through the valley, with giant waterfalls on either side and friendly cows grazing throughout the *alm*. Reaching the lake and the Alpengasthaus Wasserfälle, at 3662 ft. (1116 m.), you will take a private bus return to Mayrhofen and a bus or train back to Zell am Ziller.

Directions: Leave Zell am Ziller by train or bus to Mayrhofen in sufficient time to catch a morning private bus. After leaving the Mayrhofen train station, turn right along the road. Make your first left turn, and just before the post office, note the large sign BUS LINE—STILLUPGRUND to the right. Follow that street around, into the parking area. The bus stop is next to the

i. *NOTE: Check times and location carefully.* The forty-five-minute bus ride winds through the narrow entrance of the valley to the Gasthaus Wasserfälle, where you change for another minibus, riding deeper into the valley to the Grüne Wand Hütte, where the walk begins. (Purchase a round-trip ticket for the first bus and a one-way ticket for the second. There is a separate charge for each bus.)

Start: This walk is along a little-used road, starting at 4712 ft. (1436 m.), descending through meadows filled

Zillertal hiking sign

with grazing cows, with the rapidly flowing Stillupbach (Stillup River) on the left. After you've walked about an hour, the Stilluphaus, at 3911 ft. (1192 m.), is available for a rest or refreshment stop. Continuing, walk through and around three small tunnels leading to the lake and the Wasserfälle Restaurant. The return private buses to Mayrhofen usually leave at thirty minutes past the hour, the last bus at 5:30 P.M. After arriving in Mayrhofen, walk to the train station for the next train or bus to Zell.

Walk #4

Gschösswand Top Station to Mid-Station Finkenberg Lift, Lift to Penken, Walk to Gschösswand Top Station

Walking Easy Time: 3 hours

Rating: Comfortable

After a short ride and visit to Mayrhofen, you'll take the Penken Lift to the top station, at 5906 ft. (1800 m.), and walk along the mountain on a comfortable path to the mid-station of the Finkenberg Lift. From there you'll take the chairlift up to Penken and return to Gschösswand on the higher trail, with fabulous views of the Ziller Valley, its surrounding peaks, and summer *grunde*.

Directions: Take the train or bus from the Zell am Ziller *bahnhof* to Mayrhofen. Walk up to the main shopping street and turn right for the ten-minute walk to the Penken Lift Station. Buy a round-trip ticket to the Gschösswand Station.

Start: On exiting, follow the PENKENHAUS #22 sign on to the road under the chairlift, all the way to the Almstüberl Restaurant and Finkenberg Chairlift. Take the chairlift one-way, up to Top Station Penken.

At Penken take the Finkenberger Panoramaweg #23 to the chairlift above Gschösswand. Here you have the option of going to the Penken gondola by riding the chairlift or walking down the path for the return trip to Mayrhofen and the walk to the *bahnhof*.

Walk #5

Finkenberg to Kreuzlau to Burgstall to Schwendau to Hippach to Zell am Ziller
Walking Easy Time: 4 hours
Rating: Comfortable

Although all walks are nicer when the skies are clear, this midlevel hike can also be taken on a cloudy day. The walk begins in the village of Finkenberg after a short bus ride from Mayrhofen. Walkers will hike along the Leonhard-Stock-Weg above and along the Ziller Valley. The trail then ascends to Burgstall, eventually reaching the picturesque villages of Schwendau and Hippach. From there, the walk is on a level path along the valley floor for an easy stroll into Zell am Ziller.

Directions: Take a bus or train to Mayrhofen, transferring to the Finkenberg bus outside the train station. Buy a one-way ticket to Finkenberg, getting off at the church at Finkenberg-Dorf.

Start: Walk into the churchyard and follow the sign #26 LEONHARD-STOCK-WEG up to the right, on a narrow road in the direction of the forest. The path soon becomes a grassy carriage road and splits. Follow signs reading LEONHARD-STOCK-WEG #26 as you enter the forest on a *bergweg*. Avoid trails #26a and #26b, and continue in the direction of Mariensteig along the Leonhard-Stock-Weg. This trail continues through the forest,

A farm in Zillertal

where you take path #2 to Mayrhofen, descending to a dead-end main path (overlooking the river and SPAR market). Turn left (unmarked #12) and continue to the Zillertal Restaurant.

Walking a little past the restaurant, do *not* turn left on #2c to Zimmereben, but walk a bit farther and ascend left on path #12 to Burgstall, Schwendau, and Hippach on the *waldweg* (marked on an old hut). This trail, blazed white, is easy to follow and eventually arrives at a road. Cross and continue on path #12, to the charming community of Schwendau. After exploring this village filled with old landmark homes, walk through the apple and pear trees back to the trail marked #12. The trail leads up and around Schwendau and onto a level, red-blazed forest path for the walk to Hippach. Follow signs to Hippach and turn right at Cafe Waldegg, signed #7 HIPPACH, descending through town and making a left turn before the bridge on the path marked #1 ZILLER PROMENADE to Zell am Ziller. The next hour's walk is along this path, with the river on the right. After passing through Zellberg, turn right at the bridge and walk over the river into Zell am Ziller. In Hippach/Ramsau, it's possible to take the train or bus back to Zell am Ziller.

Walk #6

Sonnalm Top Station to Kotahornalm to Bühel
Walking Easy Time: 4 hours
Rating: More challenging

Today's more challenging hike takes you from Sonnalm, at 4462 ft. (1360 m.), the top station of the Ramsau Chairlift, up to Kotahornalm, at 5328 ft. (1624 m.), and its old snack hut, famous for local cheese, sausage, beer, and schnapps. This isolated farmhouse is an oasis sitting on a high *alm,* welcoming hikers with old-fashioned *gemütlichkeit.* The trail brings you up 866 ft. (264 m.) and finishes with a downhill trek directly to Bühel, a train and bus stop, or to Ramsau, where the walk began earlier in the morning. The descending path is not so much steep as it is long, and it will take about two and a half hours to descend 3281 ft. (1000 m.) to Bühel from Kotahornalm. This walk should be taken on a dry day and not after a wet period—the trail can be slippery.

Directions: Take the bus or train from Zell am Ziller *bahnhof* to Ramsau. Follow signs to the Ramsberg Lift. Purchase a one-way ticket to Sonnalm, where the walk begins.

Start: Walk down the path to the front of the lift station, following the sign KOTAHORN AND GERLOSSTEIN, PATH #50. This road/trail ascends to Kotahornalm, marked #50. After about a half hour, a sign directs you sharply left, up a steep trail on #50 to Kotahorn. Do *not* take it. Continue ahead up the road, the path becoming a red-blazed trail, still marked #50. Shortly, the path buttonhooks steeply up a stepped trail marked BRANDENBERG, STEINKOGEL #50. At the top a sign indicates the path to Brandenberg and Steinkogel to the right. This path also goes to the left, back down the mountain. You *must* turn right here, following the red-blazed ascending trail. The sign is movable, so don't be fooled—turn right. Shortly you'll come into a meadow. Bear right and walk up the path. Around the turn on the left is an old farmhouse, providing a warm, cozy place to rest and snack.

When ready, return down to the path and follow signs reading #51 MAYRHOFEN, remembering that your final destination is Bühel/Ramsau. Pick up the #51 Ramsau/Bühel path, descending from 5250 to 2133 ft. (1600 to 650 m.). The church steeple in the town of Hippach comes into view as you descend through the forest, arriving at a road. Follow the sign to Bühel, turning left at the dead end and walking to the bus or train station, near one another. Check your bus and train timetable, taking the first to come along for the short ride into Zell am Ziller. The bus station is on the main road, marked by the familiar **H** sign; the tiny train station can be reached by walking through a tunnel and making a left turn. *NOTE: Don't forget to hail the train—it stops by request only.*

Walk #7

Gerlosstein Top Station to Kotahornalm to Karlalm to Kotahornalm to Sonnalm, Ramsberg Lift to Ramsau (Optional Walk to Zell am Ziller along the Ziller Promenade)

Walking Easy Time: 3 to 4 hours

Rating: Comfortable

Our hike today starts at the top station of the Gerlosstein Lift in Hainzenberg, reached by bus from Zell am Ziller. You'll walk to Kotahornalm, with its quaint cabin and terrace—a perfect spot for local sausage and cheese—to prepare for a mountain trail rising from 5387 ft. (1624 m.) to the Karlalm pasture, at 5729 ft. (1746 m.), with its fabulous views of the Zillertal and the Tuxer Alps across the way. Although it's possible to continue ahead for a descent to Brandberg, Steinerkogel, and, eventually, Mayrhofen, we recommend that *Easy Walkers* return from Karlalm to Kotahornalm and take the path to Sonnalm for the chairlift return to Ramsau. From Ramsau you have the option of returning along the Ziller Promenade to Zell am Ziller or, if you prefer, taking the first available train or bus.

Directions: Bus service to Hainzenberg is limited—check the bus schedule. However, there is an early-morning bus that leaves the Zell am Ziller *bahnhof* about 9:00 A.M. for the short ride to the lift. Purchase a round-trip ticket to the top station, good for both the Gerlosstein Lift and the return Ramsberg Chairlift from Sonnalm to Ramsau.

Start: After leaving the lift station turn right. Walk in back of the restaurant and follow the upper path to Kotahornalm and its rustic restaurant and terrace. A sign directs you to Karlalm on an ascending *bergweg*, eventually entering the forest as the trail climbs up to the Karlalm pasture. Although it's possible to continue the descent to Mayrhofen, we suggest returning down the same trail to Kotahornalm, taking path #50 down the mountain to Sonnalm. A little more than halfway down, at an intersecting trail from the left, walk ahead through the gate, continuing the descent to the wagon road. Turn right, following the path directly to the Ramsberg Chairlift at Sonnalm. Take the chairlift down to Ramsau and walk into the village. Turn left and proceed on the main road for about 300 feet. Cross the road to the train station for a quick ride back to Zell am Ziller. Or walk over the railroad tracks, turn right, and pick up the Ziller Promenade for the fifty-minute walk to Zell am Ziller.

Additional Walks

If you're staying at the Sporthotel Theresa, Sigal Egger and son Stefan take guests on great hikes through the countryside.

MIEMING

Tranquil Mieminger Plateau is a sunny, agricultural plain, open to the south and protected in the north by the high, snowcapped peaks of the Mieming mountain range. With over 130 miles (210 km.) of comfortable, mostly level, signed hiking trails winding through lush meadows and picturesque larch forests, around working farms and vast cornfields, this "sun terrace" in the heart of the Tyrol is only 22 miles (35 km.) from historic Innsbruck. The dramatic Höhe Munde mountain lies to the north and, if you've hiked around the *Walking Easy* base village of Seefeld, you've trekked on the other side of this uniquely shaped mountain. Another Seefeld hike leads to the village of Mösern—with a view along the Inn River to the village of Telfs—and farther, to our new base village on the Mieminger Plateau.

Mieming does not offer high, rocky, alpine hiking. Most trails are gentle, rolling paths with little change in elevation and will appeal to walkers who prefer easier challenges. The *Walking Easy* Hotel Schwarz, with its sophisticated array of spa facilities and full-board accommodations, is the center of attraction in this area for *Easy Walkers*.

Many paths weave in and around the hamlets of the Mieminger Plateau. All trails are signed, and with the aid of the local hiking map, *Easy Walkers* can stroll and hike endlessly in this pastoral setting.

Transportation

By Train and Bus - Take an express train to Innsbruck; outside the train station, at the bus *bahnhof*, take a bus to Obermieming (about an hour's ride). Get off at the Hotel Post in Obermieming and follow the sign to the Hotel Schwarz, a few minutes' walk. Or take a local train to Telfs and a taxi to the hotel.

By Car - You can reach the Mieminger Plateau via the Inn Valley Highway—4.5 miles (7 km.) from the Telfs exit and 2.5 miles (4 km.) from the Mötz exit.

Favorite *Walking Easy* Hotel

Hotel Schwarz
Four-Star; Owners—Franz and Martha Pirktl
A-6414 Mieming; **Tel:** 52 64 52 12 0; **Fax:** 52 64 52 12 7
Internet: www.schwarz.at

E-mail: hotel@schwarz.at

The "wellness" Hotel Schwarz is a secret waiting to be discovered by Americans and *Easy Walkers* who may prefer a quality four-star, full-resort hotel offering all amenities to pamper guests. Located on the Mieminger Plateau amid cornfields and potato patches, but close enough to Innsbruck for a one-day sight-seeing excursion, the Schwarz experience includes modern spa facilities, outdoor swimming pool and gardens, tennis, children's zoo, and a new golf course at its front door. Your reservation includes a bountiful buffet breakfast and lunch, excellent dinner, and an array of daylong snacks and drinks. The Pirktl family is always attending to the comfort of their guests. It will cost a bit more, but if you want to be spoiled, check into the luxurious, family-oriented Hotel Schwarz.

Excursions

The Tourist Office (Tourismusverband Sonnenplateau Mieming–Wildermieming) is on the main street of Mieming.

> **Fax:** 52 64 61 50
>
> **Internet:** www.mieming.at

1. **Innsbruck**—See A Trail of Three Cities—Innsbruck.

   Directions: Take the bus to the Innsbruck train station, a one-hour ride.

2. **Seefeld**—See Seefeld section.

   Directions: Take the bus to the Innsbruck train station and change for a train to Seefeld, a half-hour ride.

3. **Mittenwald, Germany**—See Seefeld Excursion #2 and Walk #4.

   Directions: Take the bus to Innsbruck and the train to Mittenwald.

Mieming Walks

Recommended Map:

❖ Mayr Wanderkarte Sonnenplateau #14—Obsteig, Mieming, Wildermieming

Walk #1

Obermieming to Untermieming, through the Fiechtertal to Wildermieming to Obermieming
Walking Easy Time: 3 hours
Rating: Comfortable

This comfortable walk begins at the Hotel Schwarz and brings you down through the tiny village of Untermieming and its Gothic church, then into the countryside to Fiecht. These paths offer fabulous views of the Mieminger Plateau, and the walk continues through the Fiechtertal (Fiecht Valley), returning to Obermieming through the charming village of Wildermieming. The plateau is largely agricultural, filled with working farms and massive cornfields.

Start: From the Hotel Schwarz, walk to the main road. Cross the street in front of the Gasthof Post and pick up the path to the left of the house, walking away from the road toward Fiecht. In the rural hamlet of St. Georg, pass the chapel and pick up the wagon path signed UNTERMIEMING. After visiting the church in Untermieming, turn left at the Gasthof Steigl, following the sign to Fiecht.

As you proceed gently up the hill away from the village and into the countryside, you will see the Hotel Schwarz on the plateau to the left, framed by the Mieminger Berg mountain range. At the top of the rise, turn right following 8A PLATEAUBLICK. After a few minutes on 8A, turn left on a *forest strasse* in the direction of Telfs (the right path leads to Stams). Eventually you'll follow signs FIECHT and GERHARDHOF. At a fork in the path, continue left, descending gently toward Telfs and the Gerhardhof.

There will be an opportunity at the fork to go back to Untermieming; instead continue through the Fiechtertal on #10 to the main auto road. Cross the road, following signs up and around to Wildermieming—*not* to the Gerhardhof. This path continues through the village of Wildermieming, where you can pay a visit to its magnificent church. Pick up the bike path and walk directly back to the Hotel Schwarz. (There are three different roads going through Wildermieming, all of which eventually lead to Obermieming and the hotel.)

Walk #2

Obermieming to Wildermieming to the Gerhardhof to Telfs
Walking Easy Time: 2½ hours
Rating: Comfortable

Today you'll walk through Wildermieming, into the valley and forest to the busy town of Telfs, at 2080 ft. (634 m.), with a stop at the Gerhardhof, a delightful country inn (closed on Monday and Tuesday). The return to Obermieming is by bus from Telfs.

Start: Turn left as you exit the Hotel Schwarz, walking toward Wildermieming on a country road. Just before Wildermieming the road forks—take the left fork marked WILDERMIEMING #10A. As the road continues, you can see the Wildermieming church steeple down on your right. Follow the signs ahead: TELFS—1½ HRS. and GERHARDHOF—30 MIN. Continue to follow signs to the Gerhardhof. Eventually the road turns around and continues right and then left through the Angertal in the direction of the Gerhardhof. A sign takes you from the wagon path, up on a mountain trail to a path continuing through the forest to the Gerhardhof—a charming mountain restaurant seventy-five minutes from Obermieming.

When ready, follow the sign in front of the restaurant, TELFS—1½ HRS. It actually takes only another hour to reach the suburbs of Telfs. This path from the restaurant is occasionally marked with small signs reading *rund wanderweg*. Follow the road down through the outskirts of Telfs to the main highway. Turn right for the bus stop to Obermieming, or spend some time exploring this village before returning by postbus.

Walk #3

Grünberg Panorama Rundweg, Obsteig Lift to Grünberg, Walk to Zwischen-
simmering to Obsteig
Walking Easy Time: 2½ to 3½ hours
Rating: Comfortable

Today's hike begins in Obsteig at the top of the Grünberg Chairlift, at 4912 ft. (1497 m.). *NOTE: This lift does not operate on all days. Please check with the hotel or Tourist Office for current operating hours.*

Directions: Take the local bus from Obermieming to Obsteig. Walk through the village to the chairlift.

Start: Exiting the chairlift to your right, proceed around the Grünberg peak on the Grünberg Panorama Rundweg #31, walking around and down to Zwischensimmering, at 4321 ft. (1317 m.), where you have the option of continuing down the mountain through Holzerhütte—passing the waterfall—all the way to Obsteig. Or you can continue around the peak on #31 and take the chairlift down to Obsteig.

At the base of the chairlift you have two options:

1. Return to the main road and take the bus to Obermieming.

2. Take any one of several paths up and around to Obermieming.

Walk #4

Obermieming to Moosalm to Kohlplatz along the Engenbergweg to Arzkasten to Holzleiten

Walking Easy Time: 3½ hours

Rating: Comfortable

Start: Exiting the Hotel Schwarz, turn right and right again on the first street, walking to the *spielplatz*, or playground. Turn left, walking over the river, then right, to the Tennis Hall above Barwies. Turn right as if to Moosalm, at 2920 ft. (890 m.), but then turn right again, ascending to Kohlplatz, at 3170 ft. (966 m.). Follow the Engenbergweg on #17 and then #19, rising to Arzkasten, at 3776 ft. (1151 m.). At Arzkasten follow signs to Aschland and then to Holzleiten. Across the street from the Restaurant Holzleiten, at 3567 ft. (1087 m.), is the bus stop for your return to Obermieming.

Walk #5

Obermieming to Wildermieming to Strassberghaus on 15A and Return.

Walking Easy Time: 4 hours

Rating: Comfortable

Start: Exiting the Hotel Schwarz, turn left and walk on the country road to Brente. Pass a little chapel on your left, and walk on the path above Wildermieming, where you follow the sign #15A STRASSBERGHAUS. The path is well defined and ascends gradually on the Strassbergweg from 2855 to 3908 ft. (870 to 1191 m.). It is possible to walk down along the little river to Telfs, but that can be a long, descending hike with a bus return to Obermieming and the hotel. A more pleasant and easier return is along the same path, with new views of the plateau.

Walk #6

A Walking Tour of Innsbruck
Walking Easy Time: A full day
Rating: Gentle

The imperial city of Innsbruck, the crossroads of Europe, is a stone's throw from the famous Brenner Pass and the dramatic Dolomites of Italy. Surrounded by snowcapped mountains, it is close enough to Mieming for a comfortable, one-day city tour of its charming Old Town. A historic and cultural center, Innsbruck was the home of the Habsburgs, Austria's royal family, who were responsible for developing this capital of the Tyrol into an important architectural and arts center.

The Innsbruck Tourist Office is located at Burggraben 3, at the corner of Herzog-Friedrich-Strasse—the colorful cobblestoned main street of Old Town. This car-free zone houses shops and street cafes and is the heart of today's city walk.

Directions: Take the bus to Innsbruck through the village of Telfs and get off at the main *bahnhof* (train station) and bus station. Return to this station later for the bus back to Mieming. *NOTE: Check bus schedules before today's excursion.*

See A Trail of Three Cities—Innsbruck.

SALZBURGERLAND

BADGASTEIN

The fertile Gasteinertal (Gastein Valley) in Salzburgerland is nestled between high-mountain peaks and borders on Austria's dramatic Höhe Tauern National Park. Badgastein, the valley's social and cultural center, is perched on a steep hillside and is one of Europe's most famous all-season resorts. Gushing waterfalls and natural springs originate in this beautiful valley and serve as the core of spa activity and as a source of natural energy. The Belle Epoque architecture merges with an updated center, where winter and summer sports enthusiasts seek the pleasure of the Gasteinertal's world-famous thermal springs. In summer, ski tracks give way to hiking trails crisscrossing the surrounding mountains.

Bad Hofgastein, Dorfgastein, and Böckstein, Badgastein's sister villages, complete the infrastructure of the valley, offering a full range of cultural and sports activities. Charming country restaurants specializing in local cuisine are located throughout the 55 miles (90 km.) of hiking trails. For those *Easy Walkers* who would like to combine a hiking holiday with the advantages of world-class spa facilities, Badgastein is the base village of choice.

Near Badgastein, the valley divides into smaller valleys—the Kötschachtal, home of the village of Grüner Baum; the Anlauftal, where a little rail system enters old gold-mining tunnels, now the scene of the Healing Gallery; and the Nassfeldtal, entrance to Sportgastein, one of the most scenic alpine areas in Salzburgerland.

Transportation

By Train - Trains depart hourly from Salzburg for the trip to Badgastein.

By Car - Take the A10 *autobahn* south, exiting at Bischofshofen. Drive south, then west, on Route 311. At the junction with Route 167, head south, following signs into Badgastein and your hotel. If arriving from the south, exit the A10 *autobahn* at the Villach/Mallnitz exit (railway car ferry) and follow signs to Badgastein.

Favorite *Walking Easy* Hotel

Hotel Grüner Baum

Four-Star; Owners—Familie Blumschein

A-5640 Badgastein; **Tel:** 64 34 25 16 0; **Fax:** 64 34 25 16 25

Internet: www.grunerbaum.com

E-mail: info@grunerbaum.com

This exceptional hotel-spa and mountain retreat is located in the lush Kötschach Valley. Situated in its own quiet village, the "country-elegant" Grüner Baum specializes in a complete range of spa and health-related treatments utilizing Badgastein's hot springs. Rooms, most with balconies, are in several chalets surrounding the main house and outdoor pool. An indoor pool and whirlpool are open to all guests. Mix in a dash of gourmet dining, mountain day walks, and an attentive staff, and you have a perfect vacation setting. The hotel provides pickup service at the train station if you call ahead.

Excursions

The Badgastein Tourist Information Office is located on Mozartplatz.

> **Fax:** 64 34 25 31 37
>
> **Internet:** www.badgastein.at
>
> **E-mail:** fvv.badgastein@aon.at

Your hotel and the Tourist Office can provide information about spa treatments.

Public Bundesbus and private Lackner bus (both charging the same amount and sometimes traveling on the same routes) are available throughout the valleys.

1. **Badgastein** - Visit the **Nikolauskirche (Church of St. Nicholas)** and its Gothic frescoes and stone pulpit, along with Baroque tombs and altars. The waterfall of the **Gasteiner Ache** cascades into the center of town, with its turn-of-the-century hotels and fashionable shops.

   The seventeen thermal springs originating in Badgastein are reputedly beneficial to certain illnesses. The Healing Gallery is located in Böckstein, in the heart of the Radhaus mountain. A train runs slowly through the old tunnels of gold prospectors. Visitors can "take the cure" at Austria's leading spa with thermal water baths or enjoy a ride through the Healing Gallery.

2. **Bad Hofgastein** - At 2850 ft. (869 m.), this well-established spa village

lies 5 miles (8 km.) north of Badgastein. Visit the Gothic Pfarrkirche, built in the fifteenth century, and note many ancient turreted houses—remnants of wealthy gold-mining days in the Gastein Valley.

Directions: There are frequent buses available for the short ride between the towns, or you can walk along the river promenades. (See Walk #1.)

3. Salzburg - See A Trail of Three Cities—Salzburg.

Directions: Take a morning train for the hour ride to Salzburg.

Badgastein Walks

Recommended Maps:

- ❖ Gasteiner Wanderkarte—mit Wandernadel-Summer Panorama
- ❖ Freytag & Berndt—#191—Gasteinertal/Wagrain
- ❖ Gasteinertal Panorama mit Wanderwegen und Ortsplan

Walk #1

Grüner Baum via the Höhenweg to Bad Hofgastein, Schlossalm Lift to Kitzstein, Walk to Bad Hofgastein

Walking Easy Time: 2½ to 4½ hours

Rating: Gentle

The first part of today's walk is a good introduction to the Gastein Valley. This pleasant balcony trail is about 600 ft. (183 m.) above the valley floor. After visiting the charming village of Bad Hofgastein, you'll continue by taking the Schlossalm funicular to Kitzstein for a walk down to Bad Hofgastein, a low- to mid-level hike—a good walk for an overcast day.

If you arrive at your hotel midday and want to take a walk in the afternoon, this trip can be abbreviated by taking the two-and-a-half-hour walk to Bad Hofgastein along the Höhenweg and returning to the hotel by bus from Bad Hofgastein.

Start: Start from the village of Grüner Baum. Facing the Hotel Grüner Baum, turn left in the direction of Kaiser-Wilhelm Promenade and the Martin Lodinger Weg. Turn right at the fork, following signs to the Martin Lodinger Weg. Follow the road running adjacent to the Promenade up on the left. At the fork in the road, walk to the right over the bridge, the road occasionally marked MARTIN LODINGER WEG. Continue, but do *not* take the path up to the Gamskarkogel; walk ahead on the small, paved road. Cross the bridge by the waterfall and follow the sign left, to the Höhenweg. After about forty minutes pass Cafe Hubertus and an animal farm.

Continue in a northerly direction, *not* walking down to Gadaunern. You'll soon reach and pass through the dramatic Gadaunern Schlucht (Gorge). Follow signs down to Cafe Gamskar, eventually emerging onto a paved road and Bad Hofgastein.

Turn left, then right on the road, and walk toward the church steeple. Walk down and around to the Kirchplatz, passing the Panorama Apartment Hotel. Continue down to Kongresszentrum and the open square with the Tourist Information Office. Walk through the square toward the funicular across the way, crossing over the river and passing the large bus stop.

Hint: The meadows may be separated from the path by thin wires. Do not touch them—they are often electrified.

Purchase a one-way ticket to Kitzstein (in summer, this is the last station—the chairlift to the top station is closed). Turn left to Angertal and Hofgastein. Do *not* make a sharp left turn, through the cow fences and past a farm. Instead continue ahead in the direction of the Angertal, walking over the bridge. You'll shortly come to another sign indicating the Angertal ahead. Turn sharply left, following a small sign to Bad Hofgastein, on a trail to the road below. The road ends at a house. Follow the sign in back to Bad Hofgastein on a descending wagon path through the forest. Turn left at the road and walk down to the main road. Turn left and walk back to the Schlossalmbahn and the bus stop across the road for the return to the Badgastein *bahnhof* and your hotel.

Walk #2

Sportgastein to Nassfeldalm to Veitbauernhütte to Sportgastein to Evianquelle Restaurant (Böckstein) along the Nassfelder Wanderweg

Walking Easy Time: 3½ to 4 hours

Rating: Comfortable

Reserve the better part of the day for this rewarding hike through the Nassfeld Valley into the largest "prairie" in Austria. The walk starts at Sportgastein, after a bus ride on the Alpenstrasse toll road. The path is through the valley, past old farmhouses and barns, to the Veitbauernhütte, at 5397 ft. (1645 m.). You'll return to Sportgastein along the same path and pick up the Nassfelder Wanderweg, winding through the deep valley all the way to the Evianquelle Restaurant just outside Böckstein, for the bus ride back to Badgastein and your hotel.

Directions: Take a morning Lackner or Bundesbus from Badgastein *bahnhof* for the twenty-minute ride to Sportgastein.

Start: After exiting the bus, walk ahead through the parking area to the large NASSFELDALM sign, passing the Valeriehaus Restaurant up on your right. You'll be walking with the river on your left. This gentle path offers unobstructed views of the Kreuzkogel on the left and the snowcapped peaks of the Höhe Tauern ahead. In about forty-five minutes, passing through Nassfeldalm and by the Moaralm, a small farmhouse offering Austrian specialties, you'll reach Veitbauernhütte, a one-room farmhouse selling fresh milk and other beverages. The trail then ascends the mountain. We suggest returning on the same path, back to the bus stop at Sportgastein. Continue through the parking area onto the road, until reaching the first tunnel. To the left is the *wanderweg* trail to Böckstein, descending deeply into the valley along the Nassfeld River all the way to the Evianquelle Restaurant and the bus stop for the return to Badgastein. If you wish to continue walking, pick up the Kaiser-Elisabeth Promenade in Böckstein into Badgastein.

Walk #3

Stubnerkogel Top Station along the Otto Reichert Weg to Bockhartsee to Sportgastein
Walking Easy Time: 6 hours
Rating: More challenging

Today's full-day hike is demanding and will be challenging for *Easy Walkers*. The difficulty factor is not due to the altitude change, however, but to the rocky nature of the Otto Reichert Trail around the side of the Tischkogel. The Otto Reichert Trail is well blazed in red and white and easy to follow; however, *Easy Walkers* will be scrambling over rocks for a few hours. If you hike in late June or early July, this trail can be wet, muddy, and slippery. The views of the area are quite lovely, but you will be concentrating on your footing on the rocky trail ahead. You'll descend to the Bockhartsee, then walk up to the Bockhartseehütte, before descending to the road and the bus stop in Sportgastein.

This hike should be taken *only* by strong walkers who are capable of scrambling over rocks and can handle somewhat steep descents on a trail that can be muddy. Allow almost six hours from start to finish, taking in just a little rest time. There are *no* restaurants or rest room facilities along the way, so pack a lunch and lots of water.

Hint: *Check bus schedules, both Bundesbus and Lackner, to be sure to arrive at Sportgastein before the last bus to Badgastein—about 5:30 P.M.*

Directions: Take a morning bus to the Badgastein *bahnhof*, then walk past the railroad station to the stairs up and over the tracks to the Stubnerkogel gondola. Buy a one-way ticket and get off at the top station, at 7317 ft. (2230 m.).

Start: Walk in the direction of Bockhartsee and the Zitterauer until you come to the sign OTTO REICHERT WEG, to the right. The left path goes up and over the Tischkogel. Because of the ascent to 7875 ft. (2400 m.), we chose the Otto Reichert Weg, #132 on the hiking map. This red-and-white blazed trail stays fairly level, with no major altitude changes, but it is very rocky. Continue ahead to Miesbichlscharte, where the trail descends steeply. Follow the red-and-white blazing to the left at the fork in the path, in the direction of the lake and Sportgastein. At the lake, take the gravel road up, but before reaching the restaurant, take an unsigned trail on the left that descends down to the road, winding into the bus stop at Sportgastein. Take the first available bus to the Badgastein *bahnhof*.

Walk #4

Grüner Baum through the Kötschachtal to Restaurant Prossau to Grüner Baum

Walking Easy Time: 3 hours
Rating: Gentle

Today's low-level, gentle walk is on a forest path along the Kötschach River to Restaurant Prossau and the lovely waterfall at the end of the valley. Gently rising from 3494 to 4167 ft. (1065 to 1270 m.) at the restaurant, the trail begins to steepen as you ascend toward the waterfall and the end of the valley. Many walkers stop at the terrace of the restaurant to enjoy refreshments and the view, then return on the same path.

Start: From Grüner Baum, walk on the main paved path into the Kötschach Valley and the Höhe Tauern, the Austrian National Park. This forest trail ascends easily. After about one and three-quarter hours, you'll reach the restaurant at Prossau, with a terrace and a wonderful view of the waterfall. If you wish, continue on a trail into the forest for another half hour to the end of the valley, staying under the huge stone walls of the mountain. Return to Grüner Baum on the same shaded path.

Walk #5

Graukogel Top Station to Palfner See to Palfner Hochalm to Badgastein
Walking Easy Time: 4 hours
Rating: More challenging

NOTE: The Graukogel Chairlift may not open until the second week in July. You'll take two chairlifts to the Graukogel Top Station, at 6411 ft. (1954 m.). You'll return to the Graukogel Top Station for the trek to the Palfner See and the descent to Badgastein or Grüner Baum.

Directions: Take the bus to the Graukogel Lift Station in Badgastein. Buy a one-way ticket to the top and board the single chairlift, changing to a double chairlift rising to the top station.

Start: At the top station it's possible to ascend steeply to the Hüttenkogel, at 7320 ft. (2231 m.), for a quick view. Return to the top lift station and walk past the Graukogel Restaurant on #527 to the Palfner See, at 6805 ft. (2074 m.). On the way to the Palfner See you have the option of shortening the hike by turning right on #527 and continuing down to Palfner Hochalm, instead of walking up to the Palfner See, then down to Hochalm on #526. In either case, the walk continues down the mountain to Badgastein. It is possible to pick up the Hardt Weg just before Badgastein, turning right all the way to Grüner Baum.

Walk #6

Stubnerkogel Mid-Station along the Böcksteiner Höhenweg to Böckfeld Alm
to Böckstein to Badgastein on the Kaiser-Elisabeth Promenade
Walking Easy Time: 3½ to 4 hours
Rating: Comfortable

Today's midlevel walk begins with the Stubnerkogel Lift, rising to the midstation. You'll walk along the Böcksteiner Höhenweg, passing through Hirschkarkogel, with great views of the Gastein Valley. This path eventually descends into the village of Böckstein, home of the Thermal Galleries. From

Böckstein you'll return to Badgastein on the Kaiser-Elisabeth Promenade.

Directions: Take the bus to the Stubnerkogel Lift. Purchase a one-way ticket and get off at the mid-station.

Start: Follow path #129 on your map on the Böcksteiner Höhenweg, ascending from 5857 to 6569 ft. (1785 to 2002 m.) through Zitterauer Alm, descending to the Böckfeld Alm, at 5046 ft. (1538 m.), eventually down to Böckstein, at 3711 ft. (1131 m.). In Böckstein follow signs to the Kaiser-Elisabeth Promenade for the gentle walk back to Badgastein.

KAPRUN/ZELL AM SEE

The lakeside village of Zell am See, founded by monks in the eighth century, sits at the doorway of Austria's Höhe Tauern National Park and the dramatic, twisting Grossglockner mountain road. Kaprun, Zell am See's more charming and intimate sister village, is nestled nearby, close to the 10,509 ft. (3203 m.) Kitzsteinhorn. Here a series of cableways rise to the Alpincenter, at 8045 ft. (2452 m.), reputably the largest winter and summer glacier skiing area in Austria. The world's highest cable car support takes you to Bergstation Kitzsteinhorn, at 9938 ft. (3029 m.), where a tunnel walk leads to the Glocknerkanzel and an observation terrace facing the Grossglockner, Austria's highest mountain. The valley beyond Kaprun and the Kitzsteinhorn ends abruptly at the mammoth walls of the Mooserboden and Wasserfallboden Reservoirs, part of Europe's largest hydroelectric network, utilizing the world's largest platform funicular—the site of a *Walking Easy* hike and excursion.

Trails encircle and connect Kaprun and Zell am See, serviced by local bus transportation and lifts to scenic lookouts and trailheads. The Kaprun/Zell am See area is a complete vacation destination, offering all the water sport activities associated with Lake Zell, as well as those walking adventures preferred by mountain ramblers. What a find for the outdoorsperson who likes to do both!

Transportation

By Train and Bus - At Zell am See, transfer to the hourly Kaprun Bundesbus, leaving across from the Zell *bahnhof* (a fifteen-minute drive).

By Car - Drive to Zell am See and follow signs to Kaprun.

Favorite *Walking Easy* Hotel

Hotel Tavernhof
Four-star; Owner—Family Gschwantner
Schlossstrasse, A-5710 Kaprun
Tel: 65 47 83 01; **Fax:** 65 47 82 35 66
Internet: www.tavernhofkaprun.attavernhof
E-mail: tavernhof@netway.at
The Hotel Tavernhof is conveniently located in a quiet location, just a five-minute walk to Kaprun Center, where bus transportation to Zell am

See and area lifts are available. Breakfast is a plentiful buffet. Dinner is well prepared and includes contemporary and Austrian cuisine. This hotel has an indoor pool and is a favorite of hikers in the area.

Excursions

The Kaprun Tourist Information Office is located in the center of the village.
Internet: www.europa-sport-region.com
E-mail: kaprun@kaprun.net
You can buy a reduced-rate National Park Ticket as an incentive to use the area's environmentally friendly public transportation system.

1. **Zell am See** - Situated on the shores of a deep glacial lake, Zell am See is an important summer and winter resort, with a small but interesting Old Town to explore. The twelfth-century **Constable's Tower (Kastner-turm)** was once used as a grain silo. The Romanesque **Parish Church (Pfarrkirche)** was built in the eleventh century. The sixteenth-century **Castle Rosenberg** was once an elegant residence and is now home to the Town Hall and an art gallery. Check out the **Folklore Museum** in an ancient tower near the town square. Lake Zell, 2.5 miles (4 km.) long and 1 mile (1.6 km.) wide, offers swimming and boating facilities.
Directions: Buses run hourly between Kaprun and Zell am See.

2. **The Grossglockner Road** - The Grossglocknerstrasse, the longest and most scenic alpine highway in Europe and the gateway to Austria's Höhe Tauern National Park, is a fantastic drive of about 30 miles (48 km.), rising from 2483 ft. (757 m.) to its highest point at 8220 ft. (2505 m.). Because of the altitude rise and the multitude of hairpin turns, take the bus from Zell am See instead of driving. (See Walk #7.)

3. **Salzburg** - See A Trail of Three Cities—Salzburg.
Directions: Take a bus from Kaprun, arriving in Zell am See in time to catch the train to Salzburg.

4. **Kitzbühel** - Once an old mining town, Kitzbühel is now a fashionable winter and summer resort. (See Kitzbühel chapter.)
Directions: Take a bus from Kaprun to Zell am See and the local train to the Kitzbühel–Hahnenkamm station (about a ninety-minute trip), a few minutes' walk into the heart of town.

5. **Sigmund-Thun Klamm** - In the Ice Age the Kaprun Valley was covered by a glacier. As the glacier melted, it left behind a deep notch—105 ft. (32 m.) deep and 1050 ft. (320 m.) long—through the Sigmund-Thun Klamm (Gorge), where the Kaprun River flows into the valley. (See Walk #3.)

Directions: *Take the bus from Kaprun to Sigmund-Thun Klamm.*

Kaprun/Zell am See Walks

Recommended Maps:

❖ Freytag & Berndt—Wanderkarte—Kaprun/Zell am See

❖ Wanderkarte Zell am See/Kaprun—Fremdenverkehrsverband

❖ Kapruner Wander-un Tourenführer (Alles Da)

Walk #1

Introductory Walk—Kaprun to Guggenbichl on the Guggenhöhenweg to Kaprun Castle to Kaprun (Optional Walk, Kaprun Castle to Mayereinöden to Kaprun)

Walking Easy Time: 2½ to 4 hours

Rating: Comfortable

This midlevel walk, which can be taken on the afternoon of arrival, rises comfortably from 2494 to 2953 ft. (760 to 900 m.). You'll reach Guggenbichl about thirty minutes after ascending from Kaprun, with fabulous views past Zell am See and the snowcapped peaks of the Höhe Tauern. After walking through the cool forest, you'll descend on a trail to Kaprun Castle, with a return on the road to Kaprun. If time permits, the walk can be extended from the castle toward Mayereinöden and back to Kaprun.

Start: Walk to the *gemeindeamt* (village hall) in Kaprun. Cross the street and follow signed GUGGENHÖHENWEG #10. Walk up the street and turn left at the *wanderweg* sign. Walk over a small bridge and continue up the street to the right, to Guggenhöhenweg #10. This little-used road takes you up through the meadows in about thirty minutes to the *jausenstation* (snack bar) at Guggenbichl, perched on the side of the hill. Continue the ascent on a *forest strasse,* a wagon road through the woods. Soon path #10, the Mountain Way, ascends to the right on a red-and-white blazed path. Or you can continue ahead on the wide wagon path, meeting the #10 mountain path in about a half hour. At this point, turn left on a narrow, descending, zigzagging red-and-white blazed forest trail to the castle. A left turn on Schlosstrasse takes you back to central Kaprun.

If you wish to extend today's walk, locate path #12 to Mayereinöden near the castle, returning to Kaprun via the path along the Salzach River, found by walking toward Zell am See along the road. Turn left before the river on the Romantik Way, back to Kaprun.

Walk #2

Maiskogel Top Station to Glocknerblick to Unterberg Alm to Maiskogel to Kaprun on the Güterweg
Walking Easy Time: 2 to 4 hours
Rating: Comfortable

Today's walk is a midlevel hike from the top of the Maiskogel Lift to the Glocknerblick (an outstanding panoramic viewpoint) and back. You'll then proceed to Unterberg Alm, with a return to Maiskogel for a gentle descent on the Güterweg, through the Schaufelberg meadows, to Kaprun.

Directions: Take the Kaprun bus to the Maiskogel Lift Station and buy a one-way ticket to the top.

Start: For hardier *Easy Walkers*, try the short but somewhat steep ascent to the Glocknerblick, just to the left as you exit the lift station. You'll find fabulous views of the Kaprun Valley. Descend in the direction of Unterberg Alm, from 5479 to 5128 ft. (1670 to 1563 m.), then walk back to Maiskogel Alm on path #25 on your map. For those who prefer not to ascend the Glocknerblick, follow the sign to Unterberg Alm on a gently ascending path, returning along the same path for fresh views of the Zell am See area.

With either option, at the top Maiskogel lift station, take path #3, the Güterweg, by walking under the ski lift tunnel. Do not go down path #1 (the steeper way to Kaprun), but continue on the gently descending wagon road on #3, with the sign marked NACH KAPRUN, 2 HOURS. At an intersection with path #1, stay on #3 all the way and continue on the road as it zigzags down past the Kaprun church. Turn left at the high school, into Kaprun.

Walk #3

Excursion to Alpine Reservoirs of Kaprun and Walks at Mooserboden Dam (Optional Valley Walk)
Walking Easy Time: 1½ to 4 hours
Rating: Comfortable

Reserve a clear day for this full day's exciting excursion to view the dramatic, snow-covered Glockner mountain range of the Höhe Tauern.

Directions: Take a morning Kaprun Bundesbus to Kesselfall/Alpenhaus, the last stop, and purchase a combination ticket for the buses and funicular to the top station at Mooserboden Reservoir. These buses take you through a tunnel to Lärchwand, where you board one of the world's largest inclined lifts, large enough to take a bus up the mountain, rising 1414 ft. (431 m.). Another bus takes you past the Limberg Dam and the Wasserfallboden Reservoir, up to Mooserboden, at 6693 ft. (2040 m.); the entire trip takes less than an hour. This incredible system of reservoirs and dams provides hundreds of millions of kilowatt hours of electricity for this section of Europe. Completed in the early 1950s, it changed the face and ecology of the Kaprun Valley, and now attracts millions of tourists from around the world.

Start: After arriving at Mooserboden, walk past the monument, over the first and second sections of the dam. The views are astounding—icy glaciers and high-mountain peaks. Visit central Europe's only glacier museum. Upon returning to the main restaurant and trail signs, follow the half-hour Alpenblumenweg Path for a short walk among the alpine flowers.

Return to the bus stop for the trip back to Kesselfall/Alpenhaus and the Bundesbus to Kaprun. If it's early, you can take a gentle meadow and river walk, never far from the main road, back to Kaprun. This path, #13 on the hiking map, can be entered from the parking area on the left side of the road, at the Kessellfall bus stop. The path for this two-hour return walk descends gently and can be interrupted easily at bus stops along the way, indicated by an **H** on your map.

Walk #4

Kitzsteinhorn Alpincenter (Glacier Excursion) to Kreefelder Hütte to Maiskogel on the Alexander Enzinger Weg

Walking Easy Time: 4 hours

Rating: More challenging

The following excursion and walk at the Kitzsteinhorn, at 9938 ft. (3029 m.), with its glacier and the Alpincenter, at 8045 ft. (2452 m.), was a prime target for us. Unfortunately, a July mountain blizzard wiped out our plans, and while a few hardy summer skiers seemed to enjoy this phenomenon, all hiking trails were closed because of snow conditions. Instead we enjoyed hot chocolate, threw snowballs, and returned to the more friendly environs of the bottom station, walking back to Kaprun on a very pretty forest and meadow path along the Kapruner Ache (River), visiting the Sigmund-Thun Klamm (Gorge) on the way. This is an all-day excursion and hike, and an early start is advised.

Maiskogel Lift

Kaprun 780m.

Maiskogel 1540m.

E

Stangenhöhe

Cable Car

S

Alpincenter 2452m.

Kreefelder Hütte 2302m.

2953m. glacier

Kitzsteinhorn 3029m.

Directions: Take a morning bus to the Gletscherbahn and purchase a round-trip ticket to the Kitzsteinhorn (the return ticket to be used at the Maiskogel Lift). Take the lift to the Alpincenter and transfer to the cable car to the Kitzsteinhorn Top Station. A ten-minute walk brings you to the *glocknerkanzel,* an observation terrace where you will meet the Grossglockner, Austria's highest mountain, and other major alpine peaks in Austria's national park. You can take a summit lift to the glacier plateau to experience a glacier walk to the Hocheiserwand observation point. When ready, return to the Kitzsteinhorn Top Station and take the cable car to the Alpincenter to begin today's hike.

Start: Follow signs to the Kreefelder Hütte and the long mountain hike along the Alexander Enzinger Weg, via Stangenhöhe and the Glocknerblick, to the Maiskogel Lift. This is basically a downhill trek from 7530 ft. (2295 m.) to 5053 ft. (1540 m.) at the Maiskogel Top Station, where you take the lift down to the base station and a bus back to Kaprun.

For those *Easy Walkers* who prefer not to take the long hike to Maiskogel after the activities at the Kitzsteinhorn Top Station, the glacier, and the Alpincenter, return to the base station on the Gletscherbahn. If you have not taken the Kaprun Valley walk and visited Sigmund-Thun Klamm, this might be a good opportunity to do so. The path can be found in back of the lowest Gletscherbahn parking area.

Walk #5

Schmittenhöhe Top Station to Breiteckalm to Zeller Bergbahn Middle Station to Zell am See

Walking Easy Time: 4 hours

Rating: Comfortable

A cable car rises to the 6562 ft. (2000 m.) Schmittenhöhe, with spectacular views of the mountain ranges of the Höhe Tauern and the Kitzbühel Alps. You'll walk to Breiteckalm, then to the *mittelstation* of the Zeller Bergbahn, at 4469 ft. (1362 m.), continuing to walk down to Zell am See. However, at the mid-station you have the option of riding down on the gondola.

Directions: Take a bus to the last stop in Zell am See at the PA. Transfer to the Schmittenhöhe bus; at the lift station, buy a one-way ticket to the top.

Start: Walk behind the restaurant and up to the chapel. Follow trail #6 to Breiteckalm, at 5807 ft. (1770 m.), on a little-used jeep road. Just before arriving at the Glocknerhaus Restaurant, at 5194 ft. (1583 m.), turn left onto a meadow trail, following a sign to Zell am See. This trail through the pastures leads to the road. Turn left and walk down to the Zeller Bergbahn Mittelstation, at 4469 ft. (1362 m.). Continue walking down to Zell am See, at 2484 ft. (757 m.), on the zigzagging road, still path #6 on your map. You also have the option of taking the gondola down to Zell am See. With either option, at the bottom turn right and walk to the *bahnhof* for a visit to Zell am See and the bus back to Kaprun.

Walk #6

Schmittenhöhe Top Station, on the Höhenpromenade to Sonnkogel to Sonnalm to Zell am See (Optional Excursion to Zell am See)

Walking Easy Time: 3 hours

Rating: Comfortable

The Erlebnisweg Höhenpromenade, from the Schmittenhöhe Top Station to the Sonnkogel Top Station, is a comfortable path with numerous display boards providing historical and environmental information about the Schmittenhöhe area.

Directions: See Walk #5.

Start: At the Schmittenhöhe Top Station, at 6562 ft. (2000 m.), walk around to the back of the restaurant to the tiny chapel with its group of hiking signs. Take path #10 to the right, over the Höhenpromenade to Bergstation Sonnkogel, the chairlift top station, at 6017 ft. (1834 m.)—a fifty-minute walk. When the path forks, you have the option of taking a meadow trail that descends to the mid-station at Sonnalm. However, we suggest walking straight ahead and following the sign to the Sonnkogel Bergstation and restaurant (another five minutes). At Sonnkogel you have a couple of options:

1. Take the triple chairlift down to the mid-station.
2. Walk around the restaurant, past the lift station. Pick up the wagon road going to Schmiedhofalm then down to the Sonnalm Mid-Station, at 4518 ft. (1377 m).

At Sonnalm Mid-Station you have two more options:
1. Take the gondola to Zell am See and the bus stop.
2. Descend on the road to Zell am See and the bus stop.

If time permits, walk through the pedestrian shopping streets of Zell am See and turn down to the lakefront. Walk for as long as you wish in either direction on the See Promenade along the lake's shores. To return to Kaprun, take the bus across the street from the Zell am See *bahnhof*.

Walk #7

Glacier Walk (Excursion to Höhe Tauern in the Austrian National Park via the Grossglockener Road)
Walking Easy Time: 1 to 3 hours
Rating: Comfortable

This is an excursion to Austria's largest glacier, at the foot of the Grossglockner, Austria's highest mountain, in Austria's magnificent national park—a full day's outing with an *early* start necessary. You'll take the bus from Kaprun to the Zell am See train station, where you board a special bus, riding to the last stop at Kaiser-Franz-Josefs-Höhe and visiting the glacier for a short walk. If time permits, you can walk on the upper ridges adjacent to the glacier before returning by bus to Zell am See and Kaprun.

The Höhe Tauern looks as it did 1,000 years ago—plants and animals in a protected alpine wilderness. In the heart of the park lies Austria's tallest mountain, the Grossglockner, at 12,457 ft. (3797 m.), and the largest glacier, the Pasterze, some 6 miles (10 km.) long. With 120 peaks rising over 10,000 ft. (3000 m.) and 169 glaciers, the park is one of Europe's most beautiful and enthralling high alpine regions.

Directions: *NOTE: The following are approximate times and subject to change.* Take the 8:25 A.M. bus from Kaprun, arriving at the Zell am See *bahnhof* at 8:40. Outside the train station, transfer to the 8:53 Bundesbus, arriving at Kaiser-Franz-Josefs-Höhe at 11:04 A.M. The Grossglockner Road is one of the most famous excursions in Austria, and the best viewing opportunities are from seats on the right side of the bus.

Start: After getting off the bus at the last stop, Kaiser-Franz-Josefs-

Höhe, walk toward the glacier. A short funicular ride will take you to the bottom station for your glacier walk. At the bottom station there is a steep fifteen-minute scramble down to the glacier itself. Remember that you also have to climb back up from the glacier to the funicular base station to return to the top. *CAUTION: After reaching the glacier, follow the steps cut into the ice, holding on to the guide ropes, advancing up to the forward alert ropes.* Leave ample time to climb back up to the funicular, where there may be a wait for the ride to the top.

If time permits, note the following options:

1. The park service provides an interesting and informative twenty-minute film on the wonders of the Austrian National Park.
2. Walk along the side of the glacier. Walking distance depends on how much time is left before the bus leaves. Walk through a short tunnel leading to a wide, level path, with the glacier on your left. The Hofmanshütte is about a two-hour round-trip walk.

Please remember that you *must* be at the bus stop by 2:35 P.M. if you want to take the 2:45 bus, returning to Zell am See at 4:32 P.M. to catch the 5:25 bus to Kaprun. The next (and last bus) leaves Kaiser-Franz-Josefs-Höhe at 3:45 P.M., arriving in Zell am See at 5:32, where you change for the 6:25 P.M. bus to Kaprun—the end of a long, exciting, and memorable day in the Austrian National Park. NOTE: *Check current bus schedules.*

A TRAIL OF THREE CITIES: WALKING EASY IN INNSBRUCK, SALZBURG, AND VIENNA

The historic cities of **Innsbruck** and **Salzburg** are close enough to most Austrian *Walking Easy* base villages so that you can take a comfortable, one-day excursion and return to your hotel for dinner. **Vienna**, too far away from our base villages for a one-day excursion, is included for those *Easy Walkers* who wish to spend additional time exploring this landmark city.

INNSBRUCK

The imperial city of Innsbruck, the crossroads of Europe, is a stone's throw from the famous Brenner Pass and the dramatic Dolomites of Italy. Surrounded by snowcapped mountains, it is close enough to the *Walking Easy* base villages of Seefeld, Neustift, Alpbach, Zell am Ziller, Mieming, and Kitzbühel for a comfortable, one-day city tour of its charming Old Town. A historic and cultural center, Innsbruck was the home of the Hapsburgs, Austria's royal family, who were responsible for developing this capital of the Tyrol into an important architectural and arts center.

The Innsbruck Tourist Office is located at Burggraben 3, at the corner of Herzog-Friedrich-Strasse—the colorful, cobblestoned main street of Old Town. This car-free zone houses shops and cafes and is the heart of today's walk.

Favorite *Walking Easy* Hotel

Alpotel Tirol

Four-Star; Owners—Familie Wolf; Contact—Angelika Kleimlercher
Innrain 13, A-6020 Innsbruck; **Tel:** 512 57 79 31; **Fax:** 512 57 79 31 15
All seventy-three rooms of the Alpotel have modern amenities—updated private facilities, TV and radio, minibar and room safe—many rooms with a balcony. While its location is close to the historical part of the city, the air-conditioned rooms are particularly quiet. Underground

parking is on the premises and the railroad station is just a few minutes by taxi. An ample breakfast buffet is included, and the hotel's restaurants enjoy an outstanding reputation for local specialties. The hotel has been under the personal direction of the Wolf family for years, assisted now by Angelika, the *Walking Easy* contact.

Innsbruck—One-Day *Walking Easy* Itinerary

Directions: *If not staying in Innsbruck, take the train or bus from any nearby* Walking Easy *base village to Innsbruck. Although it is possible to take a local bus or taxi to the historic city center, Innsbruck's main train and bus station are only a few minutes' walk.*

Start: Exit the train station, cross the main street, Sudtiroler Platz, then turn right. Continue on Sudtiroler to Museumstrasse and turn left. Walk about 4 blocks to Burggraben, bearing left to the famous pedestrian streets of Old Town. Turn into Herzog-Friedrich-Strasse and walk toward the **Stadtturm (City Tower)**, dating from 1440, located on the right, just before the Golden Roof. Note the tower's imposing sixteenth-century cupola. Climb to the top for a great view of Innsbruck. Continue to the **Goldenes Dachl (Golden Roof)**, a loggia covered with over 2,500 fire-gilt copper tiles on a fifteenth-century residence. As you face the **Golden Roof**, turn left toward **Helblinghaus**, situated on the left side of the street. This fifteenth-century Gothic town house is decorated with Baroque pastel stuccos. The street continues with a variety of shops.

Retrace your steps back to the Golden Roof and turn left to the Baroque **Dom zu St. Jakob (St. Jacob's Cathedral)**, featuring Lucas Cranach's famous painting of the Madonna over the main altar. Turn right after leaving the cathedral and cross the street to the sixteenth-century **Hofgarten**. After leaving the park, walk past the columned **Landestheatre**, originally the court's seventeenth-century Opera House. Just past the theater is **Leopold's Fountain** with its equestrian statue.

Across from the Landestheatre and fountain is the **Hofburg**, the imperial palace. Visit the state rooms—guided tours in English are given throughout the day. Exiting the palace, cross the street to the sixteenth-century **Hofkirche (Court Church)** with twenty-eight bronze figures inside—the famous "Black Knights." As you exit Court Church, turn left, continuing on Burggraben, walking around to the entrance of the pedestrian street. Walk past the Tourist Office and turn left on Maria-Theresien-Strasse, the main shopping street. Continue past the eighteenth-century

Anna Column, commemorating the successful Tyrolean resistance against a Bavarian invasion. Proceed to the eighteenth-century **Triumphal Arch,** erected in honor of the marriage of Leopold II. Just before the arch, turn left on Saturner Strasse and walk directly to the bus and train station, ending your tour of the highlights of Innsbruck's Old Town.

SALZBURG

Easy Walkers staying in the base village of Badgastein can take an easy, one-day visit to Salzburg, the city of Mozart. Like Vienna and Innsbruck, Salzburg is a comfortable city to walk in and boasts an impressive list of must-see landmarks in its Old Town. Architecturally, Salzburg is a gem, with its seventeenth- and eighteenth-century houses, hotels, and shops.

Salzburg—One-Day *Walking Easy* Itinerary

Directions from Badgastein: *Take a morning bus to the Badgastein* bahnhof *and a direct train to Salzburg (a one-hour train trip).*

   Start: In the Salzburg train station, follow signs to the **i**, Salzburg Tourist Office. Purchase a **24-Hour Salzburg Card** with a city map for free use of all public transportation and free entry into Mozart's Birthplace, the Höhensalzburg Fortress, the state rooms at the Residenz, and numerous museums, galleries, and memorials.

   Walk outside the train station toward the main traffic street, turn right and board bus #5, #6, #51, or #55, getting off at the fifth stop for entrance to the **Alter Markt**, just after crossing the Salzach River. Follow crowds through to the **Alter Markt**, a square filled with street vendors and tourists. As you proceed straight ahead, note the famous Cafe Tomaselli for a mid-morning snack. Bear around to **Residenz Platz**, an open square with an impressive Baroque fountain, location of the **Residenz Palace** and **Residenzgalerie,** containing European paintings and fifteen historic rooms. Also note the location of the **Salzburg Cathedral,** with its magnificent marble facade. (The entrance to the cathedral is off **Dom Platz**.) Walk toward the large statue of **Mozart** in **Mozartplatz**, just past the eighth-century **St. Michael's Church** on your left. Sounds of music will probably welcome you to the square, as choral and instrumental musicians from around the world perform, adding to the pleasure of listening to the eighteenth-century **Salzburg Glockenspiel.** On the day we visited Mozartplatz, we heard a young violinist, a Scotch bagpiper, a trio from Moscow, and an accordionist from Hungary.

Walk back toward and around the cathedral and into **Cathedral Square** in order to gain entry to this famous Baroque church. The **Höhensalzburg Fortress** towers over Cathedral Square. Cross the large square and walk toward the railway and the castle, entering Festungsgasse and the entry to the funicular. If you've purchased the Salzburg Card, the funicular ride is free. Towering 400 feet above the Salzach River, this ancient fortress is the largest completely preserved citadel in central Europe. While on the fortress grounds, visit the **Burgmuseum** with its collection of medieval art and the **Rainermuseum**'s displays of arms and armor. Conducted tours of the fortress are given daily; check for hours of English-speaking departures.

Return from the fortress by way of the funicular, turning left immediately upon reaching the bottom station. Walk through an ornate gate into **St. Peter's Cemetery,** where Mozart and Haydn are buried. Enclosed by arcades and housing numerous artistic wrought-iron gates, it is located at the foot of the stone wall of the Mönchsberg, across from early Christian **catacombs** (tours are available). Pay **St. Margaret's Chapel** a visit before walking through the cemetery and exiting onto a long street and the eighth-century **Franziskaner Kirche**, one of Salzburg's oldest churches.

Continue past the Concert Hall, crossing Herbert-van-Karajan Platz, then turn right on **Getreidegasse**, the famous walking and shopping street—#9 is **Mozart's Birthplace** and the **Mozart Museum.** Getreidegasse leads to the **Alter Markt,** where you first started. Turn left onto the main street, then left again, crossing the bridge. Turn left on the main shopping street, a few yards to the bus stop. If you have time, detour into the **Mirabell Gardens**, designed in 1690, with its groups of sculptures, the humorous Dwarves Garden, the Maze, and the Hedge Theater.

Take bus #1, #2, #5, #6, or #55 back to the railroad station for your return, ending an exciting one-day excursion to Salzburg.

VIENNA

Vienna is an encyclopedia of architectural styles, a mix of majestic palaces, churches, culturally diverse museums, and colorfully landscaped parks. All are within comfortable walking boundaries, crisscrossed by pedestrian streets and serviced by safe, clean, convenient public transportation. Vienna is like a tray of delectable pastries—sample a few, then return when time permits a more extensive visit.

If you decide on a short visit to Vienna, please refer to "Must See" Vienna, then choose those places of interest that appeal to you, depending on the amount of time you have.

Transportation

Vienna's excellent public transportation network includes buses, trams (trolley cars), and a subway (U-Bahn). Choose any discount ticket, which can be purchased in most tobacco stores and major underground stations. All tickets can be used for all transportation lines at any time.

1. **The Vienna Card** - Take any transportation for a period of seventy-two hours, with the additional benefits of reduced rates in museums and theaters. This card can be bought at your hotel and the Tourist Office.
2. **The 72-Hour Pass** provides unlimited transportation only, for seventy-two hours, and can be bought at *tabac* shops.
3. **Single Tickets** can be purchased from a coin-operated ticket machine on the tram or bus.
4. **The 24-Hour, One-Day Pass** - This pass can be bought at *tabac* shops.

Favorite *Walking Easy* Hotels

We've located two comfortable and affordable Vienna hotels, just outside the city center. Both are part of the Flair hotel group.

Hotel Altstadt

Four-Star; Owner—Otto E. Wiesenthal
Kirchengasse 41, A-1070 Vienna; **Tel:** 15 26 33 99 0; **Fax:** 15 23 49 01
E-mail: hotel@altstadt.at

The Hotel Altstadt, tastefully renovated, is a town house in an old, aristocratic building. The four-star hotel is dedicated to personal service and is looked after by a friendly and helpful staff, supervised by its dynamic owner, Otto Wiesenthal. The Altstadt's location, close to the heart of old Vienna and near public transportation, is ideal for *Easy Walkers*. Each of its twenty-five rooms and apartments is different, offering cable TV and a minibar. A delicious buffet breakfast is included in the room rate. Ask for a quiet room on the inside court, if possible.

Hotel Carlton Opera

Three Star; Owners—Familie Dauber

Schikanedergasse 4, A-1040 Vienna; **Tel:** 58 753 02 0; **Fax:** 58 125 11

Internet: www.ping.at/carlton

E-mail: carlton@ping.at

This updated three-star hotel, in an Art Deco building, is only a stroll away from the Naschmarkt, an outdoor pedestrian mall featuring clothing, produce, cafes, and mouthwatering food specialties. Not many visitors to Vienna get to experience the tastes, smells, and flavor of this market. The Carlton Opera Hotel is a ten-minute walk to the Opera House, the Ringstrasse, and Kärntnerstrasse and is only a short walk to public transportation. Rooms are comfortable, air-conditioned, and generally quiet. Buffet breakfast is outstanding, with fresh fruits and vegetables added to a complete breakfast menu and a selection of freshly baked Viennese breads and kuchen. For reservations ask for Frau Ruth Dauber.

"Must See" Vienna

The main Vienna Tourist Information Office is located behind the Opera House at Kärntnerstrasse 38.

1. **Ringstrasse (Ring Boulevard)** - This great boulevard circles Vienna's old section for almost 3 miles. For a city orientation, board Tram #1 by the Opera House and enjoy the sights as the trolley circles the Ring. Get off at the stop of your choice to begin sight-seeing. We recommend beginning at the Hofburg Palace.

2. **The Hofburg Palace Complex** - The imperial palace of the Hapsburgs is vast. It contains about 2,600 rooms, but only 20 are open to visitors.

    a. **Schatzkammer (Imperial Treasury)** - The Imperial Treasury is reached from a stairway in the Swiss Court. You'll be dazzled by the display of treasures. An English brochure and audiotour are available.

    b. **Kaiserappartements (Imperial Apartments)** - Enter by the rotunda of Michaelerplatz under the dome of St. Michael's Gate. The emperors and their families lived on the first floor of the Chancellery wing amid ornately carved furniture. English brochures are available.

    c. **Spanische Hofreitschule (Spanish Riding School)** - Written requests for the eighty-minute performances on Tuesday through Saturday at 10:45 A.M. and 7:00 P.M. should be mailed at least two months in advance to Spanische Reitschule, Hofburg, A-1010, Vienna, Austria. Do not include the price of the tickets. Tickets for training sessions (no reserved seats) are sold at the entrance on Josefsplatz, Gate 2.

d. Vienna Boys' Choir - Mass is sung in Die Burgkapelle (Imperial Chapel of the Hofburg), through the Schweizerhof entrance, every Sunday from January through June and from mid-September through December at 9:15 A.M. Line up early for standing room. Write for tickets at least sixty days ahead of time to: Hofmusikkapelle, Hofburg, A-1010, Vienna, Austria. Do not include the admission cost. Tickets may then be picked up at the Burgkapelle. During May, June, September, and October, the Vienna Boys' Choir performs at the Konzerthaus every Friday at 3:30 P.M. Tickets can usually be obtained at your hotel.

Directions to the Hofburg Palace Complex: *Take Tram #1, #2, D, or J to Burgring. From there, locate the Hofburg on your city map.*

3. Opera House - The State Opera House was opened in 1869 as the first of the grand buildings to be erected on the Ringstrasse; it was rebuilt after World War II. English-language guided tours are offered in July and August daily at 2:00 and 3:00 P.M. (you should be at the Opera House thirty minutes before the tour).

Directions: *Take Tram #1 and exit at the Opera House. Or take the U1, U2, or U4 subways to Karlsplatz.*

4. Kunsthistorisches Museum (Museum of Fine Arts) - Across from the Hofburg Palace, this art collection of the Hapsburgs is one of the most important in the world. Plan at least three hours to view just a few of this museum's treasures.

Directions: *Take Tram #1, #52, #58, D, J, or the U-Bahn to Volkstheatre stop.*

5. St. Stephen's Cathedral - The twelfth century saw the beginning of this cathedral, the geographic, historic, and spiritual center of Vienna. Damaged over the centuries by fire, conquest, and bombings, it has been rebuilt and restored. The cathedral is filled with paintings, sculpture, and intricate altars, combining to make St. Stephen's one of the great Gothic cathedrals of the world. Climbing the 344 steps of the South Tower offers a panoramic view of Vienna, the Vienna Woods, and the Danube. The North Tower ascent is by elevator for a viewing of the cathedral's great church bell. Brochures in English are available.

Directions: Take U-Bahn line 1 or 3 to Stephansplatz. Walking from the Hofburg, locate Kärntnerstrasse on your city map and walk toward the cathedral's spires.

6. **Die Deutschordenkirche (Church of the Teutonic Order)** - On Singerstrasse, near St. Stephen's Cathedral, this Gothic church was built by the Order of the Teutonic Knights in 1395. Note its beautiful sixteenth-century Flemish altarpiece. Visit the treasury on the second floor.
Directions: Take U-Bahn line 1 or 3 to Stephansplatz and locate Singer-strasse on your map.

7. **Peterskirche (St. Peter's Church)** - Situated on Peterplatz, St. Peter's is the oldest and most lavishly decorated Baroque church in Vienna.
Directions: Take U-Bahn line 1 or 3 to Stephansplatz and locate Peter-platz on your map.

8. **Schönbrunn Palace** - This is the second-largest palace in Europe, with magnificent grounds, a zoo, and a coach museum. Located out of the city proper, it was built between 1696 and 1712. Its 1,441 rooms constitute Vienna's most impressive palace, second in Europe only to Versailles. More than forty rooms are open to the public. The beautiful Schönbrunn Gardens are also a treat. Located next to the palace, these immense gardens house the Gloriette, the Palm House, the Butterfly House, the Carriage Museum, and the zoo. A guided tour is necessary to see the apartments, available in English at 9:30, 10:30, and 11:30 A.M. (Try to make the less crowded 9:30 A.M. tour.)
Directions to Palace: Take the U-Bahn green #4 line toward Hütteldorf and exit at Schönbrunn station. Follow the signs outside to Schloss Schönbrunn.

9. **Belvedere Palace** - On Prinz-Eugen Strasse 27, located on a hill above Vienna, is another of Vienna's magnificent palaces. Walk through the lovely gardens to arrive at the palace, with its two great staircases in two buildings—Unteres and Oberes Belvedere. Lower Belvedere (Unteres) includes the Museum of Baroque Art and the Museum of Medieval Austrian Art. The Upper (Oberes) Belvedere houses the Austrian Gallery of Nineteenth- and Twentieth-Century Art and provides an excellent view

of the city from its top floors.

Directions: Take Tram D to Schloss Belvedere.

10. **Stadttempel (Synagogue/City Temple)** - At Seitenstettengasse 4, this "Biedermeier jewel" was built in 1824 and renovated in 1988, fifty years after its near-destruction by the Nazis. It was the only synagogue to even partially survive World War II.
Directions: Take U-Bahn line 1 or 3 to Stephansplatz. Walk straight ahead on Rotenturmstrasse, turning left on Fleischmarkt. Walk up the stairs at the end of the street and turn right on Judengasse, then right on Seitenstettengasse to the synagogue.

11. **Stadtpark (City Park)** - This lovely park is situated off the Parkring. On summer evenings, the orchestra at the Kursalon, an elegant cafe-restaurant on the south side of the park, plays Strauss waltzes.
Directions: Take Tram #1, #2, J, or T to Stadtpark.

12. **Prater Amusement Park** - Situated between the Donau (Danube) River and its canal, the Prater is a fun place to spend a few evening hours. The Riesenrad, a giant Ferris wheel built in 1897, is near the park entrance.
Directions: Take the U-Bahn red #1 line toward Kagran and exit at Pratersten.

13. **Wienerwald (Vienna Woods)** - Bordering Vienna on the north and west, the famous Vienna Woods are 500 square miles of green rolling hills, intersected by a network of color-coded walking paths, usually at the end of public tram and bus lines. Grinzing, at the edge of the Vienna Woods, is the home of many *heurige*, or wine taverns—a village of old, winding streets and houses built around courtyards where visitors eat, drink wine, and listen to music (designated by a green branch hanging over the front door).
Directions: Take Tram #1 toward Schottentor and change to Tram #38 to Grinzing. In Grinzing you can take Bus #38A through the Vienna Woods and up the hill to Kahlenberg. This trip takes about an hour each way.

14. **Uhrenmuseum der Stadt Wien (Municipal Clock Museum)** - Located at Schulhof 2, the museum, founded in 1690, houses a collection

of more than 3,000 watches and clocks, from primitive to the more modern.

Directions: Take U-Bahn line 1 or 3 to Stephansplatz and check the city map for directions.

15. **Dorotheum Auction House** - At this 300-year-old auction house, antique art objects, paintings, furniture, and jewelry may be viewed before the auction. It's like being in a museum, only better, because everything is close at hand for inspection. It's worth a visit if you're a lover of art and antiques.

Directions: From the Opera House on Philharmonicstrasse, walk through Albertinaplatz on to Augustinerstrasse, making a right turn on Dorotheergasse to number 17.

16. **Vienna Jewish Museum** - This expanded and newly reopened museum is housed in the eighteenth-century Eskeles Palace at Dorotheergasse 11, located near the Dorotheum Auction House. The museum contains the Max Berger Collection of Judaica, with ancient texts, scrolls, and ritual objects, as well as works and photos by Jewish artists.

Directions: See #15 above to Dorotheum.

17. **Holocaust Memorial** - Located on the Judenplatz, this new memorial is dedicated to the Austrian Jews killed by the Nazis. It is combined with the excavation of a medieval synagogue and a Museum of Medieval Jewish Life.

Vienna **Restaurant** Favorites

Comfortable, Casual, and Moderately Priced

Figlmüller - Wollzeille 5, **Tel:** 512 61 77; no reservations. Restaurants serving local cuisine can be found on almost every street in Vienna, but a favorite of the authors for schnitzel is Figlmüller (closed in August). This is a *beisel,* or wine tavern, and serves one of the largest schnitzels in Austria. A mixed salad, a schnitzel, and a glass of local wine make a great Viennese dinner.

Directions: Walk on Kärntnerstrasse, past St. Stephen's in the opposite direction of the Opera House, then turn right on Wollzeille. Follow the signs through a 500-year-old arcade to the restaurant, only a few blocks from the cathedral.

Gigerl - Blumenstockgasse 2, **Tel:** 513 44 31; no reservations. This is a small, very casual restaurant in the center of the city near Stephansplatz serving buffet-style food, typical Viennese dishes, and local wines. In warm weather the outdoor area is enjoyable.
Directions: Walk past St. Stephen's on Kärntnerstrasse in the direction of the Opera House and make a left on Heihburggasse. Take a first right turn to Rauhenststrasse, then a quick right on Blumenstockgasse.

Ma Pitom - Seitenstettengasse 5, **Tel:** 535 43 13; reservations not required. This bright, modern, airy restaurant serves excellent "designer" pizzas, many variations on the theme of pasta, and a diet-breaking tiramisu for dessert. It's away from the hectic tourist area restaurants and is a favorite with locals.
Directions: Walk past St. Stephen's on Kärntnerstrasse away from the Opera House. Turn left on Fleischmarkt and walk to the end of the street and up the stone steps, turning right on Judengasse and right on Seitenstettengasse.

Cavalière - Köllnerhofgasse 4, **Tel:** 513 83 20; reservations not required. Near the cathedral, this informal Italian restaurant specializes in pasta and is a favorite with residents of the area. A green salad and linguine with bolognese sauce is a delicious and satisfying meal.
Directions: On Kärntnerstrasse, walking away from the Opera House, turn right on Fleischmarkt and right on Köllnerhofgasse. The restaurant is on the left side of the street.

Coffeehouse and Cafe Favorites

Central - At Herrengasse 14, Central is decorated in late-Empire style. This cafe is across from the Spanish Riding School. In the nineteenth century it was a meeting place for Austria's best-known writers.
Directions: Take Tram #1, #2, D, or J to Burgring. From there locate the Hofburg on the city map. Cafe Central will be across the street.

Demel - At Kohlmarkt 14, this cafe's baroque black marble tables have seated almost every visitor who comes to Vienna. Afternoon tea or coffee with unique pastries has become a tradition with Vienna tourists. An expensive snack, but a "must do" at least once in Vienna.

Directions: From Stephansplatz, walk on Graben and make a left on Kohlmarkt. Demel is on the right side. From Herrengasse and the Hofburg complex, turn right on Kohlmarkt and Demel will be on the left side.

Landtmann - Located at Dr.-Karl-Lueger-Ring 4, the beautiful Landtmann still attracts a mixture of politicians, actors, and writers. The cafe offers coffee and pastries plus full meals.

Directions: From the Opera House, take Tram #1, getting off at the Burgtheater. The cafe is across from the Rathausplatz, just past the Parliament building.

Favorite Accommodations Index—By Town

Index

About the Authors

Chet and Carolee Lipton became enchanted with the incredible alpine trail system during their travels abroad and, over the past thirteen years, they've been walking it ever since. The Liptons authored the *Walking Easy* series to fill a need for user-friendly, day-walk hiking guides for active adults and young families.

The Liptons return to the alps each summer to research new base villages, summer day-walks, and hotels for the *Walking Easy* books, including *Walking Easy in the Italian and French Alps* and *Walking Easy in the Swiss and Austrian Alps*.

You can contact Chet and Carolee by e-mail at walkingez@aol.com or on the Web at: www.walkingeasy.com.